What Makes the EU Viable?

What Makes the EU Viable?
European Integration in the Light of the Antebellum US Experience

Andrew Glencross
Lecturer in International Relations
University of Pennsylvania, USA

palgrave
macmillan

© Andrew Glencross 2009

All rights reserved. No reproduction, copy or transmission of this publication may be made without written permission.

No portion of this publication may be reproduced, copied or transmitted save with written permission or in accordance with the provisions of the Copyright, Designs and Patents Act 1988, or under the terms of any licence permitting limited copying issued by the Copyright Licensing Agency, Saffron House, 6-10 Kirby Street, London EC1N 8TS.

Any person who does any unauthorized act in relation to this publication may be liable to criminal prosecution and civil claims for damages.

The author has asserted his right to be identified as the author of this work in accordance with the Copyright, Designs and Patents Act 1988.

First published 2009 by
PALGRAVE MACMILLAN

Palgrave Macmillan in the UK is an imprint of Macmillan Publishers Limited, registered in England, company number 785998, of Houndmills, Basingstoke, Hampshire RG21 6XS.

Palgrave Macmillan in the US is a division of St Martin's Press LLC, 175 Fifth Avenue, New York, NY 10010.

Palgrave Macmillan is the global academic imprint of the above companies and has companies and representatives throughout the world.

Palgrave® and Macmillan® are registered trademarks in the United States, the United Kingdom, Europe and other countries

ISBN-13: 978-0-230-22450-6   hardback
ISBN-10: 0-230-22450-4   hardback

This book is printed on paper suitable for recycling and made from fully managed and sustained forest sources. Logging, pulping and manufacturing processes are expected to conform to the environmental regulations of the country of origin.

A catalogue record for this book is available from the British Library.

Library of Congress Cataloging-in-Publication Data

Glencross, Andrew.
  What makes the EU viable? : European integration in the light of the antebellum US experience / Andrew Glencross.
     p. cm.
  Includes bibliographical references and index.
  ISBN-13: 978-0-230-22450-6 (alk. paper)
  ISBN-10: 0-230-22450-4
  1. European Union. 2. European federation. 3. Europe—Economic integration—Political aspects. 4. United States—Politics and government—1783–1865. 5. Political culture—United States—History—19th century. I. Title.

JN30.G568 2009
341.242'2—dc22   2009013630

10 9 8 7 6 5 4 3 2 1
18 17 16 15 14 13 12 11 10 09

Printed and bound in Great Britain by
CPI Antony Rowe, Chippenham and Eastbourne

For my mentors: Graham Howes and Fritz Kratochwil

Contents

List of Tables   x

Acknowledgements   xi

Introduction: Questioning What Makes the EU Viable   1

1 The Problem of Viability in a Compound Polity   7
    1.1 Introduction   7
    1.2 Viability as defined in relation to the 'Rules of the Game' of politics   8
    1.3 Scenarios of viability in a compound polity   15
    1.4 The theory of the compound polity and the issue of the units' sovereign status   20
    1.5 Comparing the EU with other political systems   24
    1.6 Conclusion   31

2 Developing an Analogical Comparison between the EU and the Antebellum US Republic   32
    2.1 Introduction   32
    2.2 The attraction of transatlantic comparison   33
    2.3 The caesura of the Civil War: The overlooked significance of antebellum political conflict   37
    2.4 Comparing viability in the EU and antebellum US: A question of *praxis* not preconditions   43
    2.5 Conclusion: Learning through analogy   51

3 Comparing How the Rules of the Game are Contested   53
    3.1 Introduction   53
    3.2 Viability and the conflict over the rules of the game of politics in the antebellum US   54

	3.3	Contesting the rules of the game in the EU		63
		3.3.1 Dual federalism v. joint federalism		66
		3.3.2 A constitution for popular government v. a treaty system		67
		3.3.3 A project for freedom v. a project for undefined ever closer union		69
		3.3.4 A single fault line v. multiple fault lines		70
		3.3.5 A party system and Supreme Court arbitrator v. politics of treaty reform and council arbitration		71
	3.4	Conclusion		73

4 The Struggle to Maintain a Compound System: Creating and Contesting the Rules of the Game in European Integration   74

	4.1	Introduction		74
	4.2	The construction of the rules of the game of European politics, from the ECSC to the EEC		75
		4.2.1 The Coal and Steel Community		76
		4.2.2 The European Economic Community		79
	4.3	After the EEC: Unexpected constitutionalization (ECJ), the first enlargement (UK) and democratic consolidation (Mediterranean enlargement)		81
		4.3.1 The impact of the court on the rules of the game		82
		4.3.2 British accession: Opening up the Pandora's box of domestic politics		86
		4.3.3 The Mediterranean enlargement round: Defining the Community's democratic values		93
	4.4	Maastricht and after: Questioning the purpose and nature of integration		97
	4.5	Two steps forward but how many back? European integration's dynamic equilibrium		107
	4.6	Conclusion		112

5 Contrasting and Explaining the Viability of Two Compound Systems — 113
- 5.1 Introduction — 113
- 5.2 American dual federalism (with the highest functions of government) v. European joint federalism (with the most numerous) — 115
- 5.3 A constitution for popular government v. a treaty system — 118
- 5.4 A project for freedom (the union as a means to an end) v. a project for undefined ever closer union (integration as an end in itself) — 125
- 5.5 A single fault line v. multiple fault lines — 131
- 5.6 A party system and Supreme Court arbitrator v. politics of treaty reform and Council arbitration — 138
- 5.7 Conclusion: Recognizing what makes the EU viable — 150

6 The Future Evolution of the EU Compound Polity: The Obstacles to Voluntary Centralization — 152
- 6.1 Introduction — 152
- 6.2 Dynamic equilibrium: A self-reinforcing process? — 154
- 6.3 Compound polities and the problem of representing both states and individuals — 161
- 6.4 How to manage the voluntary centralization of representation — 169
- 6.5 The political process needed for justifying voluntary centralization — 173
- 6.6 Conclusion — 180

Conclusion: Implications for EU Studies and the Debate over the Future of Integration — 182
Applying the insights of this study — 184

Notes — 189
Bibliography — 206
Index — 224

Tables

1.1	The four contested rules of the game in a compound polity	14
1.2	Defining voluntary centralization and dynamic equilibrium in relation to changes in the rules of the game	18
2.1	How the US Civil War fundamentally changed the rules of the game	41
4.1	Evolution of the rules of the game in the EU according to the logic of dynamic equilibrium	109

Acknowledgements

Evelyn Waugh believed it is only possible to write an autobiography 'when one has lost all curiousity about the future'. Acknowledgements provide the autobiography of the book-writing process but this does not for a second mean I have turned my back on the future. However, the completion of this work is the proper moment to revisit the past. My original good fortune was to be admitted to Cambridge University to read Social and Political Sciences at Trinity Hall under the wise direction of Graham Howes. A better and more congenial introduction to the study of politics in all its many guises I cannot imagine. Michael Sonenscher, at nearby King's, gave me profound insights into the history of political ideas while demonstrating the enduring value of rigorous scholarship.

At the European University Institute, where I completed the Ph.D. dissertation on which the present work is based, my *Doktorvater* was Fritz Kratochwil. His challenging intellectual promptings and stalwart support – as well as a healthy dose of wry humour – ensured this project eventually saw the light of day. The other members of my thesis jury, Alex Trechsel, Daniel Deudney and Sergio Fabbrini, must also be singled out for the probing comments and generous advice that guided the rewriting of the final manuscript. To Alex I owe a particular debt of gratitude for prolonging my sojourn in Italy thanks to a research appointment at the newly launched European Union Democracy Observatory. While in Florence, Maureen Lechleitner invariably went beyond the call of duty in facilitating my research endeavours with her ruthless administrative efficiency. Moving across the Atlantic, a special mention is reserved for Frank Plantan Jr, co-director of the International Relations Programme at the University of Pennsylvania. Joining this unique programme as a lecturer in international relations has proven a richly rewarding experience as a teacher and furnished the perfect environment for putting the finishing touches to this book.

Nonetheless it would be remiss to acknowledge only intellectual heredity as large portions of the text were in fact penned during summers and winters at my family home in Saint Cricq, France. There my parents, as they have always done, offered me the nurture for which no choice of words can do justice. My father deserves extra credit for revising countless drafts in his enduring mission to prevent me from butchering the English language. Lastly, Janou has brought me more joy than I could ever have envisaged: only with her can I turn to the future.

Chapter 6 draws in part on an article 'Consensus to Contestation: Reconfiguring Democratic Representation in the European Union in the light of Nineteenth-Century Democratization', published in the journal *Democratization*, 15 (1), 2008. This material is reprinted by permission of Taylor & Francis Ltd.

Introduction: Questioning What Makes the EU Viable

Unity impossible, collapse improbable
Timothy Garton Ash (2001)

The *sui generis* interpretation dominant in mainstream European Union studies is often accompanied by a blithe assumption that the European Union (hereafter, the EU) has the political wherewithal and willpower to keep its show on the road.[1] Hailed as unique among international treaty organizations, it has even been described by one recent commentator as the embodiment of a 'new European Dream' that 'dares to suggest a new history, with an attention to quality of life, sustainability, and peace and harmony' (Rifkin, 2004: 6).[2] If deficiencies or deficits are identified in this polity, then it is usual to think there is an institutional solution: increasing the power of the European Parliament, turning the Council into a second parliamentary chamber, having a directly elected Commission president and so forth (Sidjanski, 1992: 436–8; Dehousse, 1997; van Gerven, 2005: 375–84). But whereas studies of the 'democratic deficit' reproduce these familiar, pious suggestions for improving the EU's democratic credentials they shy away from discussing what impact they might have on the stability of EU politics. This book is precisely an attempt to assess the effects of institutional change, proposed for the sake of democratization, by identifying what makes the EU viable. In particular, the aim is to scrutinize how the EU political system has resolved various existential crises as the basis for examining what potential there is for greater centralization, in the name of democracy, of competences and representation at the EU-level. Furthermore, and more unusually, it is claimed that the best way of learning about EU viability is by contrast with the experience of political conflict between federal and state authority in the antebellum US.

There are very good reasons why the viability of the EU should be questioned. Most generally, federalism, of which the EU is a 'species' as David McKay (2001) puts it, is not considered a 'notably successful governmental form' (Filippov et al., 2004: 3). In 1991, a study of political stability in federal systems emphasized the 'glaring fact that twenty-seven of the forty-four federations formed in the past two hundred or so years have failed either by breaking apart or by becoming fully centralised, unitary states' (Lemco, 1991: 1). At the same time, the modern United States, the paragon of federal studies, has recently been described by a theorist of federalism as 'a significantly decentralised unitary state' (Chopin, 2002: 35), while a leading historian of American federalism has declared that what the founding fathers invented 'no longer exists on its native shores' (McDonald, 1988: 206). Moreover, the Belgian state, often regarded as an exemplar of successful 'holding together' federalism (Stepan, 1999), teeters on the brink of secessionary crisis. In the specific case of the EU, moreover, there exist evident tensions between and within the member states over a multitude of European issues and policy debates: institutional reform, budget negotiations, the transatlantic relationship and the question of Turkish accession. Lurching from one crisis to the next is a European speciality, complete with frantic, all-night negotiations and indecorous histrionics by heads of state. Despite the momentum of post-Cold War reconciliation, the constant economic impetus for integration and the vast amounts of goodwill among Europe's political elite, the bundle of problems facing the contemporary EU is sufficient to call into question its capacity for self-sustainability as well as for transformative change.

Although European integration has recently undergone its longest ever sustained period of soul-searching for a new institutional order – a process begun in 2001 with the flawed Nice Treaty and culminating with the inconclusive Treaty of Lisbon – the viability of European integration and the resulting EU political order remains chronically undertheorized.[3] The best explanation for this state of affairs is the prevailing uncertainty over what exactly it is that needs to be explained about European integration (Hooghe and Marks, 2008: 108). This is largely a disciplinary problem as international relations scholars focus on explaining why and how European states are integrating (Pollack, 2001), while comparative politics conducts a lively debate over how best to conceptualize the EU polity itself as a preliminary for comparison (Bogaards, 2002; Schmidt, 2006).

Where these two disciplines have tended to merge of late when studying European integration, however, is in the burgeoning use of transatlantic

EU/US comparisons to test theories of integration and policymaking or to understand convergences and divergences in democratic practices. The assumption common to these works is that regardless of the recurring claims of American exceptionalism or of the EU's *sui generis* nature, pursuing a transatlantic analogy furthers the understanding of both political systems. The analysis of the EU's viability developed in this study shares this basic assumption. Yet the aim of this book is not merely to add nuance to EU/US comparisons. Rather, the ambition is to use the US antebellum experience as a foil to address the hitherto underexplored question of what makes the EU viable as a polity. So far, the travails of US political development from the constitutional founding to the victory of the union in the Civil War have barely featured in comparative analyses of European integration.[4]

This oversight is all the more surprising in view of the rediscovery by international relations (IR) scholars of the importance of the antebellum period for modern international political thought and as a unique experiment in a states-union (Onuf and Onuf, 1993, 2006; Deudney, 1995; Hendrickson, 2003; Silverstone, 2004). This body of work signals a radical shift away from the facile assumption that the US republic merely constituted a new unit – a state, albeit federal, like any other – in the competitive system of prevailing international anarchy. Instead, these authors highlight the extent to which the original federal union, described as a 'compound republic' by James Madison, was a daring political experiment intended to function as a peace pact between the states and regional sections whereby the union would also protect each unit from the depredations of foreign powers. Nothing was set in stone about the success of this project. Ultimately the project failed although the federal republic survived, albeit in a fundamentally altered form.

Since the EU is another example of a compound polity (Fabbrini, 2001, 2003, 2005c, 2007b; Schmidt, 2006) or states-union (Deudney, 1995; cf. Forysth, 1981) it becomes clear why a contrast between the antebellum experience and the European integration process is considered such a promising avenue for understanding EU viability. Indeed, the central premise of this book is that only this comparative gambit makes possible a conceptually rigorous and analytically well-grounded theory of what makes the EU viable and what transformative change – relating to both institutions and norms – might jeopardize its viability. Nevertheless it is no easy task to compare two historical cases that are typically considered exceptional both in the academic literature and in the respective polities' self-understanding. In order to accomplish such a task, therefore, this book analyses the relation of the parts (the territorial units) to the whole (the states-union) in both compound polities as demonstrated by conflict over what is termed the 'rules of the game of politics'. This struggle is considered to be the defining characteristic of polities like the EU and the antebellum US that compound identities, competences, institutions and principles of political representation. Consequently, the adoption of this framework for understanding political conflict also reflects a decision to eschew the traditional language of comparative federalism. The analysis of viability in terms of the rules of the game of politics, it is claimed, provides a better way of capturing the complex process of *becoming* a polity. This is especially true in the context of territorial expansion, a fundamental feature of both the EU and the antebellum US; modern Switzerland, which shares certain compound features (Fabbrini, 2005c) but without the politics of territorial expansion, is thus not considered a pertinent unit of comparison here.

The rules of the game are fourfold. They consist of institutional competences, expectations about the union, competency over competences and the appropriate basis of political representation. It is this conceptual framework of the four contested rules of the game that is used to compare the evolving relationship between the union and the constituent units in the US and European contexts. However, to explore the conflict over these four dimensions of the rules of the game necessarily entails a disregard for certain constrictions imposed by disciplinary boundaries. The argument thus rests on an interdisciplinary approach, incorporating IR theory, comparative politics and historical analysis, to provide a theoretically rigorous and empirically rich explanation of the differing problems of viability in the EU and the antebellum US.

Viability is a particularly vexing question in a compound polity like the EU, which is characterized by multiple question marks over its competences, membership, legitimacy and ability to represent citizens democratically. It is this nexus of unsolved issues that is conceptualized in Chapter 1 as a contest over the rules of the game of integration politics on which the fate of EU viability rests. Hence in this book the search for what makes the EU viable does not relate to what it means for the EU to be effective as a policymaker. Rather, viability refers to one of two processes. The ability to sustain what is defined as a 'dynamic equilibrium', in which the contest over the rules of the game is managed but never transcended.[5] Or, alternatively, viability entails 'voluntary centralization', whereby contestation over the rules of the game recedes as member states acquiesce – typical for the sake of democracy – to pool more political representation and powers of decision making at the centre.

Chapter 2 discusses the growing attraction of transatlantic comparison and situates the viability argument in relation to developments in EU scholarship. It shows how existing comparative studies have failed to acknowledge the significance of antebellum political conflict and its consequences for the US compound polity. This lacuna and certain shortcomings in the theoretical approaches used to study European integration are identified as the reason why so little is known about what makes the EU viable. To overcome this neglect, an indirect analogical comparison exploring how the rules of the game were contested and managed in the early American republic and the EU is offered as a productive way of generating insights into the viability of compound polities or states-unions. Chapter 3 unfolds the preliminary contextual analysis of the EU and antebellum US before outlining how the rules of the game of politics have been contested in both. The chapter ends with a presentation of five crucial political-structural differences between the EU and US compound systems, which forms the basis for the analogical analysis concerning how the rules of the game were contested in both. These differences are called political-structural because they relate to contrasting institutional arrangements as well as variance in what is probably best described as the respective political culture[6] – the political objectives behind the project of union and cleavages between the units – of each compound system.

Chapter 4 provides a detailed analysis of how exactly the struggle over the rules of the game has taken place in the course of European integration. It reveals how the EU has adhered strictly to a model of dynamic equilibrium whereby the acute tensions over what the EU should do and how it should work have been left unresolved. Chapter 5 carries out a systematic comparison of the five differences in how the rules of the game are contested in the US and EU and what this means for the viability of the respective compound polities. This analysis demonstrates that while Jacksonian democratization led to a voluntary centralization of political life, the antebellum US experienced great difficulties in maintaining a dynamic equilibrium over slavery, an issue that could not be dismissed since territorial expansion kept it at the forefront of federal politics. Hence the centralization of political representation, as changing electoral processes allowed federal institutions – especially the President – to make a stronger claim to represent citizens, was not a sufficient condition for overcoming conflict over the rules of the game of politics.

Chapter 6, the final analytical chapter, therefore, returns to the problem of viability but with a focus on what the EU/antebellum comparison reveals about managing changes in the nature of political representation, which the democratic deficit literature identifies as the cornerstone for democratization. Democratic representation is the fundamental problem of compound polities given the need to balance the representation of component units as well as of individual citizens. In this context, the US experience is vital for understanding the threat that changes to the system of dual representation pose in the EU. The travails of the antebellum suggest that enhancing the representation of individual citizens at the expense of states is no means of solving acute cleavages concerning the objectives of political union and the amount of competences it should be granted. Indeed the prospect of greater majoritarianism in the US led to calls for the establishment of new state controls over the conduct of federal politics, a move that should thus also be expected in the EU context. By showing, finally, how difficult it is to change dramatically the goals of European integration the study argues that it is difficult to hold a sanguine expectation of voluntary centralization in Europe.

1
The Problem of Viability in a Compound Polity

> *The most unambiguous signs are now being overlooked, or arbitrarily and lyingly misinterpreted, which declare that Europe wants to become one.*
>
> Nietzsche (1990: 189)

1.1 Introduction

Viability, in its most basic sense, means the ability to exist or more specifically to survive in a particular place. As a theoretical concept it is more commonly used in economics, usually as a synonym for feasibility, than in political science. In the latter discipline it is applied to understand transition states, new political entities (such as the 'Palestinian state') or even putative states such as certain regions in Europe (Jolly, 2007), as well as for analyses of various public policies. In these types of studies, the concept is ordinarily used in a common sense way based on an analytical assessment of the effectiveness, efficiency and legitimacy of the state or policy under review. A far more specialized use of the concept exists in rational choice institutionalism, where it is applied to discover the supposed conditions for a 'viable constitution'. According to this model, as David McKay (2004: 24) explains, it is assumed that viability 'depends on the ways in which particular constitutional and institutional arrangements provide elites with incentives to stick to the rules of the game'. Finally, there exists a much grander approach that considers societal or civilization survival itself, interpreting the fate of disappeared civilizations as tragedies stemming, at least to some extent, from weaknesses of perception, action or responsibility (Diamond, 2004).

Not wanting to pursue a universalizing strategy, one that 'aims to establish that every instance of a phenomenon follows essentially the same rule' (Tilly, 1984: 82), this study does not seek to match the ambition of identifying the requirements for a viable society per se, valid throughout time. However, a common sense and unspecified understanding of viability – the blunt tool of what could be called the 'unconscious thinker' – is not appropriate for the present study either. In this book, therefore, the concept of viability is used as a Weberian ideal-type, that is, not a pure description of historical reality but 'a limiting concept with which the real situation or action is *compared* and surveyed for the explanation of certain of its significant components' (Davis, 2005: 79). This serves to underscore why a comparative perspective is used to evaluate the question of EU viability. Following James Davis, the heuristic interest of the ideal-typical approach is to explain 'why a particular historical instance was *so* and not *otherwise*' (ibid., p. 80). This means the analysis in the present study is firstly interested in how the antebellum US compound republic[1] tried to manage its endogenous political tensions and why, ultimately, it failed. The viability of the EU will be discussed, secondly, in the light of this answer, namely, if and how the EU faces similar or contrasting problems and whether it has the same or alternative means of resolving them. First, however, it is necessary to define the concept of viability as used here in relation to the conflict over the rules of the game of politics. It is this conflict that is characteristic of the EU and the antebellum US compound polities.

1.2 Viability as defined in relation to the 'Rules of the Game' of politics

In political science it is conventional to define the state analytically in terms of territory, institutions and the monopoly of legitimate violence.[2] These three facets are then used to explain the sovereign quality that is specific to the modern state: in the final analysis sovereignty equates to coercive power. But this is perhaps one of the least interesting ways of understanding the business of government; for the use of coercion is so slight in actual political practice.[3] This is of course far truer of democracies than absolutist regimes. Nonetheless as Montesquieu realized, despotism relies on the principle of fear to govern and thus it can be sufficient to use only infrequent yet symbolic brutal coercion.[4]

The fact then that political authority, as the French nineteenth-century liberal François Guizot recognized,[5] is not constituted by coercion alone means that we must look elsewhere to appreciate both why states manage to govern with minimal coercion and why sometimes this arrangement breaks down. Essentially, this means understanding why the modern democratic state is not Hobbesian. The 'beast of Malmesbury' considered the existence of a supremely powerful sovereign 'to be logically necessary in order to structure individual expectations so that contracts would be kept' (Kratochwil, 1978: 50). Thus Hobbes clearly appreciated the structuring power of expectations, which enables the symbolic and well chosen use of force to generate prudential obedience. But his model of political order as something that stems from prudential compliance generated by legal sanctions containing the threat of physical consequences is inadequate for two reasons. Firstly, because law itself cannot be equated simply to a sanction that follows a command: 'emphasis on the "legitimate" use of force, even on the part of convinced "command theorists"', as a leading international relations theorist explains, 'demonstrates that the instrumentalities of coercion cannot serve as the sole criterion of law' (ibid., p. 17). Secondly, and this is David Hume's argument, Hobbes overlooks the fact that there are other proxies for generating the expectation that contracts will be kept. As Kratochwil sums up the point, 'conventions arising out of interactions that prove mutually beneficial can structure expectations and thus allow participants to overcome the posed dilemma' (ibid.).

Discovering more about how expectations are generated without coercion is made much easier if the fetishism of sovereignty, which suggests that a limpid vertical organization of power is a precondition for successful political organization, is abandoned (see section 1.4). It is commonly assumed that sovereignty is indivisible and that in any polity there has to be an institution able to claim ultimate political authority. By implication, indivisibility also means that confederation (a compact between states, *Staatenbund*) and federation (one state with units of greater or lesser autonomy, *Bundestaat*) are mutually exclusive categories: 'there can be nothing in between' (N. Onuf, 1991: 432). Nevertheless the EU seems to be precisely the 'in-between order' (Wind, 2001: 103) that undermines such peremptory statements about the nature of sovereignty. This explains the inherent difficulties of comparing the EU with federal states that are clearly sovereign in international politics, hence the resort to neologisms such as 'economic confederation' (Forsyth, 1981), 'confederal consociation' (Chryssochoou, 1994) or 'inter-state consociation' (Costa and Magnette, 2003). Ultimately this vocabulary serves to reinforce the *sui generis* interpretation of the EU, which the analysis in this study seeks to avoid. As a third category between confederation and federation the EU also confounds traditional international relations theory, which posits an antinomy between anarchy and hierarchy to explain the distinction between international and domestic politics (Waltz, 1979).

To avoid making viability dependent on the concept of a sovereign state and the associated binary opposition between confederation and federal state, therefore, in this book the notion of the "rules of the game" provides the parameters for understanding viability. This theoretical move accomplishes two objectives. On the one hand, it gainsays the assumption that polities are only viable if they have a fixed locus for the monopoly of coercion. On the other hand, it establishes that the issue of sovereignty, while a vital part of political contestation in a compound polity, is meaningful only in relation to the broader game of politics and thus not by itself a precondition of viability.

First, however, it is necessary to specify the nature of political conflict, which is usually conceptualized in a twofold fashion: internal and external, albeit with fuzzy boundaries between them. This study argues that the early US republic and the contemporary EU exist in very similar contexts both internally and externally. In terms of the relations between the units, the goal is to maintain a democratic union free from coercive centralization and avoid disintegration. To reprise the language of comparative federalism, the EU and the antebellum US are engaged in 'holding together' as much as 'coming together' (Stepan, 1999), or to employ the neologism coined by Deudney, the units constitute a 'negarchy', a system designed to 'prevent simultaneously the emergence of hierarchy and anarchy' (Deudney, 1995: 208).[6] Furthermore, with the exception of their founding periods, they have both had to achieve this feat in the absence of a direct external security threat, which is generally considered the most effective and persuasive stimulus behind federation.[7]

This is not to say that either polity is entirely disentangled from security issues. The US had both European states and Native American tribes as potentially hostile neighbours and even became a peripheral zone of hostilities (between 1812 and 1814) within the European conflagration engendered by the French revolution.[8] In fact, the founding fathers were greatly preoccupied with America's place in the international system. One of the principal reasons for embarking upon 'a more perfect union' was precisely to strengthen America's role in international politics so as to hold more sway in matters of trade and to avoid the machinations of European monarchies (see 2.3). Modern Europe has also experienced the menace of a neighbouring hostile power and during the Cold War European Economic Community (hereafter, EEC) member states had to negotiate a position vis à vis the two superpowers when the conflict became 'hot' in the so-called proxy wars. While in the immediate post-war period mutual defence against the Soviet Union was a headache for European states seeking to integrate, this particular preoccupation quickly abated as responsibility for security was transferred to NATO. Imminent security dilemmas have, therefore, not played a permanent or even telling part in the politics of both these compound unions. This is because in both cases – and unlike in the examples of union in Switzerland or the Netherlands (Goldstein, 2001) – neither faced direct and sustained threats to political independence or territorial predation. Hence, in this study, the factors explaining viability are endogenous, that is they pertain to relations between the units and not to how the units relate to the international system.[9]

In this context, I argue that functioning democracies face at least three types of political conflict that they have to manage or surmount in order to be considered viable. The first conflict concerns the agreement among elites and between these elites and citizens over 'the rules of the game' according to which politics is conducted: without this there is no political interaction. The second arena of contestation is the debate over the role of the state, that is, the scope of public intervention in economic freedom and personal liberty (Hix, 1999). Finally, although a less precise category, conflicts arise for practical and personal reasons over such things as perceived government effectiveness, confidence in leaders, judgements about personalities and so on.

This study focuses exclusively on the first type of conflict because the problem of agreeing to the 'rules of the game' is the problem par excellence of the compound republic. This is not only because such political systems are characterized by a dual horizontal (between the executive, legislative and judicial branches of the centre) and vertical (between the union and its units) separation of powers (Fabbrini and Sicurelli, 2004; Kelemen, 2004).[10] In addition, compound polities or states-unions are political projects for certain ends. Political conflict thus arises as a result of the complex interaction between levels of government and authority as well as over the ends of the political union itself – over what kind of polity it will become; the former is a feature of ordinary federal states but the latter is not.

A proper definition of the 'rules of the game' and the conflicts associated with them is a logical priority before specifying how and why certain disputes over the rules can or cannot be managed in a compound system. The game metaphor is popular among constructivist scholars in international relations because it reflects rather well the extent to which concepts do not correspond directly with 'observational facts' but are mutually constituted by reference to other concepts within the game-structure. In addition, this approach allows for a more nuanced understanding of rules in general than is possible if rules are taken to be synonymous only with commands or imperatives. What the game metaphor reveals then are the 'institutional facts'; the other concepts used within the practice of the game to give meaning to action and which help make it explicable. 'Threatening the king in a chess game by announcing "check"', the game Kratochwil uses to illustrate this point, 'means something only with reference to the underlying rules of the game. Thus, the meaning of the move and its explanation crucially depend upon the knowledge of the rule-structure' (Kratochwil, 1991: 26).

The importance of recognizing institutional facts is equally necessary in domestic politics. This is borne out in Edward Lehman's specification of the three elements taken to constitute the rules of political conduct: '(1) the actors who are the appropriate players in the political game, (2) the prerogatives of and limitations of officeholders, and (3) the rights "of one or more set of recognized leaders attempting to gain office"' (1992: 141). None is directly observable or autonomously defined: the 'appropriateness' of actors reflects existing political shibboleths subject to flux; prerogatives will depend on constitutional interpretation and precedent; gaining office is clearly a singular practice with obvious written rules like secret ballot provisions, voting eligibility, balloting times and a myriad unspoken norms such as what candidates can promise during campaigns or which public servants they can remove once in office. The conditions constituting democracy, therefore, can only be understood intersubjectively with reference to other concepts making up the practice that is democracy – a practice whose very meaning may also evolve precisely as a consequence of this intersubjective element (Collier and Levitsky, 1997).

For the purposes of this study it is preferable to use a more inclusive definition of the rules of the political game because of the weak and often constitutionally ambiguous institutionalization characteristic of the EU and the antebellum US. More so than in its member states, politics at the EU level is constituted by institutional facts – the rules of the game – of a less visible, less sedimented nature, ones that are most evident only in the practice of politics itself. The same is true of the early American union, which Tocqueville described, in a sentence from the original manuscript for *Democracy in America* omitted from eventual publication, as 'the Union is an almost perfect entity that is not easy to comprehend' (1990, vol. 1: 279).

The absence of many conventional attributes of nation-statehood like a fixed territory or national identity discomfits many students of the integration process. The result is a tendency to exaggerate the difference and novelty of EU politics in comparison with the experience of Europe's nation states. Indeed, the supposed discontinuity between the formation of nation states and the integration process is sometimes viewed as the EU's most valuable asset because novelty and difference are thought to constitute a *Sonderweg* (peculiar path) allowing Europe to find innovative ways of overcoming crises and avoiding the traditional disputes dominant in its member states. The viability of the European polity is explained by virtue of this *Sonderweg*. Joseph Weiler argues that the principle of 'constitutional tolerance' characterizes Europe's unique political identity, so different from a 'normal' democracy – as practised in nation states – where,

> [a] majority demanding obedience from a minority which does not regard itself as belonging to the same people is usually regarded as subjection. And yet, in the [European] Community, we subject the European people to constitutional discipline even though the European polity is composed of distinct people. It is a remarkable instance of civic tolerance to accept to be bound by precepts articulated not by 'my people' but by a community composed of distinct political communities: a people, if you wish, of others. I compromise my self-determination in this fashion as an expression of this kind of internal – towards myself – and external – towards others – tolerance.
>
> (2001: 67–8)

By defining the central problem of EU politics as one of finding an agreement over the rules of the game and by understanding how this is affected by the compound structure of the political system it is possible to analyse viability as well as to set aside these Panglossian assumptions. To do this, the rules of the game, as illustrated in Table 1.1, are taken in a broad sense to refer to an agreement to be bound by certain decision-making institutions as well as less tangible norms that cannot be so readily institutionalized. These latter norms include the shared understanding over where competency over competences stands; expectations about the project of union; and finally, the agreed relationship between the two competing principles of representation, the (federal) representation of individuals *qua* citizens of the union and the (confederal) representation of individuals *qua* citizens of a territorial unit.[11] Hence rules of the game such as expectations about the union and the

Table 1.1 The four contested rules of the game in a compound polity

Rules of the game of politics	Subject of contestation
Institutional competences	What are the respective decision-making powers of the union's legislative, executive and judicial branches?
Expectations about the Union	What is the nature of the union and the project that unites its members?
Competency over competences	Where does the power to determine competency over competences reside?
Representation	What is the relationship between the representation of individuals *qua* citizens of the union and the representation of individuals *qua* citizens of a territorial unit?

agreed relationship between antagonistic systems of representation may well remain tacit in run-of-the-mill European or early-American politics and yet frame the discourse of political contestation in more fraught moments. The game metaphor thus takes seriously the problem of arguments and identities in political life, especially the self-description of polities, rather than reducing politics to a technical question of distributing scarce resources, effective policymaking or managing the conflict between rational yet divergent interests. (see Table 1.1)

Conflict arises when one of the above four elements constituting the rules of the game is in dispute. Three examples will suffice to illustrate how these conflicts arise and the form they take. Firstly, the US sovereignty debate that preceded the Civil War was a classic example of the struggle to identify who had the ultimate authority to determine competency over competences as well as to define the nature of the political bond between the states. Was the union indissoluble or was it a compact? If only a compact, who had the right to judge whether its terms had been broken? An instructive example, secondly, of how an institutional crisis can create new expectations is the infamous 'empty chair crisis'. This took the form of an institutional conflict – France's refusal to participate in Council meetings and the wrangle over farm subsidies – but was largely a debate over norms and expectations as de Gaulle refused to accept EEC competency except through unanimity. The solution was not to redesign institutions or put in place a new policy but the establishment of a new norm, which became known as the Luxembourg Compromise: 'when very important issues are at stake, discussions must be continued until unanimous agreement is reached'. This cannot be found in the parchment of the treaties and yet it is still a rule that guides the way actors play the game, notably by creating new expectations about the process of future decision making. Finally, perhaps the best recent example of the clash between competing principles of representation is the debacle of the defunct Constitutional Treaty and its successor the Lisbon Treaty. The failed referendums on both treaties posed, as never before, the problem of whether the arduous process of treaty revision, to which a vast majority of member states is favourable, could be unravelled by citizens in only one or two countries. Indeed, similar disputes, discussed in detail in chapters 3 and 5, arose in the antebellum US when states attempted to invoke popular sovereignty at the state level to nullify federal legislation.

1.3 Scenarios of viability in a compound polity

If it is not to disintegrate, therefore, a compound political system faced with this inherent conflict over the rules of the game has to respond in one of three ways.[12] Firstly, the response can be *coercive centralization* through the threat or actual use of force against a member state to enforce the primacy of the union and/or to prevent secession and the use of economic or political sanctions to do likewise. Secondly, the response can be non-coercive or *voluntary centralization* through one or more of the following systemic changes: the explicit transfer of competences to the union, an agreement to allow the union to exercise competency over competences, the redefinition of the nature of the union and its objectives to extend its purview and the strengthening of the principle of the representation of individuals *qua* citizens of the union at the expense of territorial representation. Thirdly, and finally, conflict can be resolved through a *dynamic equilibrium* that tries to reinvent the rules of the game in a sufficiently ambiguous fashion so as to create new anti-majoritarian safeguards when delegating more competences to the union, avoid specifying where competency over competences lies, leave the objectives of union unchanged by keeping certain questions off the table and maintain the balance between confederal and federal principles of representation.

The very purpose of founding a compound system in the early US and the EU is to prevent coercive centralization. This means the definition of viability in a compound system needs further refinement: it is conditional on having the ability to overcome, or manage, without recourse to coercion, its inevitable tensions. Alexander Hamilton began *The Federalist* by asking whether mankind was 'forever destined to depend for [its] political constitutions on accident and force' (Hamilton et al., 2003: 1).

In the same vein, this study wants to analyse the EU's viability in terms of the possibilities for sustaining itself or centralizing through compromise and consensus rather than the largely unknowable variables of accident (external shocks) and force (coercive centralization). For as the great nineteenth-century British liberal Walter Bagehot remarked, 'in politics we must not trouble ourselves with exceedingly exceptional accidents; it is quite difficult enough to count on and provide for the regular and plain possibilities' (1963: 285). Moreover, in the history of European integration significant steps in the process, such as the creation of monetary union or a common foreign policy, have not been the product of extreme catastrophes; there is no place here for an apocalyptic vision of conditions necessary for a viable European polity.

As discussed earlier, this study incorporates both institutional and non-institutional factors in the analysis of viability, which explains the choice of a detailed contextual examination of two similar cases. This kind of approach thus requires a more detailed *ex ante* outline of how and why scenarios of viability for compound systems differ.

The scenario of voluntary centralization is more difficult to identify than that relying on coercion. Increasing centralization is most visible in the realm of constitutional politics, where it is the product of three factors: constitutional interpretation by legal as well as political actors, statute law and a certain discretionary element in the form of the conventional understanding of competences and procedures or, in pithier terms, amendment, interpretation and usage (Bryce, 1995; vol. 1: 322–3). Beyond constitutional politics, centralization may also take place through the establishment of new political institutions, such as political parties or voting procedures, which favour the representation of individuals at the expense of the representation of the constituent units.

Gauging or measuring centralization in both a compound and a federal system is eminently possible (McKay, 2001). Various options include measuring the proportion of the budget spent by different levels of government (Pollack, 1994), legal resistance among the units to competences exercised by the centre (Goldstein, 2001) or evolution in the allocation of competences (Donahue and Pollack, 2001). What this kind of approach does not reveal, however, is the nature of the political debate that surrounds this change in the relationship between units and union: how they were justified and interpreted and what consequences this had for expectations about the future. Thus Leslie Goldstein's (2001) study of legal resistance to central authority in the antebellum US and in the European integration process revealed that the US states proved more obstreperous in their defiance of federal legal authority than the six founding EEC states did in relation to the European Court of Justice (hereafter, ECJ). But the principal weakness of this so-called member-state resistance paradox argument is that it fails to include the alternative methods whereby member states can constrict and discipline integrationist ambitions; as the analysis in Chapter 4 of disputes over the rules of the game will show, overt resistance by constitutional courts is only a small part of the *rapport de forces* between pro- and anti-integrationists.

Similarly, a constitution by itself is not a straightforward list of rules to govern, a moral textbook setting out how decisions ought to be made or a compilation of objectives to pursue. It is difficult to measure what constitutions 'do' for even their political objectives are not self-evident because sometimes they are framed not simply to achieve some goal but to prevent something happening or being discussed (Holmes, 1988). In the latter instance this is only meaningful in context. Historical experience suggests that constitutions are a *genre* of political writing or speech acts that are often intended to function negatively (to prevent something happening) as much as positively. Thus the American constitution was obsessed with finding a way of neutralizing conflict over the slave issue as well as avoiding all mention of who or what is to be sovereign – it is implicitly the constitution itself that is sovereign – to deny any one actor the right to make a claim against this settlement. More recently, the German *Grundgesetz* ('Basic Law') was framed to avoid any possible return to fascism while the French Fifth Republic sought to put an end to political instability by reinforcing the office of president.

To circumvent these problems, voluntary centralization will be understood in this study as changes to the rules of the game – due to formal amendment, convention, usage or institutional innovation – that allow the union to preponderate over the units either through an expansion of competences, the ability to adjudicate ultimately all competence clashes, increased expectations about the purview of political union or an enhanced ability to represent citizens at the expense of territorial representation.[13] These changes will be considered voluntary to the extent that the democratic constituent units have in some way acquiesced – or at least not objected to them – through their participation in constitutional politics.

Conversely, sustaining a dynamic equilibrium between the union and its units is a process of 'muddling on', whereby acute contestation over the rules of the game leads to a redefinition of the relationship between units and centre with only a minimalist transference to or creation of power at the compound centre, as illustrated in Table 1.2. It is a dynamic process precisely because it does not sanctify and seek to preserve the

18   What Makes the EU Viable?

Table 1.2 Defining voluntary centralization and dynamic equilibrium in relation to changes in the rules of the game

Rules of the game	Changes amounting to voluntary centralization	Changes amounting to dynamic equilibrium
Institutional competences	Explicit transfer of competences to the union's branches of government.	Creating new anti-majoritarian safeguards each time new competences are delegated.
Expectations about the union	Redefining the nature and objectives of the union to extend its purview.	Leaving the objectives of the union ambiguous by keeping certain policy questions off the table.
Competency over competences	Agreement to allow the union to exercise competency over competences.	Leaving the location of competency over competences unspecified.
Representation	Strengthening the representation of individuals *qua* citizens of the union at the expense of territorial representation.	Maintaining the balance between confederal and federal principles of representation.

status quo, favouring instead a recalibration of the rules of the game. Redefining or reinventing the equilibrium as opposed to centralizing is less the case of the union being unable to create new competences per se. Rather, it is taken to mean primarily a process whereby the compound union can only grant itself new competences or takeover the prerogatives of its members by appeasing the constituent units. This is achieved by granting new safeguards to frustrate action by the centre or by more integrationist constituent units (veto power), by allowing exemptions from certain areas of legislation (opt-outs, opt-ins, abstentions) or else by keeping intractable problems off the reform agenda.[14] Perhaps the most obvious difference, therefore, when comparing dynamic equilibrium with voluntary centralization is that in the former case the union will continue to struggle to claim and exercise competency over competences. In fact, the very locus of sovereignty will remain undefined. Moreover, in a logic of dynamic equilibrium, the delicate act of balancing the representation of states and citizens will continue whereas under voluntary centralization the representation of citizens *qua* citizens of the union will prevail over territorial representation.

The use of a theoretical framework that explains how compound political systems follow one of two scenarios of viability is intended to show how these systems can cope with changes in the rules of the game. Hence this approach departs from the traditional fashion in which the future evolution of the EU polity is understood in political theory. For nearly 30 years the fundamental political problem of European integration has been understood in terms of a 'democratic deficit' (Marquand, 1979). The EU is said to lack a meaningful element of democratic participation by citizens, poor accountability given the feebleness of the parliament and the absence of a pan-European public sphere. Thus the basic argument is that a more integrated EU will survive or fail according to whether or not democratic legitimacy can be established beyond the boundaries of the nation state. Consequently, the three most widespread answers to this question are concerned with whether it is conceptually plausible for democracy to transcend the nation state or whether non-electoral proxies for democratic legitimacy can legitimate a polity in the eyes of its citizens. The 'no-demos' position suggests the political bond is derived from a cultural-linguistic bond that by definition cannot be pan-European (Preuss, 1995; Miller, 2000), making the notion of a more integrated and democratic EU a very moot point. 'Post-national' theory claims that an abstract 'constitutional patriotism' can replace shared nationality in the creation of a political community, which in this case will span national boundaries (Lacroix, 2002; C. Cronin, 2003). Finally, the theory of 'output legitimacy' argues that a European polity can be constituted by the positive results of its governance regime (Scharpf, 1999).

In other words, these three responses to democratic deficit anxiety do not provide much guidance for understanding what effect institutional reforms typically discussed at times of treaty revision – chiefly greater EU competences and more supranational representation – will have upon the EU system. In addition, democracy itself remains a contested concept liable to be stretched and distorted (Collier and Levitsky, 1997), making it an unreliable yardstick for judging the viability of further integration.[15] This explains why this book proposes to shift the understanding of whether more EU integration is possible away from the argument, which will remain unresolved as long as the ontology of democracy is questioned, of whether the EU can overcome its democratic deficit. Instead, the argument developed here conceptualizes the EU as a compound polity where the rules of the game are contested by elites and institutions at the union level as well as at the unit level and, more rarely, by citizens exercising popular sovereignty. In this way, the analysis, drawing on a comparison with the US antebellum experience of this same kind of political contestation, can demonstrate the extent to which the EU can respond to the struggle over the rules of the game either through dynamic equilibrium or else voluntary centralization.

However, this book does not merely go against the grain of contemporary political theory's engagement with the EU. The treatment of the EU as a compound polity subject to acute contestation over the rules of the game also differs significantly from the way in which the EU is analysed in comparative federalism. The task of the following section, therefore, is to specify in more detail the concept of the compound polity and to justify the analogy with the antebellum in relation to certain shortcomings of the comparative study of federal systems. In particular, it is the way that the rules-of-the-game framework enables a deeper probing of the problem sovereignty poses in such a polity that vindicates this conceptual gambit. This is because sovereignty claims on the part of the units and the union alike are not just a matter of the institutional allocation of competences or of determining where *Kompetenz-Kompetenz* lies. The issue of fragmented political authority – *imperium in imperio* – is only part of the reason why the rules of the game are so contested. Sovereignty also constitutes an expectation about the nature of the political union as well as being, in the form of popular sovereignty, a crucial factor affecting the nature of political representation. It is precisely, as explained in the final section of the chapter, the two latter elements that comparative federalism struggles to take account of when analysing the EU, thereby compromising its ability to understand what makes the EU viable.

1.4 The theory of the compound polity and the issue of the units' sovereign status

In the history of political thought, the term 'compound republic' was first used by James Madison to describe the novel political structure that was intended to replace the grossly deficient Articles of Confederation (1781–9), which had hitherto bound the 13 former British colonies in America. According to Madison, the new constitution established a compound republic because it alloyed 'national' (that is central) government with 'federal' (state) government. As he explained in Federalist 39, 'the proposed constitution therefore is in strictness neither a national nor a federal constitution; but a composition of both' (Hamilton et al., 2003: 187). The union was also a compound of two different forms of political representation as both the state and the union had a claim to represent citizens; in addition, the bicameral legislature of the federal government combined both representation of the states and of the aggregate people. Thus the double vertical and horizontal system of separation of powers was precisely a product of establishing political institutions on the basis of a dual system of representation. The new admixture, however, was not fancied to be naturally harmonious, as Madison clearly saw that the states would often have a key political advantage that could frustrate the wishes of the national government:

> The State government will have the advantage of the Federal government, whether we compare them in respect to the immediate dependence of the one on the other; to the weight of personal influence which each side will possess; to the powers respectively vested in them; to the predilection and probable support of the people; to the disposition and faculty of resisting and frustrating the measures of each other. The State governments may be regarded as constituent and essential parts of the federal government; while the latter is nowise essential to the operation or organization of the former.
>
> (ibid., p. 225)

His fellow Federalist author Alexander Hamilton expressed even graver misgivings during the debates on the constitution at the Philadelphia convention. At the conclusion of the convention, he conjectured that in the absence of a strong and visionary administration, which could 'triumph over the state governments and reduce them to an entire subordination ... it is probable that the contests about the boundaries of power between the particular governments and the general government and the momentum of the larger states in such contests will produce a dissolution of the Union' (Hamilton, 1993: 11). These fears were a testimony to the fact that the compound mixture was not the product of the search for a perfect system but born of a skilful compromise designed to reconcile the more extreme proponents of national government with the intransigent advocates of states' rights: *mater artium necessitas*.

Indeed, even before the Constitutional Convention had met, in a letter to his friend Edmund Randolph dated 8 April 1787, Madison had explained the inevitability of such a compromise:

> I hold it for a fundamental point that an individual independence of the States is utterly irreconcilable with the idea of an aggregate sovereignty. I think, at the same time, that a consolidation of the States into one simple republic is not less unattainable than it would be inexpedient. Let it be tried then, whether any middle ground can be taken, which will at once support a due supremacy of the national authority, and leave in force the local authorities so far as they can be subordinately useful.
>
> (Madison, 1840, vol. 2: 631–2)

Yet Tocqueville realized that in the resulting constitutional middle ground there was an inherent political tension that ought not to be misconstrued as the relatively simple task of settling the boundaries between the union and the states. The divergent pull of competing identities, the protracted arguments over the locus of sovereignty and the expectations about the taboo areas beyond the pale of federal authority explained why the early republic was convulsed by vivacious and permanent political dispute. Tocqueville insisted that it was necessary to think of the American union as founded on an *abstract idea* (Maletz, 1998). He sensed that even if the US constitution had effectively sidestepped the thorny issue of settling the boundaries of a divided sovereignty and spelling out the highest authority by introducing constitutional ambiguity – what Bruce Ackerman (2005) calls the 'grand abstractions and cryptic formulae' – over which branch of government could do what, there remained a serious tension within the unified body politic.

The deliberately ambiguous constitutional allocation of powers thus gave rise to a protracted political struggle over the balance between state and national government. Tocqueville took this to be symptomatic of 'the great struggle which is going on in America between the states and the central power, between the spirit of democratic independence and that of a proper distribution and subordination of power' (Tocqueville, 1994: 410). The antagonism between the two fundamental principles for allocating powers – the states' retention of all non-enumerated powers (the tenth amendment)[16] and the federal government's supremacy (article six)[17] and right to make all laws necessary for the preservation of the union[18] – was at the heart of the union's politics until the North's victory in the Civil War. As the comparative scholar of federalism David McKay has put it, 'this tension between nationalism and state sovereignty dominated political discourse' (2001: 27).

But it would be misleading to interpret the political cleavage in a compound republic as merely that of competing sovereignties – the *imperium in imperio* the 'anti-federalists'[19] had railed against – because this model of political contestation suggests the possibility of a simple legal or constitutional settlement to the question of who is sovereign. From the outset, the US constitution was notorious for not specifying a single locus of sovereignty in the classic sense of ultimate and indivisible political authority. As Walter Bagehot put it, the American founding fathers purposefully 'shrank from placing the sovereign power anywhere' (1963: 218). The resulting 'dual federalism' (Corwin, 1934), establishing two distinct and in theory autonomous levels of political authority, created plenty of scope for jurisdictional conflict.

Comparative federalism has traditionally interpreted conflict concerning competences claimed by both the states and the federal government as a clash over demarcating the boundaries of the vertical separation of powers, a clash supposed to continue unchanged to this day (Goldstein, 2001; Kelemen, 2004). Yet a more recent strand of republican scholarship on the antebellum period presents the tussle over state sovereignty in the antebellum as a republican debate about the appropriate relationship of the people to their various governments (Deudney, 1995; Fritz, 2008). Thus whereas studies of federalism concentrate on the issue of divided sovereignty, republican theory is concerned with the problematic exercise of popular sovereignty – or the sovereignty of the people (Fritz, 2008). Given that a compound polity is 'a union of states and their citizens' (Fabbrini, 2007b: 3), the clash over the level at which popular sovereignty should be exercised is a fundamental cleavage affecting viability.

Until recently, comparisons with the US or other mature federal systems were not considered particularly apposite in EU studies. This initial reluctance has now receded because the EU is taken to be a sufficiently consolidated political system and so can be examined alongside other federal states (Howse and Nicolaïdis, 2001; Parsons, 2003; Kelemen, 2004; Menon and Schain, 2006). However, such comparisons highlight the common absence of an indivisible locus of sovereignty but neglect the issue of the sovereign status of the units in the EU and the antebellum US, an issue that ultimately relates to the question of the exercise of popular sovereignty. It is precisely this notion of sovereign status and its effect on viability that can be captured thanks to the framework provided by the rules of the game.

Instead of starting from the assumption that sovereignty is an indivisible whole, certain contemporary IR scholars claim that that sovereignty is better understood as 'a status, i.e., a legal standing, and thus a right to participate and engage in relations and to make agreements with other sovereign states' (Jackson, 1999: 453). More accurately, sovereignty is a claimed status, which serves 'to legitimize certain rights, duties and competences' (Werner and de Wilde, 2001: 297). Hence this conceptual move shifts the problematic state of sovereignty away from the preoccupation with the antinomy between indivisibility and fragmentation by suggesting that it is more important to appreciate what it means to make (and uphold) a successful claim to sovereign status. By definition, therefore, the successful status claim that constitutes sovereignty is above all relational: it depends on negotiating the claim to sovereign status in the face of 'audiences external and internal to the state' (ibid., p. 290).

From this perspective, what matters most for the politics of sovereignty in a non-unitary system is less dealing with competence clashes between levels of government than understanding the extent to which political units can 'rely on their sovereign status and whether relevant audiences accept their claims to sovereignty' (ibid., p. 304). In the republican tradition, the domestic audience is understood in terms of popular sovereignty (Morgan, 1988; Yack, 2001). But this same power or audience can be conceived as engaged (active) or recessed (passive), depending on whether the actual exercise of political authority is delegated or not (Deudney, 1995: 197–200). Only in the latter case, therefore, can popular sovereignty be represented by actors or institutions. Hence in anything besides a small democratic polity the politics of sovereignty is closely bound up with the mechanism of political representation, which negotiates a state's claim to sovereign status in the context of different audiences.

But in a compound polity, or states-union such as the one created at the Philadelphia convention, there is no single recessed popular sovereign to be represented (Fritz, 2008; cf. Schmitt, 1992) thereby allowing institutions and actors at both the unit and union level to invoke popular sovereignty to buttress their claims to sovereign status. Moreover, unlike in most federal states, the units in the original US federal union had a highly credible claim to the status of sovereignty both prior to and after the ratification of the US constitution (Van Tyne, 1907; McDonald, 2000). After all, the Treaty of Paris (1783) that ended hostilities with Britain recognized the former colonies as 'free, sovereign and independent states'. In terms of the rules of the game, therefore, sovereign status affects expectations about the nature of the political union and the structure of political representation, given the competing attempts to invoke popular sovereignty as both units and the union try to determine their respective sovereign status. Yet comparative federalism finds it difficult to incorporate these aspects of political contestation, as can be seen from attempts to conceptualize what the EU is by virtue of systematic comparisons with other polities exhibiting fragmented authority, whether confederations or federal systems.

1.5 Comparing the EU with other political systems

Although more than two decades ago the EEC was described as an 'economic confederation' (Forysth, 1981), the theory of confederalism has seldom been used effectively to understand the EU.[20] The contemporary preference, when using the traditional language of the state, has been to interpret the EU as a species of federalism in order to conduct comparisons with other federal systems. Recently, however, Giandomenico Majone has argued that the EU is best understood as a confederation, which is 'simply the extension of mixed government to the international level' (2006: 122). This implies that the EU is best understood in terms of its mixture and balance of different corporate bodies, whereby 'the overarching goal of this mode of governance is the defence and promotion of the interests of the component units rather than the protection of the rights and liberties of individuals' (ibid., p. 121).

Two important consequences flow from this mixture of corporate interests. Firstly, a differentiated mode of decision making according to policy field, as 'each subject matter has its own decision-making procedure according to the nature of the interest receiving special protection' (ibid., p. 128). Secondly, there is an immanent flaw in the policymaking process since previous experience of mixed government suggests that 'the corporate bodies constituting the mixed polity were less interested in making policy for the entire polity than in questions of privileges and rights' (ibid., p. 127).

Despite offering a nuanced and seductive interpretation of the integration process, Majone's theory of confederalism nonetheless overlooks the importance of sovereignty as a status and thus cannot account for certain fundamental features of conflict over the rules of the game in the EU. First of all, the identification of 'interests' as lying at the core of the EU political system neither explains how such interests are constituted in the first place nor how they come to be represented and hence protected and promoted. Ultimately, the principle of sovereignty as a negotiated status offers the best explanation for the configuration of EU architecture: the member states have an exclusive standing and right to participate in the EU system that derives from their sovereign status, notably a seat in the two principal decision-making bodies, the European Council and the Council of Ministers. In addition, they exclusively possess a set of rights, derived from the same source, notably veto powers in specific policy areas, for instance taxation, enlargement and treaty renegotiation, as well as *ad hoc* opt-outs from certain policies. This status thus clearly distinguishes the member states from mere regions, which are only offered a seat at the purely consultative Committee of the Regions. Indeed, the aim of regional separatism in Scotland or the Basque Country is precisely to accede to the sovereign status of member states.[21]

At the same time, however, the ECJ has effectively curtailed the set of rights that member states derive from their sovereign status, although obviously not the right to participate in decision making. Consequently, the EU is unquestionably no longer a pure confederation. As Majone recognizes, confederalism is premised on the fact that the unit of political representation is solely a collective one (i.e. a state, people, territory) and as such legal acts fall on those units in their 'corporate or collective capacities' (Hamilton et al., 2003: 67). This arrangement means that in a confederation individual citizens do not acquire rights against states. Yet by developing the doctrine of direct effect, which rules that European legislation creates legally binding obligations that are justiciable in member state courts, the ECJ has changed the rights associated with sovereign status (Stone Sweet, 2005). Hence it is the direct effect principle, rather than the 'supremacy' doctrine, that constitutes the revolution in the politics of sovereignty in the course of European integration because confederalism already presupposes the maxim *pacta sunt servanda*. Moreover, member states have lost their monopoly to represent their citizens in the EU political system. This right, formerly an exclusive component of sovereign status, is now shared with the European Parliament ever since the holding of direct elections in 1979 and its transformation into a co-legislator in an increasing number of policy areas following the 1992 Maastricht Treaty. This distinguishes the EU polity from historical confederations such as the US (1781–9) or the *Deutscher Bund* (1815–48) founded on indirect representation via territorial units.

Majone's confederal theory thus misses the way in which two particular aspects of the conflict over the rules of the game suggest that the EU is above all a failed confederation (Parsons, 2003). Firstly, there is the attempt, discussed in Chapter 4, to prevent the ECJ from creating more rights derived from the treaties and subsequent secondary legislation that individuals can wield against member states. Secondly, EU member states have had to defend their right to participate in authoritative decision making against the claim of the European Parliament, which seeks to become an equal co-legislator. As a result, member states have consistently refused to transform the Council of Ministers into an upper legislative chamber, which would leave the directly-elected Parliament responsible for the bulk of policymaking.

Although a previous generation of EU scholars 'eschewed comparative analysis' (Kelemen, 2003: 184), further economic and political integration, combined with the greater legislative power of the European Parliament, now makes comparison a favourite method for studying the EU (Rosamond, 2007). This holds true not only for the study of regulation and policymaking but also for the whole gamut of executive, legislative and judicial politics (Pollack, 2005). Increasingly, these comparative studies choose the language of federalism, emphasizing the similarity of institutions and policy programmes and their ability to deal with common problems of government (Sbragia, 1992; Zweifel, 2002; Kelemen, 2004; Menon and Schain, 2006; Mendez, 2007). Yet for all comparative federalism's contribution to understanding the nature of EU policymaking, this approach rests on a conceptualization of the EU that fundamentally fails to problematize the question of sovereign status within the EU system as compared with other contemporary federal systems. This is all the more surprising since federalism is understood to 'change the political status of every member of the federation ... it establishes a new *status* for every member' (Schmitt, 1992: 29). In the language of the rules of the game adopted here, the comparative federal approach fails to provide much guidance for understanding contestation over the principles of political representation as well as expectations about the nature of the union.

Certain federations with which the EU is sometimes compared are parliamentary regimes (Austria, Germany, Australia and Canada) that presuppose the existence of single people, a united popular sovereign. This feature is perhaps best reflected by the presence of cross-unit political parties in these federal systems – with the exception of the secessionist *Parti Québécois* in Canada. Moreover, in these same systems the government depends on the support of the directly elected lower houses, representing citizens *qua* citizens of the federation rather than as citizens of a particular territorial unit as in the upper houses. Thus comparisons between the above federal systems and the EU err in not addressing the implications the patent absence of a united popular sovereign has for the integration process. It is this absence that gives rise to manifold thorny quandaries of integration: bickering over the move to qualified majority voting, the continued insistence on unanimous ratification of treaty reform and attempts to prevent the extension of co-decision with the European Parliament. Such conflicts illustrate the manner in which EU member states rely on their sovereign status to dispute change in the system of political representation at the EU level.

Hence the most recent wave of comparative federalist approaches to European integration has deliberately sought to construct more pertinent comparisons with the two federal systems that differ most from the parliamentary norm: the modern US and Switzerland. As Fabbrini and Sicurelli explain, comparison with the US is attractive because 'there is no European equivalent of a political system defined by this multiple separation of powers, at once vertical and horizontal'

(2004: 232). Of course, Switzerland in fact does meet this criterion of a dual system of separation of powers – a point stressed by certain comparative scholars interested in EU politics (Blondel, 1998; Zweifel, 2002; Mendez, 2007) – but tends to be excluded for reasons of size (Fabbrini and Sicurelli, 2004).

However, both Switzerland and the modern US can be distinguished from the EU by virtue of their having a single popular sovereign that is ordinarily 'recessed', to reprise Deudney's terminology, but which periodically becomes very active indeed. In Switzerland, this is evidently the direct democracy device, the referendum, that allows Swiss citizens to collectively challenge both a law passed in parliament as well as propose constitutional amendments. Whereas the US constitution does not allow for national referendums, there the institution that mobilizes popular sovereignty is the presidency. The nature of that institution changed fundamentally in the course of the nineteenth century, transforming the contest for the executive into a competition for the popular vote rather than an indirect election of the most suitable candidate by those who should know best (Aldrich, 1995; Glencross, 2008). As a result, the legitimacy furnished by this unique connection between the presidency and the united sovereign US people has enabled various presidents to reform the modern US body politic (Ackerman, 1991, 1998) as well as overcome certain policy impasses within the legislature by mobilizing citizens directly (Schain, 2006).

Thus both modern Switzerland and the post-Civil War US have a mechanism for the direct cross-unit mobilization of citizens, which allows the federal level to represent popular sovereignty. This move denies the territorial units the ability to claim the sole right to represent popular sovereignty as an integral part of their sovereign status. Hence the struggle over the rules of the game of politics is very different in the EU because there the member states have been able to use their sovereign status to preserve their monopolistic claim over the representation of popular sovereignty within the EU architecture. In this way, EU member states have purposefully sought to counteract attempts to mimic both the Swiss and the US mechanisms for activating a single recessed popular sovereign at the EU level. This explains the hollowness of the new-fangled 'popular initiative', which would allow a million EU citizens to invite the Commission to consider legislating in a certain policy area already within the framework of its powers. The same explanation lies behind the Lisbon Treaty's introduction of a president of the European Council elected by the member states rather than directly by EU citizens. In this context it is perhaps important to remember that Belgium, the European federation that is neither parliamentary nor has mechanisms for empowering a cross-unit display of popular sovereignty, is slowly imploding.[22]

The second feature of the contestation over the rules of the game that comparative federalism does not dwell upon concerns expectations about the nature of the EU. The presence of a unilateral exit procedure in the Lisbon Treaty (Article 49A)[23] for member states wishing to leave the EU, owes its existence to member states seeking to underscore – especially to their domestic audiences – the fact that membership of the EU is fully compatible with an unaltered sovereign status. The result puts the EU at odds with virtually all historical examples of federalism since only the USSR (in theory) permitted voluntary withdrawal of a territorial unit (McKay, 1999: 126). Yet the withdrawal option is a vital part of contestation over the rules of the game in a compound polity. The possibility of exit from the EU treaty framework contrasts starkly with the US constitution, which – unlike the Articles of Confederation – was ambiguous regarding whether the union was perpetual. It was precisely this ambiguity that allowed southern secessionists to argue that since the American states retained sovereign status the unilateral right of withdrawal was by definition an integral element of this status. Without this right, the states could no longer plausibly be said to possess a sovereign status.

In other words, sovereign status affects conflict over the rules of the game – and *a fortiori* whether this can be managed through dynamic equilibrium or voluntary centralization – in a way that cannot be grasped if the focus of analysis falls solely upon institutions and the evolving boundaries between the units and the centre. What matters as far as understanding viability is concerned is to discover how the rules of the game are contested and how they are settled or not. Hence a tabularization of the transfer of competences in the course of European integration (Börzel, 2005: 221–3; cf. Donahue and Pollack, 2001: 107) only indicates a change in one aspect of integration but not whether this reflects an evolution in the nature of the project, whether it generates new expectations, settles the competency over competences question or affects the tension between principles of representation. A comparative narrative of transferred competences, therefore, is not by itself sufficient for understanding how conflict over the rules of the game can be managed.

Similarly, an examination of how institutional disputes over allocated powers are adjudicated (that is, who exercises *Kompetenz-Kompetenz*) is not sufficient to grasp where a compound polity like the antebellum US or EU stands in the spectrum between dynamic equilibrium and voluntary centralization. This is because the settlement of a particular competence issue does not necessarily entail any further consequences for the rules of the game. After all, in such situations, which arise frequently in compound political systems, the emphasis may be on 'conflict settlement, not the vindication of rights' (Kratochwil, 1978: 47). One scholar, whose pioneering contrast of antebellum contestation of federal sovereignty by state courts with similar struggles against the ECJ by national courts in Europe, thus provided a very partial account of the contestation over the rules of the game. The failure to capture the wider gamut of political contestation led Goldstein to claim that there is an 'evident paradox':

> That the nominally sovereign government of the United States of America experienced several decades of overt and even violent official defiance of its authority by the member states of the American union, while the nominally sovereign member states of the European Union virtually from the start obeyed as a legitimate higher authority the dictates of their federal union.
>
> (2001: 15)

Unfortunately, by concentrating purely on legal resistance within the respective polities, Goldstein fails to question whether member-state compliance with the EU legal regime relates to how especially thorny issues of sovereignty (such as the budget, enlargement, treaty reform) are deliberately prevented from becoming subject to resolution through judicial arbitration and hence dealt with by other means. Indeed sometimes, as in the case of the Stability and Growth Pact, the legal procedures for compliance are more or less ignored.[24]

Thus a purely institutional or competence-focused study is blind to other dimensions of political life that have a crucial bearing on contestation and (re)construction of the rules of the game in a compound polity. Here there is an obvious parallel with the US political system, whose functioning cannot be summed up by the provisions of the constitution and subsequent legislation. As Nichols observes:

> American democracy ... was never completely planned nor projected, and even in the laws and constitutions which have been its charters, it was never fully described. Certain of its chief elements were neither designed nor authorised, while some of its most effective instruments of operation have been unspecified improvisations.
>
> (1972: xi)

Nichols is referring here, among other things, to the populist innovations of Jacksonian democracy, the rise of nationally organized parties and the reconstruction settlement. These extra-constitutional innovations condition the way in which political arguments arise and how they can be settled and it is myopic to neglect them. It is exactly this kind of oversight that the present study seeks to avoid by paying attention to the broader context in which political contestation takes place in a compound polity.

1.6 Conclusion

Rather than invoking the notion of a compound system as characterized by a set of institutional features (Fabbrini, 2003, 2005a, 2007b; Mendez, 2007) therefore, this study prefers to define a compound political system as one experiencing a form of political contestation not present in other forms of state. It is precisely this experience of contestation over the four dimensions conceptualized as 'the rules of the game of politics' that provides the subject matter for the analytical comparison between the antebellum US and the contemporary EU pursued in the following chapters. The analysis identifies and explains the crucial differences in both how conflict over the rules of the game occurred and how it was managed (or not). As a result, the transatlantic analogy demonstrates the extent to which changes in the rules of the game in the EU and the antebellum US underwent dynamic equilibrium or voluntary centralization. Only once this is known does it become possible to determine what effect proposed institutional changes to the EU compound architecture will have on the viability of this unusual polity.

2
Developing an Analogical Comparison between the EU and the Antebellum US Republic

Give me another theory that would fit the facts.
Arthur Conan Doyle (1985: 462)

2.1 Introduction

Traditional theories of state-building baulk at explaining recent trends in European integration, which is why a range of scholars prefer to adopt a *tabula rasa* attitude, devising new concepts or metaphors that emphasize the uniqueness of this polity. Nonetheless this *sui generis* approach has been much criticized of late for failing to perceive the merits of comparing the EU with other non-unitary systems, as discussed in the previous chapter. It is in this context, as explained in section 2.2, that transatlantic comparison has become so attractive. However, such comparative studies of the EU and the US almost invariably focus on the modern experience of American federalism.

Section 2.3 thus takes issue with the neglect of the antebellum US experience – a time during which the very viability of the republic was at stake – when conducting such comparisons. A sketch of the historical and theoretical significance of the post-bellum settlement is presented to demonstrate why the Civil War represents a fundamental caesura in the principles and practices of the original US compound republic. By showing how the rules of the game evolved, resulting in a far more centralized compound polity, this section makes the case for why a transatlantic comparison of viability needs to focus on the antebellum period of US political development.

However, a potential complication for the transatlantic analogy pursued in this study arises from the fact that the question of viability does not fit well with the mainstream research agenda of EU studies. Hence the final section, 2.4, highlights the absence of a well-developed viability problematic in the field and discusses why this is an omission that needs to be tackled. Tocqueville is used here as an exemplar of an approach to the study of politics driven by issues arising from *praxis*. The argument contends that the generation of interesting research questions does not come from the search for universal answers but from the consideration of concrete, practical political disputes. The notion of viability is put forward precisely as one such problem of *praxis* as distinguished from the search for preconditions of successful federalism or supposed 'lessons from history' presented as path-dependency arguments. Such attempts to discover the generalizable causal effects of historical context are rejected in favour of an indirect analogy that incorporates political and historical context by examining how the rules of the game were contested and re-negotiated in the two compound polities studied here.

2.2 The attraction of transatlantic comparison

Contemporary political science often has a hard time making sense of the process of European integration and the nascent European polity. Whereas the previous great transformation in the boundaries and political nature of European societies is conventionally sketched as the transition from absolutism to liberal democracy – albeit with certain fascist and communist hiatuses – the demise of empire and the rise of nationalism,[1] no similar theoretical framework exists to explain the process of post-war integration. In many ways this stems from the fact that the idea of European unity has been formulated in irenic terms – putting an end to war – that do not transpose easily into other political objectives. Furthermore, both modern historical experience and the concepts of contemporary political thought are deeply anchored in the assumption that the nation state is the basic unit of our political world.[2]

This does not mean that the nation state has been a perennial feature of human history. Far from it, for as Niall Ferguson points out 'they are a novelty compared with empires' (Ferguson, 2001: 169). The conceptual entrenchment of the nation state, however, makes the understanding of alternative forms of polity problematic from the outset. The EU is a peculiar and uncanny object of study for the discipline of political science precisely because the democratic nation state was once widely considered the *non plus ultra* or *telos* of political modernity. In many domains, sometimes quite unexpectedly, the EU is altering the political landscape of Europe by increasing the size of the political unit beyond the nation state, thereby challenging the fundamental *national* character of European democracies (Schmidt, 2006). At the same time, the European polity often functions through bargaining (states and interest groups) or expertise rather than by argument conducted through parties, politicians and a public sphere, which puts it at odds with the democratic practices of the nation state.

Thus the existence of the EU runs counter to the founding assumptions and theories of modern political development (Tilly, 1992; Rokkan, 1999 cf. Bartolini, 2005). These classical theories were devised to explain the rise of the territorial nation state as the seemingly definitive form of modern political organization. But the historical origins of European states are rooted in absolutism, warmongering and nationalism whereas integration rests on an avowed rejection of all these traditions, and is supposed to be a means for overcoming their pernicious legacies. Moreover, twenty-first century Europe does not face the classic external stimuli for state-building: security imperatives.

Following the logic of Charles Tilly's historical-sociological analysis of state-building as a function of mobilizing coercion and capital for the sake of greater security,[3] European state-building could occur because Europe's nation states were no longer individually competent to defend themselves (or their interests) in the face of more powerful rivals. This would be analogous to the transformation, absorption or combination of cities into nation states. But in today's geopolitics it is practically impossible to isolate an imminent threat of a magnitude sufficient to provoke such a collective epiphany. A concept and enemy as vague as terror may promote enhanced police and intelligence cooperation but it cannot stimulate state-building because it does not imply the same total obsolescence of existing capacities as when, say, the 1000-year-old republic of Venice was confronted with Napoleon's war-machine.[4] In any case, it is NATO not the EU that is obliged to respond to external threats from foreign states; it is the US that for the most part, defrays the cost of making the Atlantic alliance a credible military power so that even in the absence of a discernible security threat the EU has been spared the usual state-building incentive of financing its self-defence.

European integration, therefore, challenges previously held assumptions about the nature of the modern political unit. Given the limitations of the existing conceptual vocabulary, the response from many scholars has been to reappraise how political concepts and theories could be applied to this novel regional integration. Yet in spite of the widely acknowledged need to re-evaluate concepts, the response to this challenge to the orthodoxy of nation-state centred political science has, in terms of theoretical construction, been underwhelming. The tendency is to use modish metaphors that by themselves say little of substance: 'multi-perspectival polity' (Ruggie, 1998); 'demoi-cracy' (Nicolaidis, 2004); 'post-modern polity' (Caporaso, 1996); 'new Middle Ages' (Wæver, 1996); or even 'metrosexual superpower' (Khanna, 2004). Some descriptions even spatchcock together the entire gamut of neologisms. Philippe Schmitter does so magnificently when he calls the EU 'a postsovereign, polycentric, incongruent, neo-medieval arrangement of authority' (1996: 132). Yet these are mostly hollow terms as they only raise more questions about the EU. Is postmodernism a cultural or political phenomenon? Is *demoi-cracy* an oxymoron? Is the analogy with the Middle Ages intended to be positive or negative? This hollowness greatly weakens their analytical value for assessing a problem like viability.

Political science has also borrowed the *de rigueur* metaphor used to characterize the European project of integration in legal discourse: the idea of a 'non-state'. This interpretation considers the EU an ambiguous entity that creates obligations well beyond the normal reach of international law but one which is not akin to historical, sovereign nation states.[5] The description is drawn by making a negative contrast with the history of the nation state. Normally this takes the form of a checklist of how European integration, unlike the nation state, is not characterized by state-building, imperialism or nationalism. Marc Plattner offers a nice summary of this interpretation, when he explains that the EU 'has become a federal *non*state whose decisions are accepted voluntarily by its constituent units rather than backed up by the modes of hierarchical coercion classically employed by the modern state' (2003: 53).

The gospel of uniqueness, whereby the EU is said to create new conditions for the conduct of politics, suggests the EU is apt to find new ways of solving old challenges of modern government. Disappointingly, this comes at the expense of bothering with the detail of how or why this will continue to be so: Joseph Weiler's (2001) theory of constitutional tolerance neither explains what sustains this nor where the limits of toleration lie. This *a contrario* definition of the EU is essentially retrospective and forbears from thinking about the future of this polity. Just as the EU cannot be dismissed as a viable polity because it is simply unlike the nation state, neither can its difference be used uncritically to explain its adaptability and resilience. Some scholars have nevertheless succumbed to this temptation, most recently Mark Leonard, who explains that 'to this day, Europe is a journey with no final destination, a political system that shies away from the grand plans and concrete certainties that define American politics. Its lack of vision is the key to its strength' (2005: 10). Logically speaking, this is a classic instance of question begging as the argument relies on its own proposition, the EU is unique, to support the premise that the EU will find novel ways out of its political impasses. Thus, while the notion of a non-state may highlight the novelty of the European polity as a form of modern political organization, this is not the same as constructing a sophisticated conceptual model of exactly how and why the EU polity is different from nation states and the implications this has for its political future.

It is precisely the failure of such idiographic analysis, in the context of continued integration that continues to puzzle, which has made the comparison with other political systems, especially but not exclusively US federalism, so attractive.[6] This comparative turn is a welcome development and not only because it avoids the stifling dichotomy of imagining integration as either necessarily culminating in a superstate or being frozen by the obstinacy of the nation state. Traditionally, scholars of the EU were diffident towards learning by comparison because it was thought that few, if any, productive comparisons were possible. Further economic and political integration, combined with the greater legislative power of the European Parliament, now makes comparison a favourite method for studying the EU (Pollack, 2005). This holds true not only for the study of regulation and policymaking but the whole gamut of executive, legislative and judicial politics (ibid.).

Clumsy contrasts with European federal states and consociations, however, have become less popular due to a growing awareness of the marked institutional differences between the EU and parliamentary federations or consensus democracies based on cultural and linguistic cleavages. Instead, in the hope of generating more rigorous insights, comparativists have increasingly turned their attention to the US, with its dual vertical and horizontal separation of powers as well as a historically weaker notion of statehood (Skowronek, 1982). Carrying out a transatlantic comparison flies in the face of claims of American exceptionalism as much as of the EU's supposed *sui generis* nature. Nevertheless such a move is proving increasingly popular among scholars as a way of generating insights into the functioning of both systems. This is often associated with the growing tendency to apply a positivist theoretical framework to problems of integration so as to test falsifiable hypotheses and produce replicable claims (Pollack, 2005). Thanks to their rigorous comparisons, such studies have contributed much to understanding similarities and differences in, respectively, democratic practices (Fabbrini, 2007b), regulatory politics (Majone, 1996; Kelemen, 2004), institutional decision making (Chopin, 2002) and judicial supremacy (Goldstein, 2001).

However, in these existing studies the comparison with the US is largely indifferent to the caesura of the Civil War. In fact, the conflict's role in settling fundamental questions of constitutional authority is simply not analysed as part of the comparative problematic. Thus despite the fact that it has become almost historiographically commonplace to refer to the union victory as a 'second American revolution' (McPherson, 1991), or another foundational moment (Ackerman, 1998), comparativists have hitherto not dwelt upon the emergence and importance of the constitutional debates preceding the secessionary conflict. The result is a substantial omission in the literature analysing, from a comparative US perspective, the federalization or constitutionalization of the EU polity. At the very least, as the following section shows, there is an urgent need to incorporate into transatlantic comparisons an appreciation of the complexities of antebellum political conflict against a background of perhaps the most fecund period for constitutional analysis in US history.

2.3 The caesura of the Civil War: The overlooked significance of antebellum political conflict

When searching for insightful transatlantic contrasts, comparative politics has so far largely neglected the early period of American political history. One exception concerns the study of the respective constitutional foundations of European integration and American federalism (Cappelletti et al., 1986; Spinelli, 1993; Elazar, 2001; Magnette, 2006). Focusing on the foundational origins provides a snapshot of differences that highlight the US constitutional moment – as a deliberative moment of popular engagement with constitutional issues – with Europe's treaty-based, functional approach to political union (Spinelli, 1993; Magnette, 2006). The subsequent travails of the US polity and its near-disintegration are generally ignored – albeit with one major exception (Goldstein, 2001) – with the result that EU/US comparisons overwhelmingly study twentieth-century US political history and, in the case of policy studies, especially the last few decades.

By contrast, certain scholars of international relations have recently done their utmost to demonstrate the rewards of studying the antebellum period as a way of re-evaluating the theoretical understanding of the US federal order. Whereas the realist canon treated the birth of this new nation as just an additional unit in the competitive, anarchic world of states, scholars such as Daniel Deudney, Nicholas and Peter Onuf, as well as David Hendrickson, have brought to light the security dilemma that the federal union was tasked to solve, notably that 'once independent, the American states found their precarious position in the European system a source of constitutional crisis' (Onuf and Onuf, 1993: 5).

Using this 'security liberalism' (Deudney, 1995: 225) perspective, these authors argue that the US was a novel security community whose very independence owed much to the European balance of power – France's contribution having proved so vital. Yet the desire to profit from this international order through international trade meant that 'to exploit the balance of power the United States would have to become a real power' (Onuf and Onuf, 1993: 94). At the same time, these ambitions were jeopardized by disharmony among the former colonies. Under the Articles of Confederation it was obvious that 'the balance of power among the American states was neither stable nor self-perfecting' (ibid., p. 102). Thus the American founders' 'more perfect union' sought to boost the new country's credibility among the European states, establish peace and cooperation amid potentially fractious and secessionary units as well as guarantee self-government both individually and collectively. Domestically, the twin obsessions of this republican security project were, as Deudney explains, 'avoiding the extremes of anarchy and hierarchy' (2004: 342).

These scholars furnish a fundamental insight into the theory and practice of early American politics and one that serves to counterbalance the tendency not to engage with the complexity of the compound project devised at Philadelphia. Hans Morgenthau, for instance, was unconcerned with the trepidations and theoretical speculations present at the constitutional convention. 'What the Convention of Philadelphia did', he writes, 'was to replace one constitution, one sovereignty, one state with another one, both resting upon the same pre-existing community ... the United States was founded upon a moral and political community the Constitution did not create but found already in existence' (1985: 391). In Morgenthau's reading then, the union of 13 states represents primarily a transfer of sovereignty to increase unit power in a competitive international state system rather than a scheme for reorganizing security in a manner compatible with limited government.[7]

Besides highlighting the way republican theory came to be applied to rethink the problem of domestic and external security, this recent IR scholarship has also had the merit of revealing the importance that fears of sectionalism and inter-state cleavages played in shaping the debates over replacing the Articles of Confederation. Indeed, these apprehensions lasted well beyond the convention and ratification debates precisely because 'the states' republican constitutions did not guarantee their harmonious union' (Onuf and Onuf, 1993: 130).[8] It is this feature of acute antebellum political conflict, already well documented by historians, especially McDonald (2000), that has yet to be incorporated into comparative studies of European integration and American political development. While the aforementioned IR scholars have done their best to slaughter this holy cow of erroneous historical generalizations about the early US republic, it is important to ensure that EU studies does not fall into the same trap of overlooking the significance of the antebellum period.

Thus my interest in this recent IR debate is focused primarily on what it reveals about the unsettled nature of the American union, a project with certain *explicit political objectives* and with *contested rules of the game*, rather than as 'a structural alternative to the European state system' (Deudney, 1995: 193). As Deudney explains, the US in its first 70 years of existence 'had a government but was not a state' (ibid., p. 207).[9] Rather than sketch the manner in which the rules of the game were contested in this period (the subject of section 3.2), however, it is more important to specify how exactly the American Civil War[10] changed the nature of the American union. This is because the rationale for this study is the claim that the compound characteristics of the antebellum republic, which were fundamentally altered in the aftermath of the South's defeat, makes this period the most pertinent for generating comparative insights into EU viability.

Without a doubt, the starkest depiction of the caesura represented by the Civil War is that of Forrest McDonald, for whom 'from a constitutional perspective, the truly revolutionary consequence of the Civil War and Reconstruction, one that was entirely unforeseen, was the general public's acceptance of the idea that the [Supreme] Court was the sole and final arbiter of constitutional controversies' (2000: 224). Although it is sometimes believed that from the outset US federalism established that 'state and federation would each have a common duty to obey a federal court whose task was to uphold the federal pact' (Spinelli, 1993: 269),[11] the reality, as will be shown in the next chapter, was altogether different.

Originally, the locus of sovereignty went unspecified in the US constitution; political conflict typically took the form of clashing sovereignty claims voiced by the federal and state governments alike. Furthermore, the ultimate right to judge the legitimacy of a sovereignty claim was variously thought to lie with the people of a state, the people of the entire US and the Supreme Court. In fact, the ardent advocate of states rights John C. Calhoun interpreted this struggle to define the source of sovereignty in the constitution as one between the people of the states and the Supreme Court:

> The question is in truth between the people and the Supreme Court. We contend, that the great conservative principle of our system is in the people of the States, as parties to the Constitutional compact, and our opponents that it is in the Supreme Court.
> (Calhoun, 1978: 92)

The quashing of secessionism meant that sovereignty could no longer be tenably claimed to lie with the people of a particular state, as Calhoun had proposed. Almost immediately after the end of hostilities the Supreme Court, ruling on a confederate state's claim to recover war bonds seized by the union, confirmed that secession was unconstitutional because what had been created at Philadelphia was 'an indestructible Union, composed of indestructible states' (McDonald, 2000: 218). States thus lost their claim to be able to withdraw from the union, nullify laws or unilaterally question the constitutionality of its actions.

However, the express denial of the right to invoke popular sovereignty at the state level to defy the federal government did not signify a wholesale transfer of the exercise of popular sovereignty to the federal level. Although the indirect election of senators has been abolished, relics of a system based on multiple popular sovereigns, that is, the people of the states, survive (Fritz, 2008). Hence the Electoral College is still used to elect the president, there is no constitutional option of direct democracy at the federal level and constitutional amendment cannot be achieved by federal legislators alone. It is in this context of the demise of state sovereignty and the problematic exercise of popular sovereignty at the federal level, that the Supreme Court – thanks to the Civil War – gained its status as final arbiter of the constitution. Quite remarkably, popular acceptance of this constitutional settlement has remained stalwart despite both the growing self-confidence of the Supreme Court in challenging the other federal branches (D. Strauss, 2005) and the academic clamour for diluting its powers of judicial review, a doctrine known as 'popular constitutionalism' (Tushnet, 1999), but which has not found a popular base.

Thus the failure of secessionism and the Reconstruction settlement fundamentally changed all four constitutive elements of the rules of the game of politics in the US compound system – institutional competences, expectations about the union, competency over competences and political representation, as represented in Table 2.1. Firstly, the post-bellum order redefined the institutional order of the republic by altering the status of the Bill of Rights and, *a fortiori*, the relationship between the states and federal government. In an 1833 case, *Barron v. Baltimore*, where the owner of a Baltimore wharf sued the city for Fifth Amendment 'just compensation' for conducting public works that rendered his dock useless, the Supreme Court ruled that '[the Bill of Rights'] amendments contain no expression indicating an intention to apply them to the State governments' (McDonald, 2000: 117-18). It was precisely to undermine this doctrine of non-application of the Bill of Rights to the states, especially in the South, that the Reconstruction Congress passed the Fourteenth Amendment in 1868,[12] which 'revolutionize[d] the structure of the federal union' (Kaczorowski, 1986: 940).

As Zuckert explains, 'the framers of the Fourteenth Amendment wished to apply the Bill of Rights to the states' (1992: 87). The purpose was thus to overturn the Dred Scott decision denying citizenship to non-white Americans as well as to uphold 'the privileges and immunities' of US citizens and guarantee both 'due process' and 'equal protection of the laws'. Although the Supreme Court soon afterwards blunted the revolutionary scope of the amendment by refusing to apply the 'privileges and immunities' clause against the states,[13] this amendment proved

Table 2.1 How the US Civil War fundamentally changed the rules of the game

Rule of the Game of Politics	Antebellum	Post-bellum
Institutional competences	Bill of Rights restrains the federal government, does not apply to the states	Fourteenth Amendment seeks to apply Bill of Rights to states and establishes primacy of national citizenship
Expectations about the union	Union is a compact: States can legitimately withdraw if people decide so; states are bulwark against centralized power	Union is perpetual, secession is unthinkable; centralized power can be used to promote freedom
Competency over competences	Ambiguous and contested	Unquestionably resides in the Supreme Court
Representation	Nullification doctrine: Popular sovereignty at the state level can legitimately be used to block federal legislation	Primacy of Congress; nullification unthinkable

to be the cornerstone of all subsequent citizenship and civil rights cases aimed at preventing discrimination at the state level. Equally important, the amendment reflected the fact that – contrary to the fundamentally ambiguous arrangement pertaining in the antebellum period – 'national citizenship was primary and state citizenship derivative' (Kaczorowski, 1986: 867). By establishing this hierarchy, Congress was thus able to make an unprecedented claim to possess 'the primary authority to secure the civil rights of American citizens' (ibid.). In this sense, the Fourteenth Amendment achieved Madison's original ambition of endowing the federal government with a veto over state laws,[14] albeit through a judicial device, dependent on the (fitful) cooperation of the justices of the Supreme Court, not the political mechanism he had wanted.

Thus the second element of the rules of the game of politics in the US, expectations about the political union, was likewise overhauled after 1865. The aftermath of the violent struggle to save the union brought with it a recognition of the perpetuity of the federal union: it could no longer be interpreted as a compact, from which the states could withdraw as freely as they had once entered into. This move reconfigured expectations about the nature of relations between the states by removing secession as a state threat against the federal level. Furthermore, as McPherson points out, the Fourteenth Amendment represents a watershed by dissolving 'the eighteenth-century antithesis between liberty and centralized power' (1984: 378). Whereas previously the states were automatically considered bulwarks against the tyranny of centralized government, the post-bellum period made possible the hitherto unthinkable proposition that the federal level could be a redeemer of individual rights.

Principles of representation within the compound polity, the third feature of the rules of the game, were similarly affected by the new constitutional settlement. The novel understanding of the primacy of Congress – the government of a single sovereign people – in its relations with the states was the death knell of the doctrine of nullification (a state veto of federal legislation within the former's territory). In the absence of legitimate nullification claims as well as the right to withdraw from the federal union, the exercise of popular sovereignty at the state level thus lost its ability to impact directly upon constitutional politics, except in the rare cases of constitutional amendment. Finally, after the ability to invoke state popular sovereignty against the federal level had been trumped, the reliance on a largely recessed exercise of popular sovereignty at the federal level transformed the fourth element of the rules of the game: competency over competences. Instead of the ambiguities of the antebellum arrangement, the Supreme Court, as explained above, became the uncontested arbiter of US constitutional disputes about the distribution of competences and thus sovereignty claims. This was not merely a *de facto* transformation but a *de jure* one given the tremendous expansion of federal-question jurisdiction granted to federal courts in the 1875 Judiciary Act.[15]

By virtue of the above explanation of the changes wrought by the Civil War it should become clear that it is above all during the antebellum period that the rules of the game of politics were contested in a manner resembling conflict over the rules of the game in today's EU. The two compound systems share the following characteristics: disputed competence allocations to the federal level, the expectation that units can withdraw to protect their citizens' liberties, an ambiguous sovereignty arrangement leaving the locus of competency over competences unspecified and, finally, a fundamental tension between the exercise of popular sovereignty at the state level and at the federal level. Conversely, after the Civil War, contest over the rules of the game in the US became dominated by disputes over institutional competences as expectations about the nature of the union had changed while sovereignty and the exercise of representation could no longer be questioned as before.[16]

2.4 Comparing viability in the EU and antebellum US: A question of *praxis* not preconditions

Even if there is no absolute consensus in EU studies over what is the *explanandum* (Hempel and Oppenheimer, 1948: 152), or phenomenon to be explained about integration (Hooghe and Marks, 2008), it is nonetheless evident that theoretically sophisticated studies of the EU have traditionally focused on answering the following paradigmatic question: why integrate? Or, in Moravcsik's lengthier formulation, 'how are the various choices of governments to delegate and pool sovereignty to be explained?' (1998: 8) In answering this question the dominant approaches are essentially meta-theoretical ones, which can be and are applied to non-EU contexts. Neo-functionalism has been applied to other instances of regional integration (Lindberg and Scheingold, 1971), intergovernmentalism has been extended to the analysis of other international organizations (B. Cronin, 2002), liberal institutionalism is used to explain interstate cooperation in general (Keohane and Martin, 1995), while constructivism has been used to chart how developments in international politics stem from changes in norms and practices (Koslowski and Kratochwil, 1994). Referring to the specificity or uniqueness of the EU is, unsurprisingly therefore, the standard way of impugning any one of these methods. But calling the EU *sui generis* promises to add little to our understanding of what makes the EU viable as this approach renders comparison unthinkable. Hence the study of viability pursued in this book steers a middle course between the *sui generis* case study and overambitious law-like generalizations concerning the why and how of integration, by choosing instead an approach based on examining viability as a problem of *praxis*.

The ambition behind the dominant theory-testing approach is the construction of an explanatory model through which the true nature of the EU will be revealed or, by using more restricted middle range theories, at least that of policymaking. 'Political science theory', as the leading historian of integration John Gillingham argues, 'claims to explain the alpha and omega of European integration' (2003: 487) thereby trying to uncover the gamut of interests and motives of the various identifiable actors and how these may or may not change through interaction. By adopting the same question while pointing out the shortcomings of previous answers, it is assumed that in explaining each additional nuance or deviant case one is approaching the correct theoretical model that eventually will accurately describe in its entirety the object of study. Good theory is thus supposed to supersede bad theory.[17] Disputes between advocates of competing theoretical positions focus on what other theories cannot explain. This is especially true of the old debate between neo-functionalists and intergovernmentalists which is now in the process of being surpassed by the clash between rationalists and constructivists (Pollack, 2005). Such a conflictual mode of theorizing is quite probably a legacy of IR, the discipline that spawned EU studies and which has a tradition of great debates between different explanatory methodologies.[18]

The research question of viability thus stands apart from the typical investigatory priorities of the discipline. The exploration of what makes the EU viable is a question of more immediate political concern, one that is seldom incorporated into the research priorities of EU studies. Yet answering the viability question seems at least as pressing an objective as the elaboration of a theoretical model that can eventually explain every stage of the integration or policymaking process. The latter emphasis on explaining the why behind integration is partly a consequence of the disciplinary dominance of hypothesis-testing methodology. But it is also a problem stemming from the selection of research questions. Sherlock Holmes, who thought 'it is a capital mistake to theorize before one has data' (Conan Doyle, 1985: 12) and who believed one should 'always look for a possible alternative and provide against it' (ibid., p. 550), was certainly a partisan of a positivist scientific method. Yet the cases he investigated were clearly interesting ones with much at stake: guilt and innocence as well as, in some tales, vital state secrets. Unfortunately, the research questions that dominate the field in EU studies do not always have similar high stakes.

The paradox of the EU is that in spite of its evident success compared with other attempts at regional integration it is still beset by an awesome multitude of problems: interest cleavages, the widening versus deepening debate, the wrangle over institutional reform, the prospect of Turkish membership and contested foreign policy stances. By contrast, the domestic politics of all but the most turbulent member states can seem stolid; indeed, often the most disruptive factor in national political life is the issue of integration itself.[19] It was explained in the first chapter that this disparity is due to the EU's compound nature, a characteristic the member states do not share.[20] Rather than assume that a compelling reason for more integration (another compromise or bargain, an event that changes perceptions and so on) will render these problems evanescent, it seems more appropriate to consider whether the EU is well equipped to survive in the face of recurring tensions over how to define the rules of the game of politics. The advantage here is that more specific questions can be generated in response to the initial problem of viability, such as what tensions will be exacerbated if the system of political representation is recalibrated? What policy issues can or cannot be addressed without jeopardizing the viability of the union? What is the trade-off between constitutional clarity and constitutional ambiguity?

It is precisely this type of questioning, with potentially controversial answers and evident policy implications, that is largely absent when theorizing obsesses over the why and how of integration as part of a problem-solving approach limited to a scholarly search for gaps in the existing theoretical explanations. Consequently there is an abundance of 'gap-filling' studies, each one threatening to add another turn of the screw to Stanley Hoffmann's complaint that despite being 'one of the few really inspiring political innovations of the last half-century' the literature devoted to the EU is 'so often soporific' (2005: 189).

Filling in the missing explanatory gaps, *ex post facto*, is thus no substitute for trying to reconsider the usefulness of the questions that are asked about the EU. As a counterweight to this existing dominant research framework, the intention here is to follow Alexis de Tocqueville in arguing that the first step in the understanding of politics is the selection of appropriate questions to explore. Political analysis in this sense is comparable with historical analysis, for even the most pedestrian historian can only function by asking questions of the past. Without the ability to ask questions there can be, by definition, no historical *inquiry* just a chronicle of unplotted events from among what Hayden White calls the 'unprocessed historical record'.[21]

Knowing which questions to ask, however, is not synonymous with asking the *right* questions. The canon of political philosophy was devoted to grasping the ideal: finding an answer to the question of how the body politic is best organized. But modern political science abandoned the notion of a classical catechism of inquiry into the ideal, such as Aristotle's investigation into what is the ideal constitution (although he was also interested in the best possible one), as part of a move away from asking canonical questions in favour of trying to devise *useful* ones.[22]

If not quite the first to signal this turn towards the useful, Tocqueville was certainly the most explicit proponent of this approach, which he boldly termed a 'new science of politics'. In the introduction to the first volume of his magisterial study of American democratic society, he explained that 'it is not, then, merely to satisfy a curiosity, however legitimate, that I have examined America; my wish has been to find there instruction by which we may ourselves profit' (Tocqueville, 1994: 14). By this he meant more than the facile claim that the study of American democracy could not yield a model of the perfect commonwealth.[23] Tocqueville's insight, writing as a French noble perhaps envious of American political stability yet shrewdly aware of the various causes of France's tumultuous recent history, was that to profit from the analysis of politics, one should not expect to find institutional templates with universal applicability. 'Let us look there', he wrote with his gaze fixed on America, 'less to find examples than instruction; let us borrow from her the principles, rather than the details of her laws' (ibid., lxv).

In other words, useful questions are those that tend to forsake universal answers and limit themselves instead to producing knowledge helpful to our understanding of the current situation or predicament that motivated the process of questioning in the first place. In Tocqueville's case the situation was that of a country in political turmoil, in which the gains of the revolution were still threatened by counter-revolution and the liberty promised by the revolutionaries of 1789 had been curtailed by a centralized and authoritarian state apparatus that each post-revolutionary regime had made its own. What he wanted to know, therefore, was whether the principles of democratic individualism, the 'equality of conditions' and the sovereignty of the people, which had swept away the fabric of the Old Regime without leaving anything solid in its place, were compatible with stability, prosperity and property. To find this out, he turned to America where these principles had extended furthest: 'I have selected the nation, among those which have undergone it [the 'social revolution' of democracy], in which its development has been the most peaceful and the most complete' (ibid., p. 14). Tocqueville explored American society as a result of the questions he asked of contemporary French politics. This is evinced more clearly in the rough draft of his introduction, where he explained his original motivation: 'I have not recounted all that I have seen, but I have recounted all that I believed both true and useful to be known, and without seeking to write a treatise on America I thought only to help my fellow citizens to solve a question that must interest us more keenly' (Tocqueville, 1990, vol. 1: 3).

The case of Tocqueville illustrates rather well the problem of *praxis* in intellectual inquiry. For Aristotle, the two necessary elements for leading a truly human and free existence were *theoria* and *praxis*. But whereas contemplation is the pursuit of knowledge for its own sake – with a passive result although it is not a passive activity in itself – *praxis* is the pursuit of knowledge for some end, that is to say, performing or accomplishing something in a certain way.[24] In politics, however, *praxis* does not mean the ability to determine all the possible consequences of trying to alter the world through action and it certainly does not equate to technical knowledge about which policies to apply under the circumstances. Michael Oakeshott put this latter point most bluntly: 'rationalism is the politics of the politically inexperienced' (1977: 23). His metaphor for politics, which illustrates and illuminates the notion of *praxis*, was the floating ship: 'in political activity, men sail a boundless and bottomless sea; there is neither harbour for shelter nor floor for anchorage, neither starting place nor appointed destination. The enterprise is to keep afloat on an even keel' (ibid.). Yet problems of political *praxis* can be perceived or interpreted in different ways – sticking with Oakeshott's metaphor, there will always be different proposals for keeping afloat and plenty of gainsaying regarding the evenness of the keel. Had Tocqueville, for instance, not considered the democratic revolution the providential condition of modernity, he would have been less frightened by the authoritarian distortions and monarchical reactions it gave rise to in France.

The starting point of this book, the question of the viability of the EU as a polity, is taken to be a useful question only because I believe a certain fragility and tension, not present in European nation states,[25] can be observed in the EU. If these were not interpreted as tensions, viability would be a much less interesting problem. But since the rules of the game of European politics continue to be negotiated and renegotiated it is important to discover more about this process and the implications it has for the EU as a functioning polity. One way to do this is to explore another pellucid example of similar conflict over the rules of the game: that present in the antebellum US. Yet this analogical approach ought not to be mistaken for a search for the general causal preconditions of a successful federal polity.

In fact, the comparative study of federal systems has revealed surprisingly little about what makes these regimes fail, survive or thrive, as one telling snapshot should suffice to reveal. Writing in 1991, Daniel Elazar, one of the foremost authorities on the study of federalism, was able to adopt a sanguine view on the incipient breakdown of the Yugoslav state after the fall of the Berlin Wall because:

> [I]n all the history of federalism, no federal system that has survived for at least fifteen years has abandoned federalism of its own volition ... While federal arrangements may look fragile, once rooted they become 'habits of the heart', as well as constitutional devices and very difficult to uproot.
>
> (Elazar, 1991)[26]

Such studies that focus on the universal causes of stability, centralization or disunion over the widest possible sample thus seem to have climbed the ladder of abstraction at the expense of being able to explain much about the politics of why these systems can endure. Indeed, one recent study has even tried to recast traditional understandings of the failure and success of federalism by arguing that territorial secession does not necessarily constitute federal failure as what also matters is the 'success or failure in sustaining federal values' (Burgess, 2006: 282) among the remaining units. Conclusions such as Thomas Franck's are, therefore, perhaps unsurprising in their glib generality:

> The principal cause for failure, or partial failure of each of the federations studied cannot, it thus seems, be found in an analysis of economic statistics or in an inventory of social, cultural or

institutional diversity. It can only be found in the absence of a sufficient political-ideological commitment to the PRIMARY concept or value of federation itself.

(Franck, 1968: 177)

Other attempts to draw on the historical instances of successful federal states in order to understand the future of the EU are also of limited value as they tend to rely upon a retrospective teleology presented as 'lessons from history'. This latter approach is exemplified by Larry Siedentop's recent analysis of what the reasons for the success of US federalism imply for European integration. Siedentop (2000) seeks to establish the preconditions for a successful European federation by drawing a parallel with the American union. In the jargon of political science, this approach could be described as an incomplete parallel demonstration of theory (Skocpol and Somers, 1994). Incomplete because one part of the parallel, Europe, does not yet exist, yet the assumption is that what holds true of the US will be equally valid for Europe as they are both instances of the same project of federal political union. Siedentop thus develops a theory of the factors that 'determined' the stability of the US, and drawing on this parallel story argues that the viability of European federation depends on replicating three cultural preconditions,[27] a recipe for federal success in other words.

According to this cookbook of federal politics, a stable 'United States of Europe' would depend on three common cultural traits: Christianity, English as its official language and (more obscurely) a legally trained, pan-European political class. This causal analysis of the preconditions of federal statehood, however, rests on a misreading of the history of state-building for, as Bartolini has explained, 'the elements of the nation state missing in the new European entity were not "given" as preconditions of the emergence of states in Europe but were rather "constructed" by the latter' (Bartolini, 2004: 169). In fact, one of the scholars that has dwelt most seriously on comparing institutional structures in the EU and US considers the US almost as a prototype of a supranational polity because the American experience 'challenge[s] the view that democracy requires a nation and a state to prosper' (Fabbrini, 2005a: 17).[28] Siedentop's comparative hypothesis turns the Whig interpretation of history on its head: it glorifies the American past and ratifies the failures of the European present by suggesting they are both constrained by the same historical straightjacket.

This focus on establishing causation, by identifying through comparison the general preconditions for a certain type of political regime, does not yield much in the way of convincing explanatory analysis. For instance, the claim that Christianity is inevitably a source of stability is readily open to question. It is inherently very difficult to assign any causal significance to religion across historical contexts as manifold examples can be produced to testify that it causes both one thing and its opposite. In fact, most commentators on American politics in the last two decades, and especially recent presidential elections, have lingered (particularly the liberals) on the role politically hyper-organized Christian confessional groups have had in polarizing the electorate over issues such as abortion and gay marriage. Indeed, the language used to describe this phenomenon, 'culture wars' or the 'two Americas' (Hunter, 1992; Greenberg, 2004; cf. Fiorina et al., 2004) of red and blue (in reference to the colours used by psephologists to represent the republican and democratic parties on the electoral map) suggests religion causes something other than political stability. Tocqueville, from whom Siedentop claims to have derived the preconditions of American stability[29] was perhaps the first to recognize that the spirit of religion need not necessarily be an ally of liberty. For while he acknowledged their mutual compatibility in the US, he also explained 'that the relation of religion and liberty in France [was] the exact opposite of what it [was] in the United States' (Aron, 1991, vol. 1: 199). In other words, Tocqueville was deeply sensitive to the way that historical context sundered the ideal-type dependence between free government and religion.

Hence Siedentop's search for the preconditions of federalism does not permit a proper appreciation of how the nuances of historical context affect the struggle over the rules of the game of politics. This flawed understanding of the fetter of historical constraint is also present in attempts to describe the EU as an untenable mixture of contradictory principles, which historical examples show to be doomed to failure. Amitai Etzioni represents this perspective perfectly, thanks to his conclusion that the EU's 'halfway supranationality' is such that it 'cannot be sustained and that the EU will have to move to a higher level of supranationality or fall back to a lower one' (2001: xxxi).[30] He reaches this conclusion because the EU does not meet the three supposed 'capabilities' required for a supranational union: 'legitimate control of the means of violence, which must exceed that of the member units; allocation of resources among the member units; and command of political loyalties that exceed those accorded to member states' (ibid., p. xxii). According to Etzioni, therefore, the current equilibrium is condemned to be unsustainable. Ironically, precisely the same proposition of a *tertium non datur* was touted 40 years ago. Stanley Hoffmann was certain that

> [b]etween the cooperation of existing nations and the breaking in of a new one there is no middle ground. A federation that succeeds becomes a nation; one that fails leads to secession; half-way attempts like supranational functionalism must either snowball or roll back.
> (Hoffmann, 1966: 909–10)

What this 'either, or' interpretation overlooks is the very possibility that certain opportunities exist for recasting the equilibrium in a union in permanent tension so that the halfway status – a compound polity between confederation and federal state – can be maintained.

2.5 Conclusion: Learning through analogy

Instead of seeking to identify the historical preconditions for a viable EU polity, the analysis of the contest over the rules of the game in both the EU and antebellum US is based on learning through analogy. Analogy is most often used as a term for describing the common properties of two or more objects.[31] The sense in which it is used in this study, however, refers not to properties held in common but to a 'similarity in the relation of the parts to the whole' (Hesse, 1964: 330) in two different cases: two compound polities in which the same rules of the game were contested. This meaning goes back to Aristotle, who explained in his *Poetics* that 'metaphor by analogy means this: when B is to A as D is to C, then instead of B the poet will say D and B instead of D'. To make this clearer, he added an example of this use of analogy: 'old age is to life as evening is to day; so [the poet] will call the evening "day's old-age"' (Aristotle, 1982: 81).

Tocqueville's great study of American democracy was also based on this logic of analogy through relation. He did not make a straightforward comparison between France and America, of the sort F is like A. Rather, he was interested in discovering how American society had accommodated itself to the principles of democratic equality and popular sovereignty, for he knew that this was the great struggle within French society. The comparison was meaningful, therefore, only in so far as both societies could relate to the same problem. America was no template or crystal ball in which France's future could be seen. But in case the analogy was misunderstood, and despite his careful use of language, Tocqueville thought it necessary to remind his readers that instruction not example was the purpose of his book. The present study adheres to the same logic.

The analogical reasoning that is used thus centres on seeking instruction about how the early American republic managed conflict over the rules of the game and comparing it with the EU experience. The argument here is that to appreciate the viability of the EU and the possibility that the contest over the rules of the game might lead to a more centralized polity it will be useful to understand more about how the US republic fared in managing similar disputes over the rules of the game. This approach resembles what Sewell has called 'historical perspective' (1967: 218), meaning the generation of insights rather than discerning rules of causation common to various historical cases. Developing a comparative perspective in this way, what I have conceptualized as an indirect analogy between two cases, is thus rather different from hypothesis testing, as Stretton has pointed out, because its value is above all heuristic:

> [T]he function of comparison is less to stimulate experiment than to stimulate imagination ... Comparison is strongest as a choosing and provoking, not a proving, device: a system for questioning, not for answering.
> (quoted in Lijphart, 1975: 159–60)

Making an analogy with the early American republic is not, therefore, supposed to yield a template theory of the EU's likely development. Instead, its function is firstly to provide a guide for determining the political tensions and constraints specific to this type of polity. Furthermore, if it is true that a compound polity is characterized by a disputed understanding of the rules for the conduct of politics then, secondly, it will be instructive to learn how the American union was shaped by, and responded to, this challenge. This means identifying the complex manner in which the rules of the game were contested and how and why these were resolved or not. The comparison with European integration is designed to ascertain the differences in how the rules of the game are contested and renegotiated in both polities and what this implies for their respective viability as compound systems. Through analogical analysis it is possible to show not only that context matters but also some of the actual mechanisms for why it matters. This will also provide the interpretive tools necessary for making whether transformative change in integration is a viable venture.

3
Comparing How the Rules of the Game are Contested

> *That generation which grew up with the century, witnessed during a period of fifty years the immense, uninterrupted material development of the young Republic ... there seems to be little room for surprise that it should have implanted a kind of superstitious faith in the grandeur of the country, its duration, its immunity from the usual troubles of earthly empires ... From this conception of the American future the sense of its having problems to solve was blissfully absent; there were no difficulties in the programme, no looming complication, no rocks ahead.*
>
> Henry James (1879: 142–3)

3.1 Introduction

To understand the nature of contestation over the rules of the game of politics in the antebellum US it is necessary to scrutinize the historical record of political and legal arguments in this period. What was under dispute in these moments of acute tension was the shared understanding structuring the rules of US politics: the allocation of competences to the different branches of government, expectations about the union, the exact location of competency over competences and the appropriate basis of representation. At stake was the future of the union, which depended either on the ability to renegotiate a compromise acceptable to both supporters and opponents of a more centralized government or on finding a way of overcoming states' protests for preserving autonomy. Ultimately, as section 3.2 explains, no such agreement was found and the union was held together by force of arms. Following the secessionary war, a new understanding over what the game of politics presupposes had to be found in order to buttress the victorious union.

In the EU compound polity, these same four rules of the game have been subject to repeated contestation. However, the analogical method of comparison developed in this study is based on capturing the differences between how the rules of the game were disputed in the EU and antebellum US respectively. Hence section 3.3 traces five key political-structural differences between how the rules of the game are contested in each compound polity and why this affects viability. These differences have hitherto not been granted much attention in the transatlantic comparative literature, with the singular exception of the oft-remarked absence of a European constitutional foundation for the integration project. This oversight is the result of relying upon a direct comparison between the US and EU systems. Since the observational lens in the case of a direct analogy is focused on the common problems facing both unions – for instance, dilemmas of democratization (Kelemen, 2006), centralization (Donahue and Pollack, 2001) or the role of the legislative in a separation of powers system (Kreppel, 2006) – existing comparative scholarship tends to neglect the evolving relationship between the parts and the whole in either system. Consequently, this literature rarely discusses how the contested relationship between the units and the union affects the viability of the respective EU and US compound polities.

What follows, therefore, is a list and explanatory synopsis of five crucial ways in which both compound systems differ with respect to how the rules of the game are contested and the implications this has for how such crises can be managed. Some (sections 3.3.1 and 3.3.5) concern institutional arrangements, or the structure of the respective compound system, others (sections 3.3.3 and 3.3.4) relate to what can best be described as the political culture – the political objectives behind the project of union and cleavages between the units – of each compound polity. Indeed, another (section 3.3.2) contains elements of both, which is why I have chosen to refer to all five as political-structural differences.

3.2 Viability and the conflict over the rules of the game of politics in the antebellum US

Admittedly, the application of the concept of the compound polity to the US case rests on the acceptance of a 'compact theory' reading of the early American political system, which is by no means the only and uncontested interpretation that exists.[1] Nevertheless the compact interpretation is accepted here as the most persuasive one because, as the argument will demonstrate, in practice the struggle over the rules of the game of American politics was open-ended and not consistent with the assumption that American citizens and politicians shared a common understanding of what the union was for or what competences it should have.[2] Moreover, the principal weapon in the argumentative arsenal used in the various struggles between the union and the states in this period was precisely the claim that the union was a compact between sovereign states, which gave its members the right to interpret the constitutionality of its legislation and even contemplate secession. Thus instead of being driven by a steady logic of national consolidation, the US, as a compound polity, had to find a way of maintaining a consensus over the procedures governing who had the authority to decide, what they could decide and what procedures were to be followed. Above all, the difficulty in finding such a compromise was related to the slavery issue, for all the disagreement over the eventual trigger of the secessionary conflict, is almost universally seen as the root cause of the conflagration.[3]

The historiography of nineteenth-century America is overshadowed by the seemingly endless sport of reinterpreting the founding intentions of the republic. Consensus, pluralist and progressive interpretations represent the three most prominent attempts to capture the way in which institutional design and political ideology reflected the struggle to preserve individual liberty and republican government.[4] One of the most distinguished scholars of US history, Arthur Schlesinger, has identified a recurrent and unresolved tension in American thought that is more useful for the purposes of conceptualizing the problems of the antebellum compound polity. In this dichotomy, the first republic of the new world is considered as either the product of destiny or the triumph of a unique, ongoing experiment (Schlesinger, 1977).

In the nineteenth century this tension between destiny and experiment was more than a sterile intellectual exchange. Eventually it was played out as historical drama on the battlefields of the Civil War as the experiment of the union proved incapable of fulfilling a peaceful destiny due to the slavery issue. In Herman Melville's (1991) stirring words, this was the benighted moment when 'the tempest bursting from the waste of Time/ On the world's fairest hope linked with man's foulest crime'. The next few pages set out how this tension between destiny and experiment translated itself into a struggle over the rules of the game in the American compound system. There were four elements to this conflict: institutional competences, expectations about the union, competency over competences and political representation.

American political development prior to the Civil War was dominated by debates over the meaning and application of the constitution in a period when the US grew tremendously in territory, population and wealth. After the revolution, the Declaration of Independence was immediately revered as a foundational document but the constitution had a more contentious role in public life since it elicited different interpretations and sustained vigorous party conflict. Indeed, only with the impending centennial of the constitution was the original copy of the text exhumed from its resting place in a tattered tin box and properly mounted for exhibition in the library of the State Department, whereas the Declaration held pride of place on the wall of the main reading room.[5]

The first decade of the new republic proved a tumultuous time that in many respects set the pattern for the next 60 years of political strife. What became known as the Republican and Federalist factions first clashed during Washington's presidency over the proper extent of federal power when Hamilton proposed the establishment of a national bank for servicing the public debts of the Confederation and the states (McDonald, 2000: 28-32). Here it was institutional innovation and the proper remit of federal government that proved controversial, whereas in the aftermath of the Supreme Court's 1793 decision in *Chisolm* v. *Georgia*, which confirmed the right of US citizens to bring suits in federal courts against states of which they were not citizens, the argument shifted to competency. In fact, this decision provoked a swift backlash that led to the passing of the Eleventh Amendment[6] – one of only two enacted between the Bill of Rights and the Civil War.

Partisanship within the administration between those seeking to extend the national government and those who wanted it circumscribed continued as the situation in mid-1790s Europe deteriorated, bringing with it the threat of war with France. The so-called Alien and Sedition Acts (1798) forbade defamation of the president and were viewed as a crude and anti-constitutional instrument for silencing those with Republican sympathies. In response to these measures, Madison and Jefferson drafted the Virginia and Kentucky resolutions respectively, both of which set out a compact reading of the constitution that allowed the states to claim that 'the government created by this compact was not made the exclusive or final judge of the extent of the powers delegated to itself' (Rabun, 1956: 51). According to this interpretation, the states were apt to judge the constitutionality of federal laws for themselves and could refuse to execute them if they failed to pass this scrutiny. Ultimately, state sovereignty was invoked by Madison and Jefferson as the best means of protecting individual liberty (Tipton, 1969: 24; McDonald, 2000: 38-42). What had begun as a dispute over the threat to individual freedom posed by federal law had thus evolved into another conflict about where competency over competences lay as well as which branch of government could best represent citizens' interests and hence rights.

National politicians were far from consistent in their opinions as to the limits of federal authority. It has often been remarked how both Federalists and Republicans held different positions according to whether or not they were in power. In a remarkable role reversal, Jefferson was prepared to exploit the grey area of the constitution to seal the Louisiana Purchase while his Federalist opponents – usually the standard bearers of a national vision of the republic – cried foul. But even the intoxicating power of office cannot be used as an explanation for privileging the scope of the national government, given that Jackson vetoed the rechartering of the national bank and refused to help execute a decision of the Supreme Court during his presidency (Remini, 1998a: 331-73; 1998b: 293-314). Likewise, the state actors ought not to be considered straightforward antagonists to the federal union or even consistent in their stance towards the union. For instance, the Kentucky and Virginia resolutions stimulated declarations of loyalty from several New England states who later, during the war with Britain (1812-14),[7] met at the Hartford convention that called for the nullification of a conscription bill then under review in Congress (DiLorenzo, 1998).[8]

In other words, the union also saw its institutional competences called into question – nullification was not a power attributed by the constitution. Indeed, the actual right of the Supreme Court to consider itself the final arbiter over the boundaries between state and federal government as well as the right to strike down state law remained contested throughout this period (Warren, 1913; Miller and Howell, 1956; Goldstein, 2001). Sometimes the Court was viewed solely as a mechanism for reviewing the constitutionality of federal law, that is, 'with power over cases and controversies arising under the Constitution itself, laws enacted in pursuance thereof ... but not cases arising from state laws, which were reserved to state courts' (McDonald, 2000: 78). Thus in 1809 the Pennsylvania Legislature called for an amendment to the constitution because 'no provision is made in the Constitution for determining disputes between the general and the state governments by an impartial tribunal' (Rabun, 1956: 59).

The justices of the Supreme Court were mostly steadfast in their preferences: under the initial impetus of the first Chief Justice, John Marshall, they interpreted the constitution in a way that expanded the competences of the union. Marshall's opinion in the *McCulloch* v. *Maryland* decision (1819),[9] which used a Hamiltonian reading of the constitution to describe the 'implied powers' conferred on the Federal government, is the classic demonstration of this tendency. In a case that indirectly called into question the constitutionality of Hamilton's Bank of the United States, an instrument which the constitution had not mentioned, Marshall wrote: 'Let the ends be legitimate, let it be within the scope of the Constitution, and all means which are appropriate, which are plainly adapted to that end, which are not prohibited, but consistent with the letter and spirit of the Constitution, are constitutional' (quoted in Baker, 1974: 600).

From this brief sketch of political conflict in the nascent republic it should be clear already that the struggle to define the rules of the game was more than a search for a revised and definitive settlement over *Kompetenz-Kompetenz*. Viability in this compound context did not mean discovering a philosophically sound locus of sovereignty or reasoned principle for dividing up the tasks of government between different levels. The union also had its work cut out managing expectations, primarily the South's founding expectation that membership of the US and the protection of slavery were compatible.

In fact, it was the attempt to alter this original compromise over slavery that provoked the first tremors in the compound polity; each time the conflict was linked to the admission of new states, which threatened to upset the sectional balance of power in the Senate. The proposed amendment to the entry of Missouri (1819), which would have prohibited the introduction of new slaves in addition to providing for gradual emancipation, caused an upheaval that led to the so-called Missouri Compromise (1820). Under the terms of this deal, new states would enter, like the animals in the Ark, two at a time, one slave state and one free state. Following further territorial expansion, by mid-century the Missouri deal began to unravel, thereby altering expectations. To re-establish northern expectations of containing slavery a new piece of legislation in Congress sought to outlaw human bondage in lands acquired from Mexico. However, only a new, more complex settlement (commonly known as 'Clay's Compromise') managed to quell the ire of southern leaders, but this unravelled completely with the passing of the Kansas-Nebraska Act in 1854.

This act tried to maintain the expectations of southerners that slavery's status in the union was secure but only by rewriting the existing settlement over competences. Kansas-Nebraska declared Congress, which hitherto had exercised the power to regulate slavery in territories acceding to statehood, unfit to decide the status of slavery in unorganized territories and repealed the geographical limitations imposed by the Missouri Compromise. Decision-making power over slavery was transferred instead to popular sovereignty as exercised by the local population, so-called squatter's sovereignty. However much the notion of popular sovereignty was in keeping with the spirit of American democracy and political experience it was not sufficient to re-establish consensus over the rules of the game. By calling into question the existing compromises over the containment of slavery, the Act was unable to re-establish on a firm foundation both the North's expectation that slavery would be prevented from spreading and the South's condition that the union not interfere with the 'peculiar institution' in its heartland.

Without a delicate balance between these two sentiments the future of the union was uncertain. Northerners feared their concerted efforts to limit the expansion of slavery would now prove useless and that effective national government was impossible in the absence of a new settlement that southern politicians had done their best to scupper. On the other hand, in reaction to the creation of the anti-slavery Republican Party in the wake of Kansas-Nebraska, southerners began to abjure the union. These southerners felt they could not participate in a polity where one party threatened to destroy the economic and social institution on which its distinctive 'way of life' depended; this was a prelude to the extreme forms of resistance to the union that followed.

Thus political representation, which through the states' equality in the Senate and the unforeseen development of national, non-sectional parties – a process explained in depth in Chapter 5 – contributed both to the preservation and, ultimately, the destruction of the compound polity. It was the emergence of the Republicans and their overt hostility to the extension of slavery – previously parties had done their best to keep the question of chattel slavery off the political agenda – that created the conditions for a schism leading to violent confrontation. If consensus over the rules of the game was difficult to re-invent after popular political mobilization on the slave problem it became even more so after an ill-judged judicial attempt to preserve southerners' faith in the union.

When the Supreme Court, under Chief Justice Roger Taney, came to its decision in the egregious Dred Scott case (1857), where the court had to rule on the status of a slave whose master had brought him to a free state, the survival of the union was by this time clearly under threat.

The violent clashes between pro- and anti-slavery supporters in the Kansas territory was the context in which the Court decided to consider Scott as property rather than as a citizen. With this judgment, the Court was performing an active role in the political life of the republic by making a symbolic point that slave-owners mistrustful of the union could nevertheless count on the protection of its property laws. But in doing so the Court had simply created a new political maelstrom as this ruling made slavery legal throughout the federal territories and declared Congress constitutionally powerless to determine the status of slavery in these future states, thereby threatening to void earlier compromises aimed at halting the spread of this brutal practice. Within a few years the union ceased to be a viable compound polity as unity could only be maintained by coercion.

The period immediately after the Civil War, however, is also illuminating for grasping the compound nature of the early republic because of the emphasis placed on fixing new rules of the game that would prove less contentious and thus render the union viable once again. Reconstruction, as the period is known, meant not merely the rebuilding of infrastructure, administration and commerce, to say nothing of the rehabilitation of blacks in the former slave states; it was the process whereby a new settlement to the contest of the rules for the political game was established. Whereas the antebellum period was characterized by uncertainty given the constant contestation of these rules, reconstruction meant providing a more stable political environment for the union. Historians express this tectonic shift by describing the Civil War as a 'second American revolution',[10] where the victory of the union went hand in hand with a deliberate cultivation of the ideology of nationalism. As James McPherson argues, 'the United States went to war in 1861 to preserve the *Union*; it emerged from war in 1865 having created a *nation*' (1991: viii). Militarily, as evinced by the ravaged landscape of the South, victory marked the unequivocal triumph of the union and yet this was not enough for rebuilding the polity. The war left no ambiguity as to the submission of states to the union – the compact reading of the constitution was no longer tenable as it had cost 600,000 lives – but this still did not equate to a sudden and natural epiphany as to the merits of the union.

In this sense Nicholas Butler's reflection that 'so quickly does war act as the solvent of the difficulties that had perplexed legislatures and courts and the people for two generations' (1923: 266) is a little off the mark. By virtue of its victory, the post-war union acquired a new settlement as far as competency over competences was concerned.

States lost their claim to be able to withdraw from the union,[11] nullify laws or unilaterally question the constitutionality of its acts. But other fundamental elements of the rules for politics still had to be fixed, notably the representative nature of the union and the expectations of southerners.

To win the Civil War Lincoln drew on the promise of freedom the union had inherited from the Revolution and which was enshrined in the constitutional objectives of liberty and justice. Yet even after the South's defeat, this interpretation of the union as the guarantor of republican freedom, was not adequate to meet the demands of refounding the American union. The union represented individual freedom; however this was only one part of the greater narrative that it now tried to attach itself to: the American nation. Thus in the reconstruction phase of the union there were in fact two competing visions of the Civil War and its meaning. The 'emancipationist' version is obviously that of Lincoln's rebirth of liberty leading to liberation for blacks, but there was also what historians call the 'reconciliationist' interpretation, which as Eric Foner (2001) notes, 'emphasised what the two sides had in common, particularly the valour of individual soldiers, and suppressed thoughts of the war's causes and the unfinished legacy of emancipation'.[12] The compound system devised at Philadelphia had not proved viable for the expanding republic. Postbellum, the nationalizing of the republic was one of the new features of how the game of politics was to be conducted. Instead of a war over values, the internecine struggle that had divided families was reinterpreted as a 'tragic conflict that nonetheless accomplished the task of solidifying the nation' (ibid.).

In the antebellum era the national idea represented in the political life of the union was almost entirely restricted to the revolutionary era and the period of first settlement.[13] Hence the different respect accorded to the Declaration compared with the Constitution. The volte-face after the North's victory was swift, proving the selective and often wilful nature of the forgetting and remembering needed to establish national narratives. To avoid perpetuating the tradition of local heroes, Civil War cemeteries were intended to glorify the principles on which the nation was founded, instead of persons, and landscaped accordingly.[14] Battle scenes from the war of 1812 and the Mexican war were commissioned for the Capitol even though both of these conflicts were previously thought of as the product of party politics rather than national struggles. The war with Britain had been popularly known as 'Mr Madison's War' and was further tainted because it was the launch pad for Jackson's political career, whereas the Mexican war was originally interpreted by New England abolitionists as a southern plot to extend slavery westwards. Similarly, the settlement of the West was depicted as a new act of triumphant colonization even though it was this territorial expansion that had reawakened the slavery problem in a way that the union was unable to cope with. The heroic element in American life was thus no longer confined to the revolutionary struggle. Instead it was seen as a continuous process, where man fought nature and the native tribes to conquer the land for progress and freedom, forever pushing back the frontier, which proceeded despite the union's teetering on the brink.[15]

Finally, the last element of the reconstruction of the rules of the game of politics was the definition of new expectations, and here cynicism and hypocrisy of the highest order triumphed. As arguments raged between Republicans and Democrats over Congress's plans for the South and over what the provisions of the Fourteenth and Fifteenth Amendments would actually entail in practice[16] – not to mention the local backlash against black emancipation best manifested by the sadistic practices of the Ku Klux Klan – effective government was under threat. The response to this inertia was the Compromise of 1877, which secured the southern Democrats' support for Republican candidate Hayes in the Presidential election (Foner, 2002: 564-87). This came at the cost of turning a blind eye to civil rights abuses in the former slave states, an arrangement that was to last until the 1950s. When viewed from this perspective of the rules of the game, a purely legal interpretation of the post-bellum settlement necessary for reuniting the union can be misleading. It is correct to argue, as Goldstein does that following the Civil War 'the American states ceased official resistance to federal authority' (Goldstein, 2001: 33). Yet this depiction does not account for the fact that in the Reconstruction period it was the Supreme Court that arose 'as the champion of the states against the authority of Congress' (McDonald, 2000: 221) rather than state courts and legislatures. More importantly, Goldstein's portrayal of the post-bellum settlement hardly does justice to the political struggle during reconstruction, which determined the *price* for accepting union supremacy and the abolition of slavery: the removal of federal troops, Jim Crow and Northern acquiescence to oppression of blacks by other means in the South. Reconciliation was possible, therefore, because the acceptance of the perpetuity and supremacy of the union was compatible with a large latitude for southern autonomy in social, economic and political matters.

3.3 Contesting the rules of the game in the EU

As in the antebellum US, the EU compound polity has been subject to ongoing dispute over the four rules of the game of politics: institutional competences, expectations about the union, competency over competences and the appropriate political representation of both citizens and units. A pellucid example of this multifaceted conflict over the rules of the game is the non-application in 2004 of the sanctioning mechanism, 'the Excessive Deficit Procedure', that is part of the 'Stability and Growth Pact' governing monetary union. This whole episode began as a dispute over competence allocation.

The excessive deficit procedure is designed to discipline member states flouting macroeconomic policy rules intended to keep the euro zone and its currency stable. These rules had largely been written at the behest of the German Bundesbank (Heipertz and Verdun, 2004) as a way of giving credibility to a politically risky move in a country where the currency was a symbol of economic renaissance and a return to normality. The situation changed rapidly as in 2003 Germany's public finances, heavily burdened by the enduring cost of reunification, breached the EU golden rule of a public deficit of no more than three per cent of GDP alongside a consolidated public debt no greater than 60 per cent; simultaneously France also breached the rule.

According to the rulebook, it is the Council, meeting in the configuration known as ECOFIN (the Economic and Financial Affairs Council) that adjudicates and sanctions member states breaching the pact. As a result of Franco-German opposition, however, in 2003 the Council (with only the eurozone members voting) was unable to reach a majority vote to establish a breach of the rules. Then in July 2004 the Council suspended the operation of the Excessive Deficit Procedure. A displeased Commission brought a case before the ECJ[17] contesting both the failure to recognize France and Germany's default as well as the arbitrary suspension of the infringement procedure. The Court ruled in favour of the Commission on the latter count – given the Commission's right of initiative in modifying the procedure – yet no sanctions were ever applied and the Council agreed to a modification of the pact in March 2005 (Buiter, 2006).

Here the interplay between the different rules of the game is marked since expectations, *Kompetenz-Kompetenz* and representation all entered the equation, alongside the thorny issue of competence allocation. First of all, the two bad pupils claimed that the rules were poorly devised since they did not include an element of flexibility necessary in times of economic downtown or special circumstances such as reunification. Hence the obstreperous governments challenged the appropriateness of the EU Council's competence over macroeconomic policy. Secondly, the prospect of Germany breaching the pact was originally considered outlandish – the pact was intended as a straightjacket for the notorious fiscal laxness of Greece and Italy. Since this scenario had never been envisaged, the German government felt justified in opposing a measure they had devised but not expected to face themselves. Thirdly, the French and German governments felt that the legality of the sanctions – a fine of up to half a per cent of GDP – was trumped by the legitimacy of both governments' duty to relaunch dented economies. After all, they had been elected for this purpose and not to contribute to the coffers of the EU on the basis of a decision of other member states. In terms of the rules of the game, this was an argument that the member states had a better claim to represent the interests of citizens. France and Germany were thus contesting European institutions' lack, in their day-to-day business, of a governing legitimacy based on 'authoritative democratic representation of individuals' (Kincaid, 1999: 35). Finally, the setting aside of the ECJ's verdict in this case demonstrated that the member states were not prepared to accept that competency over competences lay with the ECJ in such a controversial matter.

As a result, the member states of the eurozone allowed France and Germany to get away scot-free. The eventual resolution of the crisis involved a redefinition of the institutional rules for sanctioning spendthrift member states – a new flexibility clause was added – thereby managing future expectations, preserving a nominal European competence while also recognizing the special representative legitimacy of elected governments (Buiter, 2006). Once again, the nature of competency over competences was left ambiguous as in principle the ECJ had vindicated the Commission's contestation of the legality of dropping the sanctioning procedure, yet in practice the Council abided by its own preferences.

However, the purpose of learning about what makes the EU viable through analogy with the antebellum US experience is to understand the notable variance in how the rules of the game are contested in both polities. It is the five differences identified below that are the basis for the analogical analysis, pursued in Chapter 5, which explains the different scenarios of viability each polity faces. Furthermore, these differences provide the framework for exploring, in Chapter 6, the plausibility of voluntary centralization within the EU compound polity. In other words, the subject of political dispute – the four rules of the game – are the same in the EU and the antebellum US but the manner in which they are contested differs markedly according to political and historical context. Yet despite affecting the scenario of viability each compound polity follows, little of substance is known about the important differences in how political conflict arises and is managed in the EU as opposed to in the US.

Of course, there is one principal exception: the much noted absence of a constitutional foundation for the EU polity. Even at the very dawn of the integration process the leading Euro-federalist Altiero Spinelli recognized that this failure to build Europe upon a constitutional base would greatly constrict the possible development of this nascent polity. By choosing the alternative path of a treaty-based system, Europe was, in his eyes, fated to follow a path of pusillanimous functionalist integration because it left unresolved the fundamental issues of sovereignty and democracy (Spinelli, 1993; cf. Glencross, 2009a). The two latter questions could only be solved, Spinelli believed, by invoking a European constituent power modelled on the Philadelphia experience, the end product of which would be a legitimate constitutional blueprint for settling all future political disputes. In a similar vein, the Italian political scientist Sergio Fabbrini has recently demonstrated how the US Constitution 'furnished a language for constructing the debate on the constitutional order', thereby allowing Americans to be 'united not so much by a common interpretation of the constitution as by their efforts to justify their divergent interests using the same constitutional document' (2007a: 15). Consequently, EU political discourse lacks this unifying feature. This is exactly why the promulgation of an EU Constitution once and for all 'risks freezing an ongoing dynamic process' (Fabbrini, 2001: 63) if it is not able to produce a common method for resolving political disputes.

Indeed, it was the glaring absence of a constitutional moment that led to the fanfare surrounding the 2003 Convention on the Future of Europe, which deliberately sought to mimic the American founding. Aping Philadelphian rhetoric and symbolism, however, did not prevent the subsequent referendum ratifications in France and the Netherlands from turning the so-called Constitutional Treaty into a full-blown fiasco. In fact, this beleaboured American analogy is one reason, according to Andrew Moravcsik (2005), why the whole experiment failed. Instead of persevering in the steady, incremental logic of pragmatic treaty revisions without the baubles or garlands of constitutional foundation, the EU's change of tack promoted 'style and symbolism rather than substance'. This move upset the normal process of institutional innovation in the eyes of the wider public, Moravcsik claims, because it dressed up the quiet, modest reforms 'as a grand scheme for constitutional revision and popular democratization of the EU' (ibid.). This conceit was fashionable among the pro-integration elites but was certainly not appreciated in the same way by large swathes of voters, thereby shattering the temporary illusion that this was Europe's Philadelphian moment.

However, the fact that the EU compound polity did not come to life courtesy of a constitutional foundation is by no means the only telling difference between how the rules of the game are contested in both polities. Hence it is now necessary to outline the five key political-structural differences between the antebellum US and the EU compound systems identified as the most significant factors for explaining how and why disputes over the rules of the game evolved in divergent ways. It is these crucial differences that explain why the process of remaining a viable compound polity is not the same in the antebellum US and the EU.

3.3.1 Dual federalism v. joint federalism

As a government designed to act directly on individuals, the American union had tax-raising powers and its own agents – a system of shared sovereignty later christened 'dual federalism' (Corwin, 1934).[18] Moreover, its exclusive sphere of competence concerned the most exalted functions of government: international politics, defence, immigration, interstate commerce and monetary policy.[19] This is not the case with the EU, whose powers of execution are largely indirect, falling as they do on national legal and administrative structures, and this dissimilarity means the EU will always depend tremendously on the member states for matters such as revenue or military matériel. As Scharpf explains, this type of arrangement means 'the central government is coordinating, assisting, subsidizing and using the capabilities of subnational governments for purposes defined at the national level – but with the participation of these sub-national governments' (1995: 32).

Rather than copy the American founders' dual federalism, therefore, in which two tiers of government occupy two autonomous spheres of activity, each with their own resources and direct relationship with citizens, the European system established an almost entirely indirect form of government: 'joint federalism' (ibid.). Not only does the Commission lack autonomous tax-raising powers[20] and the obligation to run a balanced budget (Article 199 [268] EC),[21] it also relies on the member states' administrative and legal infrastructure for compliance with European-level decision making. Furthermore, the EU joint federal arrangement frames expectations about the future by enshrining the doctrine that all the powers of the union must voluntarily be conferred by the member states.[22]

In addition, joint federalism in the EU revolves around the more numerous – the *acquis communautaire* represents more than 80,000 pages of legislation and constitutes the bulk of member state law-making – yet less prestigious functions of government. This is clear from the dull panoply of its areas of exclusive competence: customs union; the establishing of the competition rules necessary for the functioning of the internal market; monetary policy for members of the eurozone; the conservation of marine biological resources under the common fisheries policy; common commercial policy. These competence areas are, needless to say, those furthest removed from the politics of identity building, such as education, foreign policy or welfare. Nonetheless the EU possesses a wide range of shared competences[23] where 'the Member States shall exercise their competence to the extent that the Union has not exercised its competence' or 'to the extent that the Union has decided to cease exercising its competence' (Lisbon Treaty, Article 2A).

Given this competence base, the EU division of competences is far more unsettled than the competence catalogue contained in the US constitution. The EU thus faces a constant struggle to justify the conferral of more competences through treaty renegotiation. Conversely, in the course of the antebellum, the struggle over competences was more a question of constitutional interpretation rather than the justification of further conferral. Indeed, the US Constitution was scarcely subject to ongoing constitutional amendment although proponents of states' rights fought a vigorous campaign for formal change to enshrine their reading of the nature of the federal union.

3.3.2 A constitution for popular government v. a treaty system

In the American case, conflicts over the rules of the game of politics inevitably centre on the constitution. As a foundational document, the constitution represents – for all its ambiguities and compromises – an original agreement for regulating the conduct of politics that is essentially timeless. With the exception of the Civil War, 'the Constitution's language has delimited and defined what should be considered as the legitimate political discourse' (Fabbrini, 2007a: 15) Even in the antebellum period, the US constitutional document became an ideological keystone of representative politics thanks to its ability to mandate – despite the filtering of popular sovereignty at the federal level by the Electoral College – a form of popular government in the shape of the presidency. Thanks to Andrew Jackson, the presidency functioned as a means for successfully representing individuals *qua* citizens of the union. Given the original adoption of the constitution by popular convention, a feature Chief Justice John Marshall would use to justify his expansive vision of the scope of federal government, the US compound system thus combined foundational and governing legitimacy.

The European union has no such bedrock. As the product of treaties subject to periodic revision, the EU is constrained in a way that is impossible under the US Constitution: sometimes there is a state of virtual suspended animation as the EU awaits the ratification of a treaty by all member states. Only states can be the contracting parties to a treaty unanimously negotiated at the elite level by the governments of the day in each member state, although ratification can be submitted to a popular vote in the member states.[24] Unlike the US Constitution, therefore, the EU treaty-based system finds it very difficult to sustain the fiction of individual consent or social contract for refounding the integration project. Moreover, the EU's unelected, collegial executive does not even offer an indirect relationship with popular sovereignty at the national level, thereby minimizing the ability of the EU to represent individuals *qua* citizens of the union. The treaty nature of the EU compound system also entails the possibility of exit, a feature that was always ambiguous under the antebellum understanding of the US Constitution, which neither specified the right to withdraw nor the right to coerce a state to remain in the union.

Yet a treaty system also offers potential opportunities, not available under the US compound system, for reconfiguring the rules of the game. This is because ongoing EU treaty reform can be a less rigid process than constitutional amendment; reform can be crafted as 'package deals', linking various policy and institutional changes together to form a new compromise. As elite-negotiated deals shielded from popular scrutiny and debate, EU treaty reform can also maintain a high-level of ambiguity about the provisions of treaty change in order to foster consensus. Such ambiguity was most in evidence during the drafting of the Constitutional Treaty, which resulted in 'a reform of EU decision-making without fundamentally clarifying the future trajectory of the European Union' (Jabko, 2007: 6), thereby satisfying supranationalists and intergovernmentalists alike. However, political contestation over the rules of the game is harder to manage – creating new problems for the viability of the EU compound polity – when such reforms are submitted to popular ratification. As Jabko explains, 'elite actors can live with ambiguity because they themselves experience the necessity of entering into strange alliances, but voters who have no direct part in complex strategies often demand greater clarity' (ibid., p. 16).

3.3.3 A project for freedom v. a project for undefined ever closer union

The first sentence of the American constitutional preamble explains limpidly – obviously harking back to the problems of the Articles of Confederation – that what is both necessary and desired is 'to form a more perfect union'. In terms of its stamp on popular conceptions of the principles of American government, however, this phrase is a very poor relation in comparison with the Declaration of Independence's trinity of 'life, liberty and the pursuit of happiness'. If there is one thing that brings continuity to the history of both theoretical interpretations and popular understanding of the US Constitution, it is the belief in the instrumentality of the American union. This is probably why the constitution, which originally only bound three million people, has also continued to be seen as a blueprint for solving problems of political organization in the rest of the world (Beyme, 1987).

The plethora of competing interpretations over whether the constitution is supposed to promote self-government thanks to pluralist checks and balances, limit democracy to protect individual rights or serve as a beacon to a corrupt world nevertheless converge on the fact that the union exists as a means to promote certain ends or values. It was this ability to connect the union to the guarantee of rights and promotion of values that allowed for the mobilization of popular support whenever the antebellum republic was convulsed by sectional crises. Conversely, Daniel Elazar and Ilan Greilsammer have made the invaluable observation that

> in many respects the process of integration [in Europe] has been the very reverse of the process in America: in Europe integration has tended to have been seen as a value in itself, confusing the means with the ends, and it is only once the process has started to produce some results that the question of the type of government, indeed the nature of the political enterprise, is being questioned.
> (Elazar and Greilsammer, 1986: 84-5)

Incremental progress in European construction – even if only a matter of inching towards ever closer union – has thus always been valued by the political elite. The reverse side of this coin is the fundamental absence of a shared idea of where the project is heading. The failed

Constitutional Treaty revealed perfectly how this project lacks a clear end. Its preamble trumpeted the member states' determination to be 'united ever more closely, to forge a common destiny' while also affirming, in seeming contradiction, that the specificity of the EU is to be 'united in diversity'.

The EU's original ends, as enshrined in the Treaty of Rome under the title of 'four fundamental freedoms', followed a strictly economic logic (free movement of goods, services, persons and capital) within the framework of a new cooperative institutional arrangement intended to bring peace to the continent. Yet this original justification has not been immutable: as part of the struggle to deepen integration, pro-Europe political elites have attempted to refocus the union on more explicitly political ends. The ambition of these elites has always been to promote supranational mobilization behind the integration project.[25] However, in addition to the difficulties of drawing on popular sovereignty to establish the EU's foundational or governing legitimacy, the integration project is hampered by the problem of justifying the enterprise itself (Morgan, 2005). Without a specified political finality, it has proved difficult to justify the EU polity vis-à-vis alternative forms of government on the basis of the 'point or purpose of a European polity' (ibid., p. 17). This justificatory problem is compounded by the ambiguity surrounding the existing level of integration actually reached, resulting in 'disagreement over the actual nature of the [integration] situation' (ibid., p. 29) among integration enthusiasts and euro-sceptics alike. Attempts to mobilize citizens in favour of integration have suffered in consequence.

3.3.4 A single fault line v. multiple fault lines

The antebellum US had a preponderant and constant cleavage between the states: chattel slavery. It is vital to note that this cleavage should also be understood more generally as the tension between two competing economic systems, agricultural production based on slavery and the manufacturing society of free labour and free soil. Subsequent territorial expansion exposed the original compromise to a stress that the constitution was not apt to bear. Clashes over the rules of the game involved more than just the detail contained in the founding constitutional parchment. More precisely, what mattered were the things that had remained unmentioned, deliberately or not: the extent of congressional power to regulate chattel slavery and its status in the new territories that would become states.[26] The result was the increasing difficulty to maintain a party system based on intersectional interests. Moreover, this permanent cleavage undermined the logic of Publius' extended republic, in which minorities were to be protected through the absence of permanent majorities. The obnoxious institution supported a way of life for a significant minority of the US population, meaning there was a constant majority living outside the slave states but which could not be translated into a quorum for constitutional amendment because this procedure required an unobtainable two-thirds vote in both houses as well as the support of three-quarters of the states.

Conversely, the EU has overlapping as well as evolving inter-state cleavages: rich and poor, big and small, free-market and *dirigiste*, federalist and intergovernmentalist; the dramatic rise in prosperity in Ireland and the economic resurgence of the UK suggest that even wealth cleavages can change in the course of barely one generation. Only territorial size is an everlasting cleavage. Indeed, in the case of state policy preferences, the position of a member state can even be subject to change from government to government. This suggests there is more room for negotiating compromises as states can hold different positions according to the issue at hand – again increasing the possibility of packaged reforms – and the government of the day. Knowing full well that financial or security prospects can change, as well as future membership and competences, member states may be less intransigent in maintaining positions that could ultimately prove harmful under different conditions. As a result, in the EU compound system there is less risk of playing a zero-sum game of politics than in the US single-cleavage system. This multiple cleavage structure makes for a powerful and enduring obstacle to centralization but one which at the same time does not sanctify the status quo and prevent it from evolving. Neither was true of the American case.

3.3.5 A party system and Supreme Court arbitrator v. politics of treaty reform and council arbitration

Tocqueville held that the Supreme Court was a forum for adjudicating disputes between the states and the union. In part this was exactly what the founders had wanted. But another reason why the Supreme Court came to exercise this power was that the states proved less able to influence federal politics than expected, notably because they could not impose instructions on senators nor sanction those who were thought to act against state interest (Riker, 1955). As a judicial body, the Court's decisions can only refer explicitly to principle and precedent, not expediency. Moreover, as a non-representative institution it upholds first and foremost an ideal (the constitution) rather than an identity (nation or citizenship). This explains why, however august the institution and however wise the justices, it offers a very imperfect solution to legal disputes stemming from – or concealing – political conflict over the rules of the game, especially against a backdrop of clashes over expectations or representation.

Given the Court's imperfect nature for resolving the gravest political disputes over the rules of the game, in the antebellum period the task fell mostly to the various party systems of this era. Frederick Grimke's reflection on the purpose of political parties was never truer than when applied to the early American republic: 'parties take the place of the old system of balances and checks. The latter balance the government only, the former balance society itself' (quoted in Hofstadter, 1970: 266). Since party politics was predicated on representing individuals *qua* citizens of the union, the inevitable result was a certain centralization of political life, at least in terms of debate and organization. As a result, parties became vectors of voluntary centralization albeit for the sake of finding sectional balance.

In the EU the adjudicating role over the rules of the game is normally played by the Council of Ministers supplemented by the European Council, which provides the impetus for major initiatives in policy-making and institutional change, more than by the Court of Justice. As explicitly political bodies, both Councils are more sensitive to public opinion and more legitimate than a judicial body when it comes to finding compromises that affect interests and identity in the member states. This is because these political actors represent citizens' interests and identities directly. They can, in principle, be held accountable for their decisions and explain them to their constituencies in a way that judges cannot. When the rules of the game are contested, the appeal to a judicial institution may vindicate one party but it is unlikely to provide a useful way of redefining the rules in a way that is acceptable to all. Yet the EU compound system nonetheless relies on the ECJ to remedy the problem of 'incomplete contracting' whereby the member states cannot define in advance all the treaty obligations they pledge to uphold (Pollack, 1997). In this way, the ECJ still has a major impact on the rules of the game. Indeed, the greater the ambiguity deliberately left unaddressed in treaty reform, the greater the likelihood that the court will be obliged to pronounce judgments capable of affecting the rules of the game.

Hence EU political debate differs greatly from the partisan politics of the antebellum US, which served to mobilize citizens and aggregate their preferences. In the absence of both a meaningful relationship between popular sovereignty and the policy output of the EU and an 'authoritative democratic representation of individuals' (Kincaid, 1999: 35) at the EU level (besides the emasculated parliament) European and national elites have increasingly resorted to grounding the EU project in another way: referendums. Referendums, on treaty reform and for acceding member states, are now often seen as the best tool for linking citizens with the European project as a whole (Auer, 2007; cf. Dehousse, 2006), thereby substituting the traditional function of political representation. However, referendum politics are far from ideal means for mobilizing national public behind the integration project itself, let alone current EU policies. Besides the reluctance of national elites to contest the institutionalization of the EU polity in domestic politics (van der Eijk and Franklin, 2004; Mair, 2005), national electorates are torn between 'first-' and 'second-order' voting, that is, between signalling domestic party allegiance and expressing preferences on the issue of integration itself (Glencross and Trechsel, 2007). In the absence of agenda-setting and governing pan-European parties, therefore, the EU lacks probably the single most effective means of communication with a broad public as well as a means for redefining the ends of the union to legitimize greater integration. This state of affairs constitutes a singular barrier against unwanted voluntary centralization.

3.4 Conclusion

This chapter first sketched the nature of the disputes over the rules of the game in the early US republic in order to characterize the nature of the arguments deployed in this period of acute political contestation. Despite facing the same pattern of conflict over the four different rules of the game, the EU experience of contestation, it was pointed out, is far from identical. The manner in which the rules of the game are contested differs in both compound systems. Its manifestation is five differences, deemed 'political-structural', affecting both how the rules of the game are disputed and the problems each compound polity faces in remaining viable. Yet before embarking on a comprehensive analogical analysis of what these differences entail for viability in the respective compound systems, it is necessary to explore in depth how the process of European integration has so far remained viable. This is the task of the next chapter.

4
The Struggle to Maintain a Compound System: Creating and Contesting the Rules of the Game in European Integration

> *The Union is an accident, which will last only as long as circumstances favour it.*
> Alexis de Tocqueville (1994: 416)

4.1 Introduction

Had he lived today, Tocqueville would probably have made the same remark about the EU. The precariousness of this political system is well known but nevertheless this chapter retells the story of integration, albeit in a brief and idiosyncratic way. While the broad narrative is a familiar one, it is less so when recounted as the contest over the rules of the game within the scope of maintaining a viable compound political system. Rather than furnish a new theoretical claim to explain why integration took place, therefore, the chapter describes the important steps on the road to 'ever closer union' in terms of how these moments challenge, reinterpret and reproduce the rules of the game of EU politics.

Integration as a label for innovations in intergovernmental action in Europe was carefully chosen. It avoided the static connotation of cooperation and the transcending one of unification, indicating instead 'the construction of a new entity that represented more than the sum of its participating elements' (Stråth, 2005: 264). Normally the process of integration is recounted, in political science, with a theoretical slant explaining why – unwittingly as well as knowingly – the nations of Europe embarked on this path. Usually the aim is also to quantify how much power has been transferred to the European entity and the repercussions this has on the concept and survival of the nation state as well as democracy. The present chapter is not intended as a discussion of the accumulation of EU power and its implications. Instead, the analysis reveals an evolution of the rules of the game according to a logic of dynamic equilibrium rather than of voluntary centralization. This conclusion, despite the evident progress of integration, is drawn from the continuing inability of the EU to settle basic questions of competence, functioning and purpose. Furthermore, despite various attempts to endow it with its own democratic legitimacy, the EU and its institutions have not become the dominant locus for the representation, or indeed mobilization, of European citizens. The member states have retained a preponderant role in both political representation and setting the agenda of democratic politics: the exercise of popular sovereignty remains firmly entrenched at the national level.

4.2 The construction of the rules of the game of European politics, from the ECSC to the EEC

Coal and steel were the raw materials of the first project of European integration. The European Coal and Steel Community (ECSC) was intended to pool and supervise the use of these sinews of war. It makes more sense, however, to understand the ECSC as a supplement to the Paris Peace Treaties of 1947, which had dealt with all the claims against former Nazi allies and co-belligerents but not Germany itself (Judt, 2005: 121-2). Allied-occupied Germany posed at least two great problems for reintegration into post-war Western Europe: the persistence of French claims over the *Ruhrgebiet*, Europe's most industrialized region,[1] and the quandary of what role West Germany would play in the Western defensive alliance against the Soviet bloc.

Yet when looking at the history and philosophy of integration at its origins it would be misleading to summarize the process as simply a successful peace project and, with regard to the Soviet menace, an aborted security one. Two other objectives were equally at the forefront and cannot be subtracted from the irenic and defensive component. The countries prepared to unshackle themselves from a strict pursuit of state sovereignty also desired economic prosperity and the preservation of liberal democracy. Trade barriers and preferential national economic arrangements hampered the former, whereas the permanent mobilization for war was also considered to sap the strength of the latter (Deudney and Suveges, 2005). Thus the only dimension of the rules of the game that emerged prior to the actual treaty negotiations on the ECSC were these four expectations about the purpose and nature of integration as well as a peace project. Therefore, integration was a mechanism for providing security against German resurgence, for stimulating economic growth and strengthening domestic liberal democracy.[2] The other dimensions of the rules of the game, competence allocation, competency over competences and representation would only be settled with the signing of the treaty itself.

4.2.1 The Coal and Steel Community

The question of the status of the *Ruhrgebiet* industrial powerhouse had preoccupied France since the end of the Great War, reflecting fears of permanent economic and military inferiority (Gillingham, 1991: xi).[3] The second obstacle to the rehabilitation of West Germany was French resistance to US pressure for German rearmament to counter the Soviet threat. This had become the first order of the day in Washington's transatlantic policy following the deployment of US troops to the Korean peninsular. The signature of the ECSC Treaty in 1951 provided the political framework for settling the Ruhr problem and established a precedent for Franco-German cooperation which, it was hoped, would furnish an analogue for the rearmament issue. The ECSC resolved the Franco-German security problem by creating more than merely institutions tasked to decide and manage matters of economic policy in common. Its competences were very marginal compared to the ordinary business of government – the goal was a common market in coal and steel. Nonetheless the ECSC's institutional architecture provided the blueprint for the future European Economic Community. Its triumph though was the creation of new precedents and expectations regarding the conduct of international politics on the European continent.

The ECSC's institutional design reflected the compromise between federal and confederal visions of political unification,[4] which in turn led to the establishment of functionalism as the philosophy of the government of these institutions, although the concept itself predates the integration process (Mitrany, 1943; cf. Haas, 1964). Already in 1952, when the ECSC was launched, there was a hybrid of supranational (the High Authority, whose sole remit was the general European interest, and the Court of Justice) and intergovernmental (the Assembly and the Council) principles. This tension survives to this day and is one of the key components of how European politics functions and is contested as integration enthusiasts try to expand the power of supranational institutions while intergovernmentalists take a stand for the shibboleth of national sovereignty embodied by the veto. Another, equally long-lasting, tension can be found in the commitment of the Community, as enshrined in the articles of the treaty, to both free market policies (outlawing cartels and state aid)[5] and social protection (Article 2 refers to 'safeguarding the continuity of employment'). The compatibility or not between these two objectives continues to be the platform for discussion when the left/right cleavage is transposed to the European level (Hooghe and Marks, 2008).

Indeed, even the problematic nature of democratic representation and accountability in European institutions can be traced back to the ECSC. The Community's Common Assembly was an emasculated representative assembly, which monitored the work of the executive, leaving the right of initiative to the High Authority and the right of assent to the Special Council of Ministers. Moreover, the Assembly's relationship with the people it supposedly represented was indirect since its members were selected by the national parliaments of the member states. A Consultative Committee was also created to represent the views of producers, consumers and workers. Their decisions were non-binding and members were selected by the Council on its own understanding of representativeness.[6] This marked the beginning of the ambivalent and often instrumentalized status of civil society actors within European integration.

The detail of Community institutions, procedures and policy is not the main story, however, at least not when it comes to the construction of the rules of the game of politics in Europe. What matters for the scope of this study is the way the ECSC served to determine expectations about the nature of the integration process. In beginning this very process, the ECSC laid the foundation stone that shaped the future contours of the integration project. Two basic precedents with long-lasting effects emerged from the establishment of the ECSC. Firstly, the Franco-German relationship, reflecting Churchill's prescient plea in his 1946 Zurich speech,[7] was to be the locomotive of integration. This engine was to function through West Germany's overriding commitment to make integration work, including at the price of certain economic concessions and the acceptance of French political leadership.[8]

Secondly, the method of integration was to be the achievement of political objectives through management of the economy: the functionalist logic of integration. The genius of this process was not merely the ability to find a proxy for furthering political ends thanks to 'spill-over' effects from one sectoral field of the economy into others that would create new needs for supranational administration and encourage supranational political entrepreneurs. Functionalism's primary benefit within the ECSC architecture was that it allowed the member states to stay in control of decision making while habituating them to cooperation and consensus. As Altiero Spinelli, the great Italian champion of a federalist Europe, noted 'the entire functional establishment was founded on the hypothesis that the power to decide would actually remain in the hands of the government of the member states, while the European bureaucracy would create a solidarity of common interests and rules, thus conditioning in growing measure the decisions of the governments' (Spinelli, 1966: 23).

Functionalism as the politically palatable doctrine of integration was greatly reinforced by the failure of the European Defence Community (EDC), which was voted down in the French National Assembly in 1954. After the initial problem of restraining West Germany had been adequately surmounted, the Soviet menace posed a new security dilemma, which revealed the limitations of the solution of the former. EDC was France's proposal to settle the issue of West German rearmament in the wake of the US strategy of global communist containment, which required that Western Europe strengthen its own capacity to resist a hypothetical Soviet invasion. The French establishment was fearful of West Germany's integration into NATO as an autonomous military power. Yet the US exerted tremendous pressure on its allies to find a new agreement for defending Western Europe that would allow for a German military contribution.[9]

In this context EDC was intended as a hybrid supranational-intergovernmental analogue to the ECSC. The project called for a European army comprised of national battle units 'grouped into multinational Army Corps whose command, general staff and tactical and logistic support echelons were also to be integrated' (Fursdon, 1992: 231). Troops would fight wearing a common uniform, something an initial French proposal (the Pléven Plan) had baulked at. These corps would come under the control of a nine-member board of independent commissioners, itself a joint decision maker alongside another council of ministers. The unanimity principle applied to key matters such as the budget and equipment programmes, thereby endowing France with a clear control over the size and scope of German rearmament.

Reasons for the failure of the EDC – despite blandishments from Washington – are not important for this story as it is the simple fact of failure itself, which had the greatest consequence on the framing of European politics (Parsons, 2003: 67-89). The collapse of the common defence project spelt the demise of the daring proposal, known as the European Political Community, steered through the ECSC Assembly by Belgian Prime Minister Paul-Henri Spaak. This plan envisaged a federally integrated political union – with a directly elected assembly and a senate representing national parliaments – that would oversee the working of the EDC (Griffiths, 1994).[10] Hence with the ambition of integration acutely attenuated to sector by sector functionalism – the logic of the EEC Treaty – the project of unifying Europe became an open-ended process without a clear end in sight. This is still the case today, as evinced by Joshka Fischer's call in 2000 for a debate on the EU's political finality, something neither the Constitutional Treaty nor the subsequent Lisbon Treaty could settle. More concretely, the first treaty of European integration established rules of the game in terms of institutional competence allocation and the nature of political representation. The logic of functionalism determined the conferral of competences: the integration process would abstain from encroaching upon the high politics of the sovereign nation state and would be incremental rather than based on an original, extensive competence catalogue. Secondly, concerning representation, there was to be a hybrid institutional and decision-making structure mixing the principles of confederalism (intergovernmentalism) and supranationalism (federalism). Furthermore, new expectations emerged, notably the open-ended nature of the integration process – there was no consensus on the final destination – and the assumption that France and Germany were to cooperate to provide the impetus for taking the European project further.

4.2.2 The European Economic Community

Certain existing aspects of institutional design, competences and decision-making rules were reinforced by the terms of the Treaty of Rome[11] but these were coupled with the development of new expectations. Finality, for instance, was singularly missing from the new treaty. Whereas the ECSC treaty had a shelf life of 50 years (Article 97), the Rome treaties had no such time limit, thereby enshrining integration as something that can take an unspecified time to arrive at an undefined destination.[12] What now framed the trajectory of integration was a new treaty commitment to 'ever closer union' meaning that even if the process was to be slow and tortuous, it was at least expected to be unidirectional: forwards never backwards.[13] This expectation lay at the heart of the refusal by the other five members – in spite of their acquiescence to many other French demands – to grant France the option of withdrawing from the customs union if the economy suffered badly (Moravcsik, 1998: 144).

The hybrid nature of the system of government was further enshrined in the core EEC institutions. These reproduced the essential design of the ECSC with a supranational executive, an intergovernmental decision-making body that would in the future, however, sometimes use qualified majority voting rather than unanimity, an independent court and a representative assembly lacking legislative powers. Yet whereas the ECSC regulated solely steel and coal companies and member states, the EEC treaty created a legal framework – notably the free movement of citizens – that touched physical persons directly. This difference, as shown below, was of vital importance for the subsequent constitutionalization of the EEC treaty by the ECJ.

In the driving seat of integration was the Commission, given its monopoly on proposing new legislation and its mission to express the common interest of the Community. Yet the institutions of the EEC deliberately forsook the classic distinction between executive and legislative powers, preferring instead to blur these two competences. Since the Council can only act on a proposal from the Commission, which in turn can only be amended by unanimity (EC Article 189a [250]), this provides a built-in system of mutual cooperation which 'keep[s] the intergovernmental ingredient under the control of the supranational one and *vice versa*' (Cassesse and della Cananea, 1992: 78; cf. Majone, 2005: 42-63).

As outlined above, one of the founding expectations of integration was 'the pursuit of the national economic advantage of all parties' (Milward, 2000: xi). Implicit in this assumption is that for European integration to be seen as effective and legitimate, it has to deliver tangible results on economic growth. As Milward explains, 'West Germany was the pivot on which the increases in foreign trade, investment and prosperity turned' and the common market 'was the one durable way that had been found' (ibid., p. 223) to make this pivot lever upwards the economies of its erstwhile adversaries. But Thatcherism *avant la lettre* this was not; the EEC maintained the ECSC's ambiguous dual commitment to laissez-faire alongside social protection. The free market created by the EEC was not supposed to disrupt the level of social protection available in the various member states. In fact, a social fund was established, with unemployment at historically low levels, for the limited purpose of 'promoting within the Community employment facilities and the geographical and occupational mobility of workers' (EC Article 123 [146]). Social policy, therefore, was clearly established as a *possible* area of European cooperation.

Tony Judt rightly calls the EEC Treaty 'for the most part a declaration of future good intentions' (Judt, 2005: 303) because of its tendency to signpost certain goals without necessarily providing for their realization. This is most obviously the case with regard to the twofold ambition of completing the free market for capital, goods, services and people, and orchestrating the common economic and monetary policy sketched out originally in EC articles 103 to 108 [99-110]. Both goals were subsequently the basis of two further treaties, the Single European Act (1986) and Maastricht (1992) respectively: these two jump-starts in integration have their origins in the founding document. Thus the EEC, more so than the ECSC, underscored the projective nature of integration, asserting explicit policy goals such as common economic and monetary management or the commitment to reducing regional inequalities that implied significant political consequences. Important to note, however, is the fact that as with the case of social policy, these promises were not accompanied by any certainty that these were politically feasible.

The choice of deferring decisions, pending a new consensus or sudden external impetus for forging ahead, was not limited to the most ambitious and sovereignty-eroding goals. Even the process of moving towards qualified majority voting in the Council on trade negotiations with third parties or price-setting on agricultural goods was fudged until a later date. This was symptomatic of the kind of treaty agreement the EEC represented, and which was to become the established norm for later ones. Moravcsik calls these 'framework documents'. In outlining how the customs union would be followed by the introduction of Qualified Majority Voting (QMV) for external negotiations and competition policy, the Treaty of Rome thus fixed 'institutional procedures through which rules would be elaborated rather than specific rules themselves' (Moravcsik, 1998: 152). Unlike the ECSC, known to lawyers as a *traité de règles*, where what matters is the application of rules contained in the treaty, the EEC is a *traité de procédures* (or *traité cadre*) (Soulé, 1958) outlining the procedures by which the Community can eventually adopt policies. Hence integration is a project with certain farsighted goals, sometimes actively pursued and at other times in abeyance. As a result, member states have squabbled repeatedly, as shown in the rest of this chapter, over how the rules of the game determine member state influence or control over future decision making.

4.3 After the EEC: Unexpected constitutionalization (ECJ), the first enlargement (UK) and democratic consolidation (Mediterranean enlargement)

There is a tendency in the political science textbook account of integration history to present the EEC[14] as the natural next step in the creation of a supranational polity. This is what John Gillingham sardonically refers to as 'the New Testament version of ECSC: bigger [sic], better, and accessible to all believers' (2003: 74). Undoubtedly, the two decades that followed the signing of the Treaty of Rome were not fallow ones. Yet this period was marked by the continuing struggle to maintain a consensus over the rules of the game – a highly contingent process that belies description as a smooth progression towards closer union.

The framework provisions of the new treaty needed to be transformed into concrete policy action and so began the work of the EEC institutions. Unexpectedly, it was the ECJ, which on paper perhaps stood out least from the four major organs of the proto-polity that made some of the most dramatic changes to the rules of the game. The two decisions in the *Van Gend en Loos* (1963) and *Costa* v. *ENEL* (1964) cases were the vital instruments for 'fashion[ing] a constitutional framework for a federal-type structure in Europe' (Stein, 1981: 1). However, the Court of Justice had been 'expected to play a marginal role ... in part because it was expected to resolve only minor, intra-organizational disputes as it had in the ECSC' (Moravcsik, 1998: 155). Under the ECSC, the Court could not consider actions brought by individuals nor did it have the power to interpret the treaty; the EEC treaty reversed both these provisions. Thus the precedent of the ECSC proved very misleading for understanding the impact the court would have on European politics.

4.3.1 The impact of the Court on the rules of the game

Although the ECJ had already been created by the ECSC treaty, it was able to establish itself as a dominant actor in the shaping of the rules of the game only after the EEC Treaty (EC Article 177 [234]) gave it the power to interpret the treaty per se, as well as subsequent legislative acts, and not just the legality of the actions of European institutions as under the ECSC treaty. In reality though, member states expected the court to deal with disputes arising under articles 169 and 170 [226 and 227], which enabled the Commission or a member state respectively to bring a suit for a state's failure to fulfil treaty obligations. Indeed, article 173 [230], allowing the ECJ to rule on the lawfulness of acts of the Council and Commission, suggested a role as a bulwark against potentially *ultra vires* EEC legislation. However, article 177 associated the right to interpret the treaty with the competence to make a 'preliminary ruling' at the behest of a domestic court 'if it considers that its judgment depends on a preliminary decision' on a question of European law. This power enabled the Court to have a tremendous effect on the rules of the game.

The two historic cases that are the starting point of any EU lawyer's studies were actions brought by a Dutch company importing chemicals,

Van Gend en Loos, and an Italian citizen, Flaminio Costa, respectively. At stake were three serious questions concerning sovereignty: did the EEC treaty confer rights to persons moral and physical against their state? Who decides when a state has broken its treaty obligations? What happens when member state law and European legislation conflict?

In the *Van Gend en Loos* case, the firm took the Dutch government to court for not respecting the EEC treaty's provision forbidding increases in customs duties on imports from member states. Since article 177 instituted a procedure for national courts to seek a preliminary decision on questions concerning the interpretation of the treaty, the Dutch tribunal (the *Tariefcommissie*) referred the matter to the ECJ. The Dutch government argued, firstly, that the ECJ had no jurisdiction in this matter as, according to EC articles 169 and 170 [226, 227], only the Commission or a member state could bring a charge of treaty infringement before the court. Secondly, as the case concerned 'the effect in Dutch internal law of an international treaty', under the practice of customary international law it was affirmed that the enforcement of treaty obligations 'must be determined exclusively by Dutch constitutional law' (Stein, 1981: 5).

The court ruled that individuals' rights were best protected by allowing them to take their grievances to the ECJ. 'To confine', it argued, 'the guarantees against infringement of article 12 [forbidding new import duties] by the member states to the procedures under articles 169 and 170 [action by the Commission or member states] would remove all direct legal protection of the individual rights of their nationals' (*Costa v. ENEL*). Furthermore, the analogy with standard international law was not pertinent because: 'the Community constitutes a new legal order of international law for the benefit of which the states have limited their sovereign rights, albeit within limited fields, and the subjects of which comprise not only Member States but also their nationals' (ibid.). This ruling established the norm of 'direct effect', meaning that treaty provisions created legally binding obligations that were justiciable in the member states.[15]

A subsequent ruling, *Van Duyn* (1973), adjudicated on the clash between a directive providing for free movement of persons and the British government's refusal to give work permits to members of the Church of Scientology. The ECJ found in favour of *Van Duyn*'s suit against the UK authorities, who had yet to implement the directive, extending thereby the *Van Gend en Loos* decision to cover directives as well. These two cases changed the rules of the game, therefore, by ensuring that European legislation has to be transposed into domestic law and that individuals have the right to see that this is done. Thus the responsibility for overseeing compliance is not the preserve of the Commission or the member states. Henceforth, national courts would play an important role in integration by highlighting the member states' failure to comply with European law and allowing citizens to seek redress thanks to the ECJ.

In *Costa* v. *ENEL*, the ECJ treated a question of conflict of laws, which had been elided in the *Van Gend en Loos* case. In effect, Costa became a proxy for settling the clash between federalist principles and confederal ones, at least in the legal arena. Although the court pronounced the 'primacy' of European law over its national counterparts, this did not entail a definitive settlement of the competence over competences issue. Nor did it simplify the identification of a locus of ultimate authority. By reading the EEC treaty in this way, the ECJ only increased the member states' desire to design the procedures for future decision making so as to control the outcome by making it virtually impossible to reach decisions except via consensus. Likewise their wariness towards adopting new policies that would transfer more power to the Community was heightened.

Costa makes an unlikely European founding father. Yet the court ruling that followed his tenacious pursuit of a dispute arising from his failure to pay an electricity bill almost seems to entitle him to a place alongside Monnet, Schuman or Hallstein – at least in terms of the number of times his name is cited. Contesting the Italian government's nationalization of the electricity industry – he owned shares in an electricity company, Edison Volta – Costa claimed the plan infringed EEC provisions on such things as monopolies, state aid and new restrictions on competition. It was the lower (magistrates) court in Milan, the *Giudice Conciliatore*, that seized the ECJ of the case and asked for a ruling. Once again the member state in whose jurisdiction the claim began denied the admissibility of this request and thus the supranational court's authority to offer a ruling on what was a matter of domestic law. The ECJ judges were at pains to point out that the EEC treaty could not be understood as a normal instrument of international law that states could avail themselves of by selecting for themselves which aspects to comply with. In their famous opinion, 'by contrast with ordinary international treaties, the EEC Treaty has created its own legal system which, on the entry into force of the Treaty, became an integral part of the legal systems of the Member States and which their courts are bound to apply' (*Costa* v. *ENEL*).

Italian nationalization of the electricity industry was not overruled by the ECJ; nor did the judges ever seriously consider deeming it unlawful despite asserting the primacy interpretation. Treaty restrictions on state aid and the right for the Commission to be consulted on state measures possibly distorting the operation of the common market did not, in the court's opinion, create individual rights. Instead of dictating government policy, the court's groundbreaking ruling sought to make a point about the evident contradiction between committing oneself to the creation of a common market and having domestic laws override these rules: 'the executive force of Community law cannot vary from one State to another in deference to subsequent domestic laws, without jeopardizing the attainment of the objectives of the Treaty' (*Costa v. ENEL*).

In another landmark case, *Internationale Handelsgesellschaft* (1970), the court returned to the primacy doctrine and reiterated the superiority of Community law by declaring that it also trumped constitutional law and traditions. The judgement coolly announced that 'the validity of a Community measure or its effect within a Member State cannot be affected by allegations that it runs counter to either fundamental rights as formulated by the constitution of that State or the principles of a national constitutional structure' (*Internationale Handelsgesellschaft*). What the ECJ (always acting with the support of the Commission) did, therefore, was less to settle permanently questions of sovereignty than force EEC members to recognize that treaty ratification had serious ramifications on the exercise of their authority.

These court decisions, however, did not trickle down into the broader public consciousness of citizens in the member states. Thus awareness of the existence of this 'quasi-federal' (Stein, 1981: 24) legal order is limited to a small and learned elite. Even today, the primacy of the European legal order remains controversial. Whereas the Constitutional Treaty affirmed the principle of primacy in full view at the start of the document (Article I-6), the Lisbon Treaty is far coyer and has buried reference to primacy in a declaration contained in the final act. In fact, the doctrine of primacy was met by resistance even from national judiciaries. The most notable contrariness came from France, whose *Conseil d'État* (Chief Administrative Court) twice defied article 177 and point-blank refused to accept a request from a lower administrative court for an ECJ preliminary ruling.[16] Only in 1989 did the *Conseil d'État* recognize EC legal supremacy, although France's highest court of appeal (the *Cour de Cassation*) had done so in 1975.[17]

Thus in the two decades following the signing of the EEC, the ECJ established that European-level decisions were not to be superseded by subsequent domestic legislation. Changes of heart reflecting changes in national policy or preference could not derail integration: the principle of *lex posterior derogat priori* does not apply. Ever closer union is a truly binding principle founded upon a system – article 177 – for binding the governments of the member states from within their domestic jurisdictions.[18]

Thanks to the ECJ, law has functioned as a mask for politics but it is clear that politics continues nonetheless because the Court's ability to 'federalize' the European Community by acting as a final arbiter over the conflict of laws has not been taken with equanimity by the member states. Armed with the knowledge that European legislation takes precedence over domestic law and that this conferred rights on individuals, states revised their expectations about the integration process and sought less to defy European authority than to pre-empt its unwanted consequences. Supremacy of European law, therefore, is almost meaningless without a proper understanding of how the politics of integration severely constrains the spheres in which the Community can consider itself supreme. Hence the acceptance of the principle of primacy has certainly not been accompanied by a settlement over the issue of where competency over competences lies.

4.3.2 British accession: Opening up the Pandora's box of domestic politics

Ever closer union was not an exclusionary principle.[19] Article 237 of the original treaty spelled out the expansionary design of the EEC: 'any European State may apply to become a member of the Community'.[20] More than ever, European integration became a subject of domestic political debate, both rational and hysterical, as existing and prospective members debated the merits of enlargement. To determine the effect this had on the rules of the game it is worth studying in detail the political contestation engendered, both within the EEC and at the domestic level, by proposed British accession. What matters is why enlargement proved so problematic, how the issue was eventually resolved and what were the future consequences.

Great Britain proved reluctant to participate in the early Franco-German initiatives of European integration. It snubbed the ECSC and, after declining to join the EEC, had constituted a European Free Trade Area (EFTA) of its own in 1960, which brought together seven states.[21] British participation in the EEC nevertheless loomed large given its size (in 1962 almost as populous as West Germany), military might and solid historic commitment to liberal democratic principles. Besides, the death throes of empire and the dismantling of the system of imperial trading preference were forcing a major rethink of national economic strategy and positioning in the world economy. Only a year after the launch of EFTA, the Macmillan government began negotiations for belatedly entering the community. Eventually, Britain would be allowed to join following two French vetoes and a special French referendum on the question.

Negotiations during Britain's candidature were a drawn-out affair that revolved largely around concessions needed to fit Britain into Europe's agricultural policy. Technically, this was the biggest sticking point because it meant Britain would be switching from 'a system of low market prices and high farmer subsidies to the Community system of artificially sustained higher prices' (Lindberg and Scheingold, 1970: 230). It is important to note that the negotiating table was not a two-sided affair in which the EEC six were dealing with Britain as united protagonists. At stake was in fact the emerging equilibrium about the details of European agricultural policy itself, notably the Franco-German bargain on supported prices for certain foodstuffs. When conducting the negotiations, therefore, 'the Community faced the dual problem of reaching an agreement with the British and at the same time reordering their own relationships' (ibid., p. 229).

The same was true of other bones of contention. British admission went beyond setting conditions for Britain's entry into the game of European politics; enlargement threatened to rewrite the rules of the club itself. The EEC members realized the extent to which expansion placed a question mark over the viability of the community. This is why, besides the technical aspects of agricultural policy or the status of the Commonwealth and EFTA in the customs union, they also made 'conjectures about where the British would stand on given issues' (ibid.) to assess the long-term cohesion of the bloc. The discrete aspect of the negotiating process over agriculture and commonwealth trade was separate from and not necessarily related to broader expectations about how the UK would behave as a member. Lindberg and Scheingold make this point by referring to 'two sets of negotiations – one explicit and the other tacit' (1970: 232). Whereas economic policy was the subject of formal talks, tacit negotiations involved 'penumbral problems' about where the Community would be heading if it expanded to include Britain and its northern fellow-applicants. Indeed, France's need to resort to the veto can be read as 'a sign that the Commission was manipulating a consensus' (ibid., p. 245) on the issues undergoing formal negotiation.

Expectations about the future were crucial since the EEC six were at that moment discussing a radical proposal, known as the Fouchet Plan, to redesign the institutions and purposes of the integration project (Parsons, 2003: 132-5). This plan owed its existence to de Gaulle's triumphant return to French politics, which post-dated the EEC treaty but whose institutions he nevertheless sought to impose his stamp on. The Fouchet Plan was a canny move that called for furthering integration by creating a 'Union of Peoples' that would 'reconcile, co-ordinate and unify the policy of Member States in spheres of common interest: foreign policy, economics, cultural affairs and defence' (Article 2, Fouchet Plan II). It was clever because at the same time as it proposed new areas of joint action it made all of these dependent on unanimous agreement and lacked any supranational institutions; clearly it aimed to curtail federalist aspirations or at least prevent any developments contrary to French interests.

Fouchet's plan collapsed before de Gaulle announced his veto. In the absence of a settlement for the rules by which Europe would forge ahead on the path of integration the possibility of enlargement became more threatening. This fear can be seen in de Gaulle's public justification of the veto, in which he specifically identified the potential clash between widening the EEC and strengthening integration. Drawing on his geopolitical perspective and his obsession with securing an independent foreign policy, he prophesied that as a bloc of 11 or more 'it is to be foreseen that the cohesion of its members, who would be very numerous and diverse, would not endure for long, and that ultimately it would appear as a colossal Atlantic community under American dependence and direction, and which would quickly have absorbed the community of Europe' (quoted in Nicholson and East, 1987: 31).[22] In other words, expansion did more than jeopardize the current agreement over the rules of the game on competence issues such as agriculture or customs union; future projects of integration could not be realized if the community grew too heterogeneous. A second British application soon followed in 1967, which was again rebuffed by de Gaulle for near-identical reasons after negotiations lasting barely a few months. It is the expansion of the EEC in 1973, however, that provides the next most telling development in the rules of the game of European politics, for it is the moment when referendums emerge as a crucial factor in the integration process.

In terms of diplomatic negotiations, the key to successful British accession lay in deliberately linking together widening and deepening to prevent the former hindering the latter. This policy was agreed upon at The Hague Summit of 1969 as the 12-year time frame for completing the three initial stages of integration drew to a close. Prior to enlargement, the six sought to settle the unfinished business of devising a system for financing the Common Agricultural Policy (CAP) and sketch an outline of the next phase of integration. The subsequent financial package, which allocated to the Community funds from levies on food imports and the common tariff on industrial goods as well as a proportion of VAT receipts, was then presented to the new members as an *acquis communautaire*. Likewise, the decision to begin foreign policy cooperation and implement an eventual economic and monetary union agreed upon at The Hague was considered a definitive blueprint for closer union, which Leigh aptly calls 'an insurance against any drift to Atlanticism following the entry of Great Britain' (Leigh, 1975: 158).

British accession is also a story of two referendums, one French and one British; the first decided the fate of the application[23] and the second, held two years after joining, determined whether or not Britain should remain in the Community. These referendums – although here the discussion focuses purely on the British one – demonstrate well the desire to legitimate the integration project through domestic political debate and the problems this give rise to, especially the difficulty of justifying a supranational polity. Once referendums are used, the fate of integration is strictly tied to the mobilization of public opinion, which has had a profound impact on the construction of the rules of the game.[24]

Edward Heath's Conservative government conducted negotiations with the EEC to a successful conclusion, formally joining in 1973 after parliamentary ratification.[25] The UK, at a time of poor economic performance and relative political instability, held two general elections in 1974. In the first of these, the Labour Party pledged to renegotiate the terms of accession to the EEC, which were still highly controversial especially because progress on the regional fund, which would reduce Britain's net financial contributions, was at a standstill. In the second election, Labour promised to hold a referendum on the results of this renegotiation to determine Britain's continuing membership – a line more consistent with its original opposition to the treaty under the previous government. In the end, the renegotiation resulted in the adoption of a 'financial mechanism' for refunding excess gross contributions but with a plethora of strings attached so that 'with hindsight it seems unlikely that it was ever intended to be effective' (Denton, 1984: 121).[26] This cosmetic change was sufficient to allow the then Labour Prime Minister, Harold Wilson, to let the people return their verdict on the EEC. The final result was 67 per cent in favour, with a turnout of around 64 per cent.

Predictably, the referendum debate aroused strong feelings as Commonwealth and Atlantic attachments proved resilient. Yet the content of the debate, which mostly revolved around sovereignty and Britain's position in world affairs, is perhaps less consequential than the referendum's overall effect on British party politics. This most stable of twentieth-century party systems, unsullied by wartime collaboration unlike much of the continent, was nevertheless unable to cope with the new cleavage issue of European integration. To start with, the constitutional innovation of inviting voters to decide a single question for themselves was unprecedented in parliamentary history. For only the second time in the history of parliamentary democracy, cabinet collective responsibility was waived[27] and both major parties were divided into pro- and anti-common-market camps. Thus the referendum device itself was 'a way of circumventing internal party splits' (J. Smith, 1998: 56). These had already been apparent in 1972 when the law ratifying British entry was passed with the aid of pro-European Labour parliamentarians. The implosion of the Labour Party on this issue intensified when it came to power, to the extent that Wilson was forced to concede a referendum to mollify his anti-European critics inside as well as outside parliament. At the grassroots level, hostility to continued membership was very pronounced: in a special party conference on the subject, the party voted two-to-one for rejecting the renegotiated terms. 'The country thus witnessed', in George's pointed description, 'the spectacle of a Labour Government recommending to the people in a referendum a line of action that it was official Labour Party policy to oppose' (George, 1998: 93).

With parties splitting before the vote and then reuniting afterwards, the net result was that the referendum 'resolved few of the tensions surrounding Britain's membership of the EEC or the failure of elites to deal with the question within traditional party frameworks' (ibid.). An extraordinary measure was thus used to deal with a new political issue that would keep recurring in the future and yet which cut across the traditional left/right party cleavage. The British precedent would be followed in many other member states, thereby illustrating the self-perpetuating character of the referendum when used as a palliative for internal party strife. Nevertheless this is typically how referendums are used on questions of integration: 'in all EC countries disagreements over European unification do not occur between the main political parties but within them' (Franklin et al., 1994: 469).[28]

The temporary suspension of party cohesion on a recurring issue only defers an intraparty resolution on the matter; the exercise is cathartic but this purging of emotions hardly precludes them from reappearing and so the patient is not cured in any meaningful sense. Hence their use has added a new twist to the rules of the game, as a supplementary element to the struggle between the principles of supranational and intergovernmental representation. In particular, since traditional domestic party politics struggles to provide a meaningful way of legitimizing further integration, referendums have increasingly come to be seen as a more promising way of legitimizing European construction. Rather than depending on indirect legitimation via national representative politics (Moravcsik, 2002), referendums entail using direct democracy at the national level to legitimize treaty reform. However, the mechanism remains confederal or intergovernmental since it in effect provides states with a second veto option over treaty reform, which can cause havoc with the process, as happened when voters in Denmark (1992), Ireland (2001), France and the Netherlands (2005) and Ireland (2008) rejected treaty reform. More so than the introduction of direct elections to the European Parliament, therefore, it is the staging of referendums that has fundamentally disrupted the 'permissive consensus' (Norris, 1997) whereby citizens formerly showed little interest in the politics of integration.

Apart from the predictable outpourings of Atlanticist stalwarts and those nostalgic for imperial grandeur, the content of the UK referendum debate is notable for two further reasons, indicative of the way referendums on integration matters enter the public sphere. Firstly, it reveals the difficulties of selling integration to a mass public and, secondly, it demonstrates the extent to which it leaves fundamental political problems unresolved. Rabid, if articulate, opponents of the EEC like Enoch Powell had it easy: their appeal for a no vote was a loud argument about sovereignty and special bonds with the Commonwealth. Those who wished to remain in the Community, on the other hand, had a harder time expressing a finer argument, which stayed clear of sovereignty and identity debates. Instead, as Michael Steed observed, the yes campaign revolved around 'the familiar bread-and-butter issues of a British general election' (1977: 130-1). Quite literally since food prices were a primary electoral concern at a time when world prices for many foodstuffs had risen above the EEC stabilized price. In the government's pamphlet advocating continued membership, the emphasis was thus placed squarely on 'food, money and jobs' (Butler and Kitzinger, 1976: 291). Indeed, the expectation of economic growth thanks to integration is apparent every time new treaties are subject to national consultation. Progress in the integration project is thus intended to be relevant to citizens through its positive effect on economic life-chances.[29]

Owing to the difficulty of justifying integration as something other than a means of securing peace and economic growth, referendums have proved no better than ordinary domestic party politics in settling questions of sovereignty raised by closer union. Neither seem able to provide the voting public with a clear understanding of the implications integration has for national sovereignty – in large part because treaty ratification entails the sanctioning not of a simple structured system of government but a complex and often opaque project with a high propensity for future changes (Jabko, 2007). For instance, the Danish opt-out on cooperation in Justice and Home Affairs has proved to be of little value in safeguarding sovereignty in this area as Denmark's participation in the Schengen open-border agreement means it is obliged to opt back in to most legislation in this area (Adler-Nissen, 2008). The UK is another case in point. Given its historical and insular detachment from continental Europe, as well as its stringent doctrine of parliamentary sovereignty, it would seem sensible to expect strong assurances or clarifications about what integration entails for UK sovereignty so that any transfer of power would be sealed with the stamp of incontrovertible democratic legitimacy.[30]

These were not very forthcoming in the 1975 referendum, however, as the government preferred to debunk popular myths by going on the record to state that 'to say that membership could force Britain to eat Euro-bread or drink Euro-beer is nonsense' (Butler and Kitzinger, 1976: 298). At the very least, the assurances proffered on sovereignty matters revealed only a partial picture of how the EEC works. The government's advice to sceptics was to remember that 'it is the Council of Ministers, and not the market's officials, who take the important decisions. These decisions can be taken only if all the members of the Council agree. The Minister representing Britain can veto any proposals for a new law or a new tax if he considers it to be against British interest' (ibid.). What this overlooked is the use of QMV in decision making, as well as the more fundamental point about the constitutionalizing role of the ECJ in creating a binding legal order.

Hence the existence of a new legal order came as a shock to a large section of the British public when a landmark constitutional case, pertaining to a dispute over Spanish fishermen's right to fish in UK waters, was referred to the ECJ in 1990. In *Factortame* (the Spanish fishing company) v. *Secretary of State for Transport*, Lord Bridge explained why ECJ jurisprudence enabled the House of Lords to strike down an act of parliament that contravened European legislation:

[I]f the supremacy within the European Community of Community Law was not always inherent in the EEC Treaty, ... it was certainly well established in the jurisprudence of the European Court of Justice long before the United Kingdom joined the Community. Thus, whatever limitation of its sovereignty Parliament accepted when it enacted the European Communities Act was entirely voluntary. Under the terms of the Act of 1972 it has always been clear that it was the duty of a United Kingdom court, when delivering final judgment, to override any rule of national law found to be in conflict with any directly enforceable rule of Community Law.

(quoted in MacCormick, 1999: 79)

This verdict spelled out much more clearly the way in which the integration process bound Westminster sovereignty – notably by abolishing the principle of *lex posterior derogat priori* – than the government's promise that veto power in the Council was a barrier against the unwanted erosion of powers. Thus neither domestic party politics nor referendums have so far provided satisfactory means for legitimizing the transfer of institutional competences from the domestic to the supranational level. Moreover, the continuing use of such referendums to try to achieve this goal also illustrates the manner in which supranational representation has failed to establish itself at the expense of national representation. Consequently, in the EEC years, the issue of competency over competence remained highly ambiguous as expectations about the nature of the union and its implications for member state sovereignty were not overhauled.

4.3.3 The Mediterranean enlargement round: Defining the Community's democratic values

One thing that the first enlargement round neither called into question nor changed was the Community's self-understanding about its values. Expectations concerning the purpose of integration were not subjected to serious revision. What evolved during the Mediterranean enlargement (Greece in 1981; Spain and Portugal in 1986), however, was that the Community found itself emphasizing the liberal-democratic element of its values in a hitherto unprecedented way. In the preambulatory text of the Treaty of Rome, the founding six had declared themselves 'resolved by thus pooling their resources to preserve and strengthen peace and liberty'. But this was a somewhat awkward, coy acknowledgement of the baneful collapse of liberal democracy during the thirties and forties. As the Community welcomed new members with their own fragile histories of liberty and democracy, however, the strengthening of liberal democratic practices became an explicit goal of integration.

This new emphasis on democracy, rights and the rule of law became part of the official conditions for membership of the future EU.[31] Eventually, the turn towards a justification of integration in terms of nurturing democratic values in Europe was instrumental in persuading the EU-15 to take the momentous decision of healing the artificial rift between east and west in 2004.[32] But there was also a downside to all this celebration of using integration to complete the democratic transformation of post-authoritarian regimes. The rhetoric of democracy was turned against the process of closer union itself as member states, public opinion and commentators took it in turns to lambaste Europe's 'democratic deficit'.[33]

The formal Greek application for admission to the EEC was submitted immediately after the successful British referendum. In fact, the government of national unity had declared its intention to apply less than a month after the fall of the junta provoked by the Turkish invasion of Cyprus and the spectre of all-out war with Turkey. Without the democratic revolution there could be no Greek accession. After the military coup in 1967, the EEC had frozen the Association Treaty (signed in 1962, which established a customs union and acknowledged that Greece would eventually be considered for admission, economic progress permitting) and in the intervening years European institutions refused all Greek demands for normalizing relations. The Europeans' treatment of Greece as a pariah state – including the suspension of loans that were part of the association agreement – singled them out from the conciliatory stance of Washington who 'carried on "business as usual" with the Athens regime' (Siotis, 1983: 58).

This commitment to supporting the return of democracy was made more explicit still after the Commission returned its verdict on Greece's bid for membership. Citing concerns over the country's readiness to join the common market, the Commission dismissed talk of prompt admission. Instead it proposed a pre-accession period, of unlimited duration, during which time fundamental economic reforms would be carried out. Unimpressed by this recommendation, the Council of Ministers believed these economic hurdles were 'overshadowed by political considerations of the same kind as those harboured by the Greeks themselves: fear for the future of the newly restored Greek democracy' (Torbiörn, 2003: 50). On the unanimous decision of the Council (1977), the Greek application was separated from the Iberian applications, owing to France's fears of unmanageable agricultural competition if Greece, Spain and Portugal joined simultaneously. Greece's application was thus fast tracked leading to full admission in 1981.

Confirming the importance of this enlargement for the Community's self-image, Roy Jenkins, the outgoing president of the Commission, welcomed the new member by emphasizing that 'democracy is at the heart of the Community' (EEC, 1981, vol. 1: 10).[34]

Spain and Portugal shed their autocratic regimes at almost the same time as Greece did, although these odious regimes had lasted far longer. As in the Greek case, the undemocratic nature of these countries had led to their isolation from the political project of ever closer union – trade agreements were the only form of negotiation the EEC members would countenance. Even then the nine were not prepared to ignore the brutal means of repression commonly used in Spain and Portugal. Thus in 1975 negotiations with Spain on a new trade agreement were broken off as a protest against the speedy trial and execution of five men accused of murdering members of the security forces. An attempted military coup in 1981 demonstrated the precariousness of free institutions in Spain, but Iberian accession was greatly delayed by continuing problems with the British rebate dispute and Greece's insistence on a new aid package as its price for accepting wider Mediterranean membership. Once again, for all the rhetoric used to justify enlargement, internal disputes have a great impact on enlargement negotiations, as widening the Community is invariably tied to new deals concerning the rules of the game.

In the 1986 enlargement, as would happen in 2004, the addition of new members with a standard of living well below the average of the ten meant that questions of migration policy and redistributive politics were paramount. The first was settled by the ten's willingness to compromise on one of the fundamental freedoms of the Treaty of Rome, free movement of persons, by introducing a seven-year transitional period during which mobility would be restricted. This served as a precedent for a similar temporary period of restricted labour mobility imposed on the 2004 enlargement countries. Financial issues were settled once Britain was awarded a fixed, no strings attached, 66 per cent rebate on gross contributions and an Integrated Mediterranean Programme of economic assistance was agreed upon.

Nevertheless the Mediterranean enlargement as a whole was far more than a set of what Harold Wilson had earlier termed 'squalid wrangles' about agricultural prices, fish quotas or regional funds. Nor was the admission of three fragile new democracies a simple recognition of the superiority of the EEC nine's values. Rather, they served as a mirror for the existing members' own troubled political histories (with the major exception of Britain), thereby embodying the previously tacit principle that liberal democracy in Europe is mutually self-sustaining and cannot be achieved in isolation. Thus enlargement placed the practice of democracy at the centre of the integration project. Yet by announcing itself as a mechanism for engendering and protecting liberal democracy, the Community was soon subject to a critical questioning of whether this regime in fact matched up to the democratic credentials it extolled so much. It was this new concern that prompted so much soul-searching in the build-up to the Maastricht Treaty as new analyses suggested that the integration process suffered from its very own 'democratic deficit'. Already at the time of the introduction of direct elections to the European parliament in 1979, David Marquand – generally credited with the coining of the term – fretted that in a future with fewer opportunities for using the national veto:

> [A] national parliament will no longer be able to hold its government to account for what the Council has done. The resulting 'democratic deficit' would not be acceptable in a Community committed to democratic principles. Yet such a deficit would be inevitable unless the gap were somehow to be filled by the European parliament.
> (Marquand, 1979: 65)

Marquand's prediction of a growing resentment over the divergence between democratic principles and institutional practice was correct – but not entirely for the same reasons as he first imagined. The Single European Act of 1986 had reintroduced QMV into the rules of the game following the hiatus after the empty chair crisis while the parliament was granted few powers to check the Council's decisions. Yet the deficit was not only the product of QMV or the unexpected impact of legislation removing non-tariff barriers to establish the common market and the weakness of a parliament devoid of pan-European parties. Even with the national veto, the ability to hold governments to account in national legislatures is attenuated because, although the latter can sanction a government for not using the veto, once the Council has endorsed legislation national parliaments cannot subsequently overturn it. This was what the Factortame case proved.

Hence the critique of the democratic failings of the European polity was linked to the hoary debate over sovereignty and the legitimate powers of the EU.[35] However, the question of how much sovereignty ought to be pooled was in turn part of and a stimulus for a wider debate, which dominated the next decade of integration, about the nature and purpose of the European project. The extent to which sovereignty had to be pooled depended on what integration was supposed to achieve.

With the fall of the Soviet empire and the prospect of more enlargement, the need to offer answers to these questions proved even more pressing, thereby setting in motion a process that would once again revisit and challenge the rules of the game as they had developed since the Schuman declaration.

4.4 Maastricht and after: Questioning the purpose and nature of integration

In the first 40 years of integration, the political struggle between supranational (federalist) projects and proponents of a states-based intergovernmental cooperation was a constant background feature. Clear indicators had been placed by national leaders to mark the limits of federalist ambitions, such as the rejection of the EDC, the empty chair crisis and Margaret Thatcher's infamous Bruges speech warning of the menace of 'a European super-state exercising a new dominance from Brussels' (Thatcher, 1988). In addition, the creation of the biannual European Council (1974) strengthened the states' control over the agenda-setting of integration.

The three enlargement rounds and the Single European Act prior to Maastricht (1992) had done little to warrant a new pan-European discussion and clarification of where member states and public opinion stood on the issue of the nature of the European polity. Despite the Paris summit's promise in 1972 to transform, by the end of the decade, 'the whole complex of the relations of Member States into a European Union' the plan was quietly shelved. A 'solemn declaration on European Union' was pledged at the Stuttgart European Council in 1983 but it was left to the federalist group within the European Parliament to devise an institutional blueprint, the Spinelli Draft Treaty on EU, for a more consolidated European government. But with the exception of a successful vote in the Italian parliament, this draft treaty was studiously ignored by the member states. In fact, the significance of this supranational/intergovernmental tension – perhaps as a result of the ECJ's landmark rulings that somewhat unexpectedly produced a binding Community legal order[36] – seemed to have paled in comparison to the time of de Gaulle's first vetoing of British accession. For at this earlier moment John Pinder spoke of the clash between 'Monnet's Europe against the Europe of nation states; federalism against nationalism; in the last analysis, order against chaos' (Pinder, 1963: 159). *Pace* this doomsaying, integration had not faced such a simple antinomy; a *modus vivendi* was quite workable in the middle ground between these two extremes, as shown by Europe's ability to evolve from the 'euro-sclerosis' of the seventies to the dynamism of Jacques Delors' completion of the single market.

The collapse of the Soviet Union and communist regimes in its satellites, however, signalled a possible new departure for European construction, thereby rekindling the debate concerning how much sovereignty was to be pooled and why. With the arrant collapse of the German Democratic Republic and the possibility of unfettered enlargement to the north and east came the old spectre of German hegemony in Europe. Reunification severed 'the neat balance between German economic power and French military power' (Laffan, 1996: 24). In this new geopolitical context, the expectation was that economic preponderance would translate into political power, which led to a reconsideration of the politico-security arrangement for supervising this economic giant. To redefine the arrangement a new Franco-German agreement was needed. The plan sought to allay French fears of unmanageable German political influence, while also serving as a vehicle for furthering French ambitions by transforming Europe into an economic bloc capable of forcing the Americans 'to sit down and negotiate the shape of the world economic order' (Gillingham, 2003: 234).

In this way German reunification was tied to the abandonment of the Deutschmark and the creation of the single currency.[37] But while the currency that would eventually be christened the euro was at the heart of this latest design for closer union, the treaty that spawned it, the Maastricht Treaty, was in itself a much broader enterprise, as evinced by the symbolic change of name to 'European Union'. Besides the proposed monetary union, Maastricht was intended to clarify the nature and distribution of European competences, create the conditions for new policy innovation and try to address the problems of legitimacy and democratic accountability for which the EEC had recently been stigmatized. This was done with an eye to the future: as in the previous enlargement rounds, the member states wanted to have a fixed, timetabled project of deepening before another expected wave of new members joined the union.

Although the Maastricht Treaty endowed the European project with a new name suggestive of a more consolidated polity, this new treaty also reflected a certain watering-down of integrationist ambitions. Whereas the Single European Act's first article had mentioned the objective of 'making concrete progress towards European unity', the Maastricht preamble referred only to 'a new stage in the process of creating an ever closer union among the peoples of Europe'. This was also a much narrower version of political union compared to that contained in Altiero Spinelli's 1984 draft treaty, which among other things envisaged a quasi-sovereign parliament and a set of fundamental rights. Conversely, however, it was more expansive than the Fouchet Plan's proposed 'union of states' and it deftly sidestepped the conventional labels of federation and confederation, which were either too integrationist or too lukewarm for reaching a consensus. In particular, the UK blocked all attempts to introduce the expression 'a union with a federal purpose'; the f-word was similarly taboo for the Labour government that negotiated the Constitutional treaty a decade later.[38]

The treaty did, however, retain the integrationist expectation that this was only another step in an ongoing process: the text was called a 'treaty on European Union', amending the Treaty of Rome, not a treaty *establishing*, once and for all, a EU. In fact, there was a special provision (article N) for convening an intergovernmental conference in 1996 to revise the treaty in order to achieve its objectives – this reflected the disappointment of certain federalist member states with the Maastricht compromise. It also allowed certain contentious issues to be shelved until a future date.

Maastricht was thus a new departure as it sought to establish a comprehensive institutional framework (called the 'pillar' structure) to allow potential political union to complement economic integration. Economic and monetary union, which created the conditions for a reunited Germany's expanding economic ties in post-Soviet Europe, could not exist in splendid isolation. At Germany's own insistence – Chancellor Helmut Kohl believed that domestic support for such an ambitious and controversial move had to be legitimated by concrete advances in the political side of European construction[39] – it was to be accompanied by a political mechanism for common decision making in foreign policy (the second pillar) and justice and home affairs (the third pillar). Unlike the clear goal of European Monetary Union (EMU), 'the negotiations on political union were completely open-ended' (Moravcsik, 1998: 447). Admittedly, these discussions were parasitic to those on EMU – Moravcsik calls them a 'sideshow' – but their importance for the rules of the game is incontrovertible, which is why they shall be discussed in some detail.

One of the landmarks of the provisions for political union was the somewhat curious definition of the union's own principle of democracy. Stung by the ferocity of criticism levelled at its democratic shortcomings, especially when seen as meddling in domestic affairs, and pressured by the UK government, European leaders decided to react by adopting a practice called 'subsidiarity' in order to 'enhance further the democratic and efficient functioning of the institutions' (Preamble). This principle is supposed to respect democracy by ensuring that political decisions 'are taken as closely as possible to the citizen' (Preamble). Somewhat unusually for a principle espousing democratic credentials, the origins of subsidiarity can be traced back to the social teachings of the late nineteenth-century Catholic church. According to this teaching, subordinate groups within society are considered better placed to empower individuals and assist them in leading meaningful lives (Millon-Delsol, 1992).

In the EU, subsidiarity was envisaged as the expression of a strong claim that 'member states are not prepared to accept an unlimited extension of Community competences' (Dehousse, 1994: 125). There was a twofold purpose behind making the proximity of decision making a yardstick of the EU's democratic legitimacy at a time when the treaty expanded competences into nine new specific policy areas alongside the invention of the second and third pillars.[40] The hope was both to show citizens that the EU lived up to its own professed values and to give states a way of preventing an unwanted transfer of powers to the European level. In the end, neither of these objectives was fulfilled. Subsidiarity did not convince Europe's citizens that the new union was committed to democratic principles, while in reality other methods were used to safeguard national sovereignty on vital issues. The introduction of this principle has thus done nothing to temper clashes over what policymaking authority the EU has (competence catalogue) and who should decide the limits of this authority (*Kompetenz-Kompetenz*).

From the very beginning, the difficulty with the subsidiarity principle was 'that it is not really a problem of competence' (Dehousse, 1994: 110). Defining and demarcating union competences is the subject of other articles spelling out the areas in which Europe can legislate and the procedures by which these decisions can be taken. Moreover, in areas where the union has exclusive competence subsidiarity does not apply; the *acquis* is similarly shielded from any *ex post facto* challenge. Thus subsidiarity was designed to apply to those areas of policy where the EU has non-exclusive competence but where the principles of primacy and direct effect mean that there can be no permanent derogation from European legislation once adopted. Instead of serving directly to create a competence catalogue, subsidiarity uses an effectiveness and efficiency criterion to determine the level of government action by comparing the costs and benefits of Community action with those of the nation state:

> [T]he Community shall take action, in accordance with the principle of subsidiarity, only if and in so far as the objectives of the proposed action cannot be sufficiently achieved by the Member States and can therefore, by reason of the scale or effects of the proposed action, be better achieved by the Community.
>
> (Article 3b)

This raises the obvious question of whether or not such a principle is justiciable by the ECJ, the body charged with overseeing the union's adherence to this principle, because 'what will ultimately be needed is a ruling on the compared efficiency of both types of measure' (Dehousse, 1994: 114). In other words, the Court would have to assess a (potentially hypothetical) comparison between the merits and demerits of government action at two different levels. Obviously this is very different from hearing a case about trespassing competences if only because competences have a basis in the treaties whereas efficiency and effectiveness belong to the realm of pure interpretation. In 1994 a leading EU lawyer delivered a sceptical verdict on the usefulness of this principle. 'As a general guideline in favour of decentralization', he wrote, 'I would argue that its direct utility as a legal instrument is limited. As it currently stands in the Treaty, it will not readily be used by the Court of Justice' (ibid., p. 124).

This prediction has proved to be entirely correct. Subsidiarity has not been invoked to counteract competence creep at the EU level nor has it been used as a shield for national policy prerogatives. In only two cases has the ECJ been compelled to 'give an explicit opinion in respect of the principle of subsidiarity' (Magnette, 2005: 54); in both instances the Court ruled against the state opposing European action. When, in 1996, the UK tried to use subsidiarity as a means of annulling a directive of fixing a maximum 48-hour working week (health and safety of workers falls under QMV) the Court ruled that subsidiarity 'concerned the need for Community action, rather than the nature or intensity of that action' (Búrca, 1998: 223). Given that the treaties endowed the EU with powers over workers' health and safety, the ECJ dismissed the UK's claim without asking for any 'demonstration of any of the reasons behind the Council's conclusion that levels of health and safety in this field should be raised across the Community' (ibid., p. 224).[41]

Thus the introduction of the subsidiarity principle was tactical: on paper it allowed for what seems to be a credible commitment to democracy without undermining in practice the exercise of EU competences. Paul Magnette shows the cynicism behind this choice, explaining that because the concept of subsidiarity itself was deliberately extrinsic to conventional federal political systems this 'made it particularly adaptable and allowed difficult debate on establishing a list of powers to be avoided. On its own it brought no clear response to preoccupations linked to the division of powers' (Magnette, 2005: 53). Unsurprisingly, the question of competences continues to raise its head at every subsequent treaty amendment. As a mechanical or neutral test for determining competency, subsidiarity thus confirms Bagehot's point that 'no important practical question in real life can be uniformly settled by a fixed and formal rule' (Bagehot, 1963: 280).

Control over the division of competences – the kernel of the ubiquitous struggle between federalist and confederalist visions of integration – has thus been maintained by other, more subtle means. From the member states' perspective, especially the more euro-sceptic ones, such control was even more necessary than before as with the treaty on EU 'the Union's competences seem to cover everything, or almost' (Magnette, 2005: 11). This argument thus differs from Karen Alter's assertion that 'the nature of the ECJ has not changed, nor have the tools the member states have to influence judicial politics' (Alter, 1998: 122). While the first part of this statement is indubitably true, the second does not seem to correspond to the subtle shift in the rules of the game of European politics designed to prevent the accrual of competences at the European level.

Besides the traditional veto power, still pertinent in matters such as tax policy, Maastricht saw three innovations for limiting the process of pooling sovereignty and preventing unexpected surprises.[42] The first method was the infamous UK opt-out negotiated by John Major's government. These covered two areas: the third stage (the single currency) of EMU (Protocol 11) and the social charter (Protocol 14). In the first, Britain was granted the right not to join as well as the possibility of joining consequently on a separate parliamentary decision. Under a second protocol, Britain obtained a derogation from the implementation of the Community Charter of Fundamental Social Rights of Workers into European law. These deals marked an important new departure, for instead of blocking an undesired new policy, a member state chose simply to withdraw from its provisions.

The second method of limiting the transfer of competences for the foreseeable future was the introduction into the amended Treaty of

Rome of specific clauses prohibiting harmonization in certain fields of law. In the fields of education (Article 126), vocational training (127), culture (128) and public health (129) [now 149-52] the EU was only permitted, by QMV, to 'adopt incentive measures, excluding any harmonization of the laws and regulations of the Member States'. In doing so, the EU set limits to its own supremacy by declaring harmonization in certain domains to be illegal.

Finally, the third and perhaps most unusual – certainly the most abstruse – method was the creation of a three pillar structure – to give the impression of the elegant symmetry of a Greek temple – as the framework for governing this nascent political union. Each pillar is governed by its own set of rules and objectives. The genius of the pillar structure is its ability to partition the intergovernmental and supranational components of EU decision making. Of course, when unanimity is required in the first pillar (on taxation, social security, treaty reform and the admission of new members) the EU remains an intergovernmental organization at heart. In the second and third pillars, however, the EU's intergovernmental nature is reinforced because these areas are deliberately shielded from the EU's supranational institutions: Commission, Parliament and Court.[43] Here is how. The Commission has a limited right of initiative on legislation in the second and third pillars, while the presidency of the Council and a Council-appointed High Representative represent the EU's foreign policy to third countries. The Parliament, as opposed to its co-decision power in many areas of the first pillar, has only a consultative role in both pillars, while the legal instruments for action 'are ad hoc legal instruments, are not of a legislative nature and escape jurisdictional control' (Magnette, 2005: 42). Thus they differ from those in the first pillar, meaning that the ECJ has no involvement in overseeing their application and enforcing compliance. Such measures, writes Stone Sweet, were 'an acknowledgement on the part of the member states of the ECJ's capacity to pre-empt the EU-legislator and the national parliaments' (2005: 54).

In this way the continuing tension between federalism and confederalism was neither neglected nor resolved. Rather, the existing settlement was reworked into a new institutional package that promised to satisfy neither camp fully and yet still represented at the same time some progress, for the federalists, and safety for the less integration-minded. No competence catalogue was defined; no primary locus of Kompetenz-Kompetenz was specified. This hybrid arrangement, albeit with a few minor modifications, is still the model for integration today (Calleo, 2001). Magnette captures this ambivalence perfectly, when he notes of the Constitution that 'having decided not to decide between the two competing models, governments have also preserved the fundamental hybridity of the European system' (Magnette, 2007: 1071). This formula – deciding not to decide – expresses succinctly the logic of dynamic equilibrium at play in European integration.

The alternatives to subsidiarity – most notably the pillar structure – used to prevent a slide towards thicker federalism made the union far more complicated than its predecessor by multiplying the different rules applicable in different policy fields. This had the perverse effect of making the union more opaque, less comprehensible in comparison to nation states and seemingly more democratically unresponsive. Anticipating this consequence, Maastricht tried to counterbalance it with the creation of a European citizenship, granting the right to vote in European and municipal elections in other member states and diplomatic representation in third countries, as the first step in building a common identity.[44]

In addition to these symbolic moves, the Maastricht Treaty also tried to foster European-level social policy – a possibility envisaged by the original Rome treaty but not acted upon – in the hope this would make the EU more legitimate in the eyes of citizens. This was to be achieved by the Protocol on Social Policy, which expanded the use of QMV in this policy field. It was a classic compromise given the 'impasse between British unwillingness to expand majority voting to social policy and France's refusal to sign a treaty that did not do so' (Pierson, 1998: 132). Indeed it was a double compromise. The UK was exempted from being subject to the expanded QMV competences of the Community in these aspects of social policy; while promoters of a welfarist version of integration were rewarded with the introduction of QMV into only the least controversial areas of social policy.

The social protocol to the Maastricht Treaty, allowed the Council to invoke QMV in five areas already included under the Treaty of Rome: health and safety at work, working conditions, information and consultation of workers, gender equality in the labour market and the integration of those excluded from the labour market. Since the most contentious categories of social policy it covers, such as social security, employment protection and employee representation, are decided by unanimity this marked no great expansion in union competences. Moreover, under article two of the protocol, 'the provisions of this Article shall not apply to pay, the right of association, the right to strike or the right to impose lock-outs'. Not only was the tax revenue necessary for funding social transfers still dependent on unanimity but the policy areas where regulatory measures could be used as proxies for creating a European system of social protection were likewise subject to unanimous decision making. This was the most lukewarm manifestation of 'social Europe' that could be passed off as a step in the right direction. Thus the protocol on social policy affected neither institutional competence allocation nor expectations about what the union is for, leaving unaltered the arrangement that 'issues of redistribution are off the table while those having to do with economic liberalization are on the table' (Sbragia, 2000: 236).

The combined efforts of the Commission's identity-building programme and the new Maastrichtian political order (with some added social policy spice) were not sufficient to convince Germany's Constitutional Court that the time of a pan-European democracy had come. In a startling decision, following a case brought by German Members of the European Parliaments (MEPs) claiming the treaty violated Germany's Basic Law (*Grundgesetz*), the Constitutional Court of Europe's most pro-integrationist country declared that the union's democratic deficit placed definite limits on the constitutional transfer of powers away from the member states (Wieland, 1994). Rejecting the complainant's claim that the QMV principle was antithetical to Germany's Basic Law provision on the democratic character of political authority, the court nevertheless found that 'should the Bundestag transfer too many of its competences, too much state power would be legitimated only indirectly; as a result, the Democracy Principle would be violated' (Boom, 1995: 183). Although it did not specify what might constitute an illegal transfer of sovereignty, the Court based its judgment on the fact that the union's democratic credentials were too weak as things stood to permit an empowered federal Europe well beyond the qualified extension of powers under the Maastricht Treaty. In particular, the court singled out the absence of 'a constant, free exchange of ideas leading to a common public opinion, transparent and understandable (to the ordinary citizen) objectives of public authority, and the possibility of every citizen to communicate in his native tongue with public authorities to whom he is subjected' (ibid.).

This decision is an important marker rather than a cavil. It represents a line in the sand signifying that political integration can only go so far if the institutional framework of indirect representation through the Council, with a weak Parliament and public sphere, is maintained. Of equal importance, the criteria it specifies for democracy are so exacting as to suggest the implausibility of breaking through the indirect paradigm of legitimation in anything except the long term.

The judges 'characterised the European Union as a *Staatenverbund*, or "league of states", which involves Germany in membership of supranational organizations but not the membership of a European state' (Duff, 1994: 61). According to this interpretation, as Stone Sweet explains, the process of integration must progress through intergovernmental control for 'at the community level, the German government negotiates and authorises, by treaty law, whatever there is of EC governance; at the national level, the Bundestag legitimizes and transposes these authorizations in national law' (Stone Sweet, 2004: 93).

Thus the German court's vision of the current nature of the European project and the conditions under which dramatic further integration would be justifiable suggest a double bind that will work to keep the union in its halfway house position beyond an ordinary international organization and yet well short of a consolidated federal system. The impediments to deeper integration outlined in legal and political theory were, in fact, quite neatly mirrored by developments in the real world as voters had their own say on the treaty. Maastricht nearly knocked one of post-war Europe's most influential political leaders off his presidential perch, while the continent reeled from the first ever popular rejection of a treaty.

French President François Mitterrand gambled his remaining three years' mandate on a treaty referendum, announced as a true Gallic *coup de théâtre* the day after Danish voters rejected the treaty. Dividing the opposition was part of the explanation for this dramatic departure but the desire to have France lead Europe in this new era of political integration was paramount. The result, *le petit oui*, with only 51.05 per cent in favour unmasked the perils of seeking popular support for an elite-engineered political project deliberately chosen to remedy the indifference shown towards economic integration. Public acquiescence to top-down initiatives could no longer be taken for granted, signalling, therefore, a clear need for stronger justifications regarding the merits of a deeper political bond between member states. The Danish 'no' to Maastricht (by a 50.7% majority) was another blow to the ambitions of integrationists. It revealed a new problem: that of accepting the democratic verdict of a national electorate when they rejected a treaty. An emergency meeting of the European Council was called, which 'categorically rejected any renegotiation of the treaty' (Duff, 1994: 55). The alternative was to give Denmark certain public assurances that would placate the treaty's opponents in a subsequent referendum campaign. Contestation hinged on several key issues: the single currency, defence, levels of social and environmental protection and the right to attribute citizenship. Under a protocol of the treaty the Danes already had the possibility of being exempted from the third stage of EMU, the single currency stage. At the subsequent Edinburgh summit, the member states reaffirmed the status of this opt-out and also specifically addressed other Danish concerns: they would be allowed to forbear from participating in 'decisions and actions of the Union which have defence implications' (EC, 1993: 23), the right to set the bar of social and environmental protection higher was confirmed and nationality was affirmed to be 'settled solely by reference to the national law of the Member State concerned' (ibid.). These new guarantees were enough to save Maastricht. On 18 May 1993, 56.8 per cent of the Danish population returned a 'yes' vote. But the Danish referendum experience – confirmed by subsequent treaty rejection at the hands of Irish (twice), French and Dutch voters – begs the question as to what kind of political legitimacy referendums can confer on pooling more sovereignty if there is a correct result that must be obtained in spite of initial reluctance.

The Maastricht Treaty, therefore, was successful in creating a new and irrevocable step in integration but at a price: opts-out had to be given to certain countries, new methods of intergovernmental control were introduced, the UK pursued an unabashed anti-federalist agenda, France was unmasked as an ambivalent integrationist since elite enthusiasm was not matched by public opinion and citizens' democratically expressed verdict on treaty reform was shown to be nugatory when negative. Yet despite the name change, EMU and the creation of the pillar system, the new treaty failed to specify the political finality of integration, thereby leaving expectation about the nature of this project unchanged. Nor did it alter the delicate balance between confederal and federal principles of representation or clear up the ambiguity over competency over competences. Thus the EU compound system remained firmly located in the middle of a spectrum between international organization and federal state. In sum, this evolution conformed fully to the logic of dynamic equilibrium not voluntary centralization.

4.5 Two steps forward but how many back? European integration's dynamic equilibrium

Several decades of integration have been surveyed in this chapter.[45] Instead of trying to explain actor preferences (and preference formation) and the reasons for negotiation outcomes, the analysis has concentrated on bringing to light what effect treaty reform and other developments such as enlargement and court rulings had for the rules of the game of the compound European polity. Special emphasis has been placed on the evolution of these rules: that is, the way institutional competences, expectations about integration, competency over competences and representation were affected. Evolution is used here in its etymological sense of 'unfolding'. Biologists sometimes refer to the concept of punctuated equilibrium when explaining the process of evolution. This refers to moments of rapid evolution followed by lengthy periods of stasis, which revises the gradualist notion of the development of species. Superficially, the story of European integration seems to fit this punctuated model: the various treaties serve as convenient markers for new steps towards closer union separated by periods of standstill. But the suggestion that during a moment of progress sufficient advances are made to make the past an irrelevance is erroneous. From having traced a series of recurring tensions and omnipresent unsettled questions, it should be clear that the integration process is not a simple dichotomy between stagnation and progress. Integration is a process with an eye on the future but also constant glances over the shoulder to the past.

Rather than interpreting integration as a gradual process of progress, like a species' adaptation to a particular environment, I have tried to present the story as one of subtle – and sometimes unexpected – development without the guidance of an invisible hand or intelligent design. By definition, therefore, this story has not been that of the steady maintenance of the existing status quo, otherwise there would be no unfolding. The integration progress has been conducted in the context of a series of great unknowns (for instance, how institutional actors would behave, the consequences of enlargement, the outcomes of referendums). The end result is that the compound European polity has proved resilient but without resolving the two basic tensions between different visions of the institutional nature of the EU (confederal or federal) and its policy purpose (free trade or social protection). In addition, the lingering uncertainty over whether integration is also supposed to serve as a security community is no nearer to being settled than at the time of the collapse of the EDC treaty. This ability to manage fundamental tensions without choosing between different visions of integration while also designing and implementing new projects of integration is exactly what I have termed *dynamic equilibrium*, as illustrated in Table 4.1.

Table 4.1 Evolution of the rules of the game in the EU according to the logic of dynamic equilibrium

Rules of the game	Changes amounting to dynamic equilibrium
Institutional competences	Greater competences conferred but new safeguards introduced: Opt-outs, the principle of subsidiarity, insulating the second and third pillars from the Commission and ECJ.
Expectations about the union	Founding objectives remain: Prosperity, peace and democracy. Enduring ambiguity over others: Social policy and security policy still only possibilities. No final end point to integration specified.
Competency over competences	Despite principle of primacy, location of competency over competences ambiguous. ECJ denied this role in second and third pillar and ignored when Germany and France broke Stability and Growth Pact.
Representation	Introduction of supranational co-decision compensated by maintenance of national vetoes in first pillar. In the absence of European parties and successful indirect legitimation, national referendums used to sanction treaty reform according to confederal principle of representation.

To conclude this overview of the European compound polity's dynamic equilibrium it is necessary to make a few points about the Constitutional Treaty and its successor, the Lisbon Treaty. These documents close the circle rather neatly as they both mimic the Maastricht Treaty's sidestepping of fundamental tensions yet nevertheless introduce certain new innovations allowing for a greater *possibility* of governing in common.

The Lisbon Treaty thus belongs to this logic of dynamic equilibrium because it too fails to transform the EU into a compound polity where the rules of the game have become subject to voluntary centralization. From the outset the 2005 Constitutional Treaty, whose contents are for the most part reproduced in the Lisbon Treaty, was encumbered with the relics of previous compromises and failures. The three essential tasks that the Nice Treaty had made no progress on concerned establishing the role of national parliaments, clarifying the legal status of the Charter of Fundamental Rights promulgated in 2000 by a special convention (it reiterated the European commitment to high social protection but its legal status was unclear)[46] and the division of competences (Dehousse, 2005).

Integrating the national parliaments into EU decision making serves a twofold purpose. Firstly, it is intended to act as a system for monitoring the hitherto feckless subsidiarity mechanism as it gives the member states enhanced power to challenge legislation if a third (a quarter in certain areas) of the parliaments decide that EU action fails to comply with the subsidiarity principle. Parliaments have also been granted the right to take the Commission to the ECJ for breaches of the subsidiarity principle. European institutions will have to transmit legislative drafts to domestic parliaments and ensure that 'the reasons for concluding that a Union objective can be better achieved at Union level shall be substantiated by qualitative and, wherever possible, quantitative indicators' (Lisbon Treaty, protocol on subsidiarity, Article 5). The second purpose behind linking parliaments to European governance is to improve citizens' faith in the mechanism of democratic control over the EU. This comes not only from the regular transmission of information from European institutions to domestic legislatures but also in the procedure for allowing a national parliament to veto a move to QMV (Lisbon Treaty, Article 48) under the 'simplified revision procedure', which makes this fundamental change possible without treaty renegotiation. By tying the transfer from unanimity to QMV to parliamentary life the assumption is that this will generate domestic party debate, which if successful will confer the direct democratic legitimacy lacking in a distant and indirect Council decision.

The Charter of Fundamental Rights was adopted as a way of killing two birds with one stone: to provide a corpus of common values as the basis for a putative European identity and to incorporate a bundle of social and economic rights to maintain the political pressure for a 'social Europe' with a regulated market. It forms the basis for a positive vision of integration as opposed to deregulation. Needless to say, this charter was only integrated into the Constitutional Treaty after a hard-fought compromise that diluted its possible implications for the harmonization of social policy. The charter only applies when countries implement European law (Lisbon Treaty, II-111. 1), meaning that it cannot create rights for individuals except in those areas where the EU is already competent. In case this declaration of rights leads to pressures for expanding their applicability, the wary member states have specified that it 'does not extend the field of application of Union law beyond the powers of the Union or establish any new power or task for the Union' (Lisbon Treaty, II-111.2).

Under great pressure from the UK and Ireland, each controversial article referring to economic and social rights, which come under the banner of the union's rights of 'solidarity', has been qualified by the clause 'in accordance with the rules laid down by Union law and national laws and practices'. Thus in these areas national practice is granted equal status with EU measures so as to prevent the latter trumping the former. Moreover, in case this clause does not guarantee enough against unwanted judicial activism special provisions 'governing the interpretation and application' have been added. Uniquely, these deliberately target the judiciary because 'the explanations drawn up as a way of providing guidance in the interpretation of the Charter of Fundamental Rights shall be given due regard by the courts of the Union and of the Member States' (Lisbon Treaty, II-112.7). The explanations themselves are designed to restrict all attempts to make these rights engender a common social policy through the back door. These safeguards have been reproduced verbatim in the Lisbon Treaty but the real novelty of the new treaty is the fact that the UK successfully negotiated an opt-out from the provisions of the Charter. No big bang in the construction of a social Europe has thus occurred. Rather, the delicate compromise between free marketeers and interventionists has, albeit in new circumstances, prevailed – although this is yet to be tested by the ECJ's interpretation of the Charter. Hence it is a dynamic situation and not a continuation of the status quo.

Allocating sovereignty through a neatly drawn division of competences has also remained off the agenda. Although the pillar system is replaced with three categories of exclusive, shared and complementary competences, alongside the 'coordination of economic and employment policies' and the Common Foreign and Security Policy (CFSP), there are hundreds of articles laying out the conditions for how the EU conducts its business in these areas of competence. As in the Maastricht Treaty, the emphasis is on proceduralism – with decisions and negotiations going back and forth between the many institutional actors – to prevent the establishment of an internal hierarchy among the institutions. The consensus outcomes that proceduralism encourages serve to avoid giving the impression that one of the conflicting principles of supranationalism or intergovernmentalism has triumphed. They are kept in check through neither being able to declare itself superior.[47]

Regarding the issue of who determines competence, the Constitutional Treaty was far more explicit than ever before about the source of EU competences. The principle of conferral establishes that the member states confer certain competences to the EU while retaining those not conferred. At the same time, the possibility of conferring more competences is made somewhat easier through the creation of so-called bridging clauses (Lisbon Treaty, Article 48) that enable the European Council to introduce QMV in areas subject to unanimity (except for military and other defence matters) without the need for treaty renegotiation. That this is to be done within the context of a unanimous decision with the possibility of a national parliamentary veto shows the member states' ability to retain control over the conferral of powers. The opportunity for a more federal system exists but it is dependent on the full consent of all member states and their parliaments.[48] It would be wrong, therefore, to describe this as no improvement on the status quo ante because the new conferral mechanism means that any such transfer of sovereignty will be based on unequivocal consent by each national democracy after a proper debate on its merits.

4.6 Conclusion

This chapter analysed the evolution of the rules of the game in the EU compound polity, revealing that integration has hitherto undoubtedly followed a logic of dynamic equilibrium. Voluntary centralization, that is, the unanimous agreement of all member states to increase the scope of EU competences, change the objectives of integration to include redistributive social policy, accord the EU competency over competences or increase the federal basis of representation within its architecture, has proved an elusive grail. Perhaps the most important process of centralization, the creation of an autonomous and binding legal order as interpreted by the ECJ, was less voluntary than stealthy or surreptitious, as can be seen by the immediate opposition it raised as well as various subsequent measures to limit the extension of competences via ECJ interpretation. From this analysis it is appropriate to conclude that the EU is only viable to the extent that it can keep reproducing a dynamic equilibrium between conflicting visions of its nature and purpose that shy away from voluntary centralization of power. The following chapter establishes why this conclusion is further tenable by analogy with the experience of the antebellum US compound system in which, ultimately, neither a dynamic equilibrium nor voluntary centralization was possible.

5
Contrasting and Explaining the Viability of Two Compound Systems

And what should they know of England who only England know?

                               Rudyard Kipling (1940: 221)

5.1 Introduction

Studies of European integration that dwell primarily on the successful constitutionalization of European law (Weiler, 1999; Goldstein, 2001; Stone Sweet, 2004) are apt to offer a partial representation of what makes the EU viable. Viewing the EU in terms solely of successful integration through law does not reveal much about the viability of this polity; it paints a picture of the increasing reach of EU legislation without revealing the recurrent and intractable conflicts over what the EU is for and how it should be constituted. This enthusiasm for a legal rather than political understanding of the EU compound polity has a parallel in the study of the US federal union. Until Reconstruction, scholars tended to see the US Constitution as 'giving existence to government and prescribing and limiting its powers, rather than as the basic structure of the polity, not consciously constructed but growing organically through history' (Belz, 1969: 111). Yet once the difficult struggle against secession had ended and the compromises necessary for re-establishing the union were in place, the constitution was more likely to be read 'in essentially political terms' (ibid., p. 123) as the role of parties, leaders, interests and unwritten norms became more obvious.

This chapter pursues a similarly multifaceted and critical interpretation of the legal and political orders of the EU and antebellum US compound systems. To accomplish this, it contrasts the consequences of the differences, already identified in section 3.3, in how the disputes over the rules of the game took place within both polities. The objective is to use these differences to explain why the European compound system has so far maintained a dynamic equilibrium between confederalism (intergovernmentalism) and federalism (supranationalism), and why in the US this ultimately was not possible, leading to an open conflict that paved the way for eventual centralization. Inevitably, this discussion compresses both the political history of this period as well as abundant historiographical disputes.

So far, what can be called the viability debate has been conducted from two perspectives (see section 2.4). One approach tends to deliver perfunctory dismissals of successful further European integration because of certain missing social and political 'preconditions' necessary for a more federal organization. The other is convinced that the EU's limbo position between international organization and federal state is by definition a structural anomaly that cannot be maintained. The former approach, which identifies the deficiencies in Europe's proto-federal momentum, explains what the EU *cannot* become; the latter suggests that it *has* to become more federal in order to survive.

Given the limitations of these formulations for explaining what makes the EU viable, it is more fruitful to consider – by analogy with the US example – how integration has continued to prove resilient in the face of acute political contestation and, extrapolating from this, to discuss what potential it has to do so in the future. As explained in section 2.5, this contrast between two different compound systems is an exploration of the 'similarity in the relation of the parts to the whole' in the contest to define the rules of the game of politics in both cases. What matters in this analogical analysis, therefore, is the way in which differences in how conflicts over the rules of the game erupted and were managed, giving rise either to voluntary centralization or dynamic equilibrium. Investigating the five major differences thus yields a new interpretative paradigm for understanding how the EU functions best and the possible limits of integration. This analysis suggests that the EU is only viable as a halfway house between confederalism and federalism given its structural problems of generating democratic legitimacy by enabling citizens to determine what kind of integration is warranted.

5.2 American dual federalism (with the highest functions of government) v. European joint federalism (with the most numerous)

In theory, original US 'dual federalism' resulted in two separate levels of government, whose conflicts took the form of legal disputes about respective competences and compliance between state and federal law. Yet to determine the precise effect of this dual structure upon the US compound system it is instructive to examine how these disputes arose and how they were settled. States notably protested about their exposure to certain suits in the federal courts, their ability to treat Native American tribes, specific acts of Congress and eventually the problem of fugitive slaves. Sometimes judgments that impinged upon the states' assumed prerogatives were either never enforced or simply disobeyed. On a few occasions, the states even determined themselves competent to decide on the constitutionality of an act of Congress.

Resistance was not simply a matter of judging where the weakness of the federal government permitted state forbearance from compliance.[1] States waged a juridical and political struggle to protect the autonomy of their sphere of government. The first amendment to the constitution after the Bill of Rights was the product of Georgia's stubbornness in refusing to accept the 1793 ruling (*Chisolm* v. *Georgia*)[2] that federal courts could hear out of state creditors' suits against a state. This protest succeeded in persuading Congress to pass an amendment granting the states sovereign immunity against suits in law and equity. Significantly, this is the only antebellum example where the constitution was revised as a result of state defiance.

Another method of contestation in the US compound republic was the use of nullification to declare acts of Congress invalid if the state legislatures or a special state convention deemed them unconstitutional. The two great nullification controversies concern the so-called Alien and Sedition Acts' restriction of civil liberties in 1798 and South Carolina's hostility to the imposition of tariffs on imports of manufactured goods in 1832. In the first case, two states challenged the federal government's constitutional right both to claim jurisdiction over the aliens residing in a state and to make seditious libel a federal offence (McDonald, 2000: 41). Under the constitution of 1789 no specific power had been granted to the federal government over aliens except regarding laws of naturalization and an amendment specifically protected free speech. In these circumstances Kentucky and Virginia upheld the right not to comply with these federal laws, claiming in effect a veto over this unconstitutional extension of federal sovereignty.[3] Thus the sovereignty of the states, although a commonplace ideology – 'almost everyone spoke of the Union as "our confederacy", of the Constitution as a "compact"' (Stampp, 1978: 28) – was a residual possession, infrequently invoked and not an active component of American constitutional government.

Whereas the US constitution was ambiguous enough about certain elements of sovereignty to allow for a compact reading of the origins of federal power, it clearly enumerated those areas of government that were the prerogative of the federal branch. These are what James Bryce called 'the highest' functions of government,[4] covering international politics, trade and defence. The states had accepted this fundamental division of competences but sometimes believed it was necessary to protest when the federal government went beyond what they saw as the letter of the constitution. The United States' original dual federalism, therefore, was designed primarily to ensure that the states forbore from trespassing on competence areas assigned to the federal level. A leading constitutional scholar once illustrated this point by remarking that 'federal law often says to the states, "Don't do any of these things", leaving outside the scope of its prohibition a wide range of alternative courses of action. But it is illuminating to observe how rarely it says "Do this thing", leaving no choice but to go ahead and do it' (H. Hart, 1955: 194).[5]

Hence in the antebellum compound system, the federal government, endowed with the highest functions of government, had the power to interpret the general good as it saw fit and seek its own solutions for promoting it. The only formal state check on this was via representation in the Senate. Conversely, the EU is constituted so that the member states have at least a say and sometimes a veto both on what the European general good is supposed to be in the first place and what policy action is called for. In this way the European nations have deliberately sought to avoid a confrontation akin to nullification, which is *ex post facto*; they seek instead to establish more powerful *ex ante* barriers against centralization.[6]

Under the EU's system of joint federalism member states are constantly in a position where they have to decide whether or not to grant an extension of competences, change the rules for decision making or contribute more resources. Thus their power of supervision is acute, active and continuous. In the last chapter it was seen how the evolution of the rules of the game of integration invariably tied the expansion of the EU's potential competences to a new framework for retaining national control. Among the best examples of this process are the creation of the intergovernmental second and third pillars at Maastricht and the Lisbon

Treaty's parliamentary veto on the abandonment of unanimity in certain policy areas, to which can also be added the ingenious catalogue of opt-out and protocols. In this way European countries have found a fuzzy middle ground between granting competences and surrendering the highest functions of government. Hypertrophied institutional proceduralism under the EU's co-decision provision (a joint-legislating process involving the Council and the Parliament, which can include up to 30 different stages) in the first pillar, further balances federal and confederal legislative power. Contentious legislative acts bounce back and forth between Council and Parliament even requiring, as a last resort, inter-institutional negotiation through a special conciliation committee. In this way, the legislative process is designed to prevent an institutional hierarchy that would undermine compromise.

It is correct to observe then, as Heckly and Oberkampf do in their comparison of US and European federalism, that 'as the geographical area and the competences of Europe expand, it appears more and more necessary to give a larger place to negotiation and compromise' (1994: 171). What they do not dwell upon though is the equally significant point that the evolution of federalism in the US did not necessitate the creation of new institutional or decision-making procedures for building consensus. The fact that growth of the federal centre was possible using the existing architecture proves the importance of *how* the federal and confederal tension over competences is settled: either through parties and popular mobilization as in the US case or via interstate negotiation and the creation of new institutional rules as in the EU. In the EU's joint federal system this tension is managed by increasing the procedural probabilities of consensus, while allowing for safeguards against unwanted competency expansion.

This means that the EU's ability to issue authoritative instructions regarding legal harmonization in the first pillar is not necessarily an indicator of a nascent strong state. Rather, the ability of a weak centre to act in this way to harmonize large swathes of legislation is to a great extent a product of its joint federal structure, which promotes consensus and leaves open alternative means of resistance should integration prove politically unpalatable to a certain member state. In fact, this system of checking and compromising is exactly the paramount virtue that the great theorist of American states' rights John Calhoun believed existed in the US system. According to Calhoun:

> It is, indeed, the negative power which makes the constitution – and the positive which makes the government. The one is the power of

acting; - and the other the power of preventing or arresting action. The two, combined, make constitutional governments.

(quoted in Forsyth, 1981: 121)

The dual federal nature of the US compound republic, in which the union exercised the highest powers of government, however, turned out to be a brittle instrument for compromise. Nullification could only ever be a reaction to federal legislation, meaning its effectiveness was highly uncertain. In addition, the inherent difficulties associated with amending the constitution meant that an alternative method of resolving conflicts between the states and the union was necessary: political parties. This was very much an unexpected development as the founders held that one of the chief merits of an 'extended republic' (Hamilton et al., 2003: 255) was to minimize the possibility of rule by party.[7] Yet as shown in section 5.6, it was nationally organized parties, linking national leaders with state politics as vectors for compromise, that was the key to the US compound system's survival amid serious political tension about the proper scope of federal government.

Thus the contrast between joint and dual federalism reveals that the EU member states have more influence over the extension of union competences as well as greater leeway for negotiating compromise legislation than the units in the US compound system. Most notably, EU member states have not had to resort to ultimately futile attempts at nullification or bandying around threats of withdrawal. Consequently, the joint federal structure is one of the principal reasons why the process of dynamic equilibrium prevails over voluntary centralization in the EU.

5.3 A constitution for popular government v. a treaty system

In the European compound polity international treaties are the means by which policy powers are granted to the EU and new rules are devised to allow for potentially more European-level decision making. The purpose of this section is to explore the impact of a treaty system on the debate over the rules of the game of politics by comparing it with the US experience of a constitutional political order. This difference has far-reaching consequences for how popular mobilization can be used to support voluntary centralization.

In the absence of a formal constitution and 'constitutional moment' of pan-European participation, it is nigh on impossible to sustain any fiction of a social contract that links European citizens, individually or collectively, to the integration process. Individual consent is not really part of the edifice of European government, where all important decisions are filtered through representatives of the national governments usually deciding behind closed doors. Inter-institutional compromise is the order of the day for less controversial subjects, thereby minimizing the impact of the European Parliament, which has the best claim to be able to link policy to popular consent; in any case turnout for European Parliament elections is abysmally low. The insignificance of the explicit democratic participation of individuals in eventual policy choices is the reason for academic attempts to justify the system on other grounds: most notably from the policy outputs it produces rather than the democratic inputs it receives (Scharpf, 1999). Indeed it is even argued that since the EU is not a nation state with an extensive set of competences the deficit of democratic participation should not be of such paramount concern.[8]

Individual consent, however, or at least the fiction of such consent, is not indispensable to government (Hume, 1994: 192). Originally, in fact, the electoral system for choosing the president was intended to preclude the possibility that the head of the federal government would be tied to the majority of individual preferences.[9] Nevertheless in the early American republic it was still possible to invoke a collective fiction, a first person plural pronoun (best symbolized by the 'we hold these truths to be self-evident' of the Declaration of Independence) that expressed a common desire to pursue a political project together.[10] This notion of a collective popular granting of authority – rather than the acquiescence of each state – to create the union was famously used by Supreme Court Chief Justice John Marshall to explain the origins of the federal government in *McCulloch v. Maryland* (1819). Referring to the state conventions, special assemblies convened to debate and ratify the proposed constitution, Marshall declared:

> From these conventions the Constitution derives its whole authority. The government proceeds directly from the people ... The assent of the States in their sovereign capacity is implied in calling a convention, and thus submitting that instrument to the people. But the people were at perfect liberty to accept or reject it; and their act was final. It required not the affirmance, and could not be negatived, by the State governments.
>
> (quoted in Baker, 1974: 595)

Although the federal government lacked the ability to determine its own competences – amendments required the approval of three-quarters of the states in addition to a congressional vote – sovereignty could at least be plausibly located in the people collectively instead of in the aggregation of individual states. For in a unique constitutional moment, the people had proved themselves to be the 'constituent power' by electing representatives with the special design of ratifying the constitution. Thus, as Peter Onuf has persuasively argued, the supporters of the federal Constitution used the notion of a constituent power as a means of resolving the twofold problem of sovereignty and legitimacy:

> Neither the states nor Congress should be considered 'sovereign', insisted supporters of the new regime ... The recent history of state constitutional development emphasized the distinction between the sovereign people – the constituent power – and their governments ... Americans should be able to distinguish between the source of legitimate authority and the various governments charged with its exercise.
>
> (Onuf, 1991: 667)

The popular ratification of the US constitution – which in Gordon Wood's words 'seemed to have legitimized the revolution' (Wood, 1969: 342) – was to prove a fundamental rhetorical and conceptual resource during the nullification crisis over tariffs. On the floor of the US Senate, Daniel Webster and Robert Hayne clashed over the question of whether the union was a treaty-like compact between sovereign states. It was the 'popular' or 'people's' conception of the constitution espoused by Webster that provided a counter-argument to South Carolina's compact interpretation of the constitution during the lengthy tariff dispute begun in 1828. President Andrew Jackson in his 1832 Proclamation on the nullification crisis resorted to this image of popular participation to justify his ferocious attack on South Carolina's presumed right to declare a federal law unconstitutional:

> The people of the United States formed the Constitution, acting through the state legislatures in making the compact to meet and discuss its provisions, and acting in separate conventions when they ratified those provisions; but the terms used in its construction show it to be a government in which the people of all the states collectively are represented.
>
> (Elliot, 1836, vol. 4: 589)

Thus the American union's founding moment established an initial direct connection between federal government and popular sovereignty. Moreover, popular legitimacy was not restricted solely to the foundational period as the development of mass politics during the Jacksonian era effected a connection between executive government and the people. In spite of the founders' designs to create obstacles to populist presidentialism, by the time Jackson sat in the White House he was able to claim, in his Proclamation, that:

> We are ONE PEOPLE in the choice of the President and Vice President. Here the States have no other agency than to direct the mode in which the vote shall be given. The candidates having the majority of all the votes are chosen. The electors of a majority of States may have given their votes for one candidate, and yet another may be chosen. The people, then, and not the States, are represented in the executive branch.
>
> (ibid.)

Jackson was deliberately cavalier with the electoral reality of presidential elections. In certain states the legislature continued to select voters for the Electoral College without a poll of voters[11] and in 1824 he himself had won a plurality of both the Electoral College and the popular vote but still lost out to John Quincy Adams. However, Jackson was correct in his assertion that the electoral mechanism provided for a strong representative bond between the president and the people. The will of the individual states, as Jackson, the great populist, realized, did not carry the same influence since Electoral College votes were weighted according to population. Moreover, the development of a cross-state system for mobilizing public opinion and participation prevented the states from acquiring a monopoly over agenda-setting and speaking in the name of the people. In this way, the practice of American politics was by mid-century much less anti-majoritarian – a point that typically escapes the attention of students of twentieth-century US political development (Fabbrini and Sicurelli, 2004) – thereby already laying down the conditions for eventual 'radical nationalization of the political process' (ibid., p. 243) in the twentieth century.

Such a feat of collective, cross-national representation is impossible in the present EU compound polity. The legitimacy of the actual EU political actors is only indirect and certainly not pan-European: none of the commissioners are elected, the members of the Council as members of national governments are elected principally for national representation, while the Parliament, whose members are drawn from the ranks of national parties, is a dull sideshow to domestic political debate. Since national and European electoral cycles are out of kilter there is also little possibility of having a majority of both member state governments and of MEPs belonging to the same political family.[12] Hence the treaty system denies the EU the ability to use a popular collective bond, stemming from an electoral mandate to govern, as a political resource in its struggle against member state reticence. Direct democracy is a potential shortcut towards popular government to the extent that it can be used to determine and even initiate public policies. This has been the case in Switzerland, where the extensive use of referendums for initiating or deciding policymaking issues has served as an outlet for popular mobilization, leading to a centralization of political debate.[13] However, member states have resisted the introduction of this method of mobilization – which *inter alia* would cause institutional upheaval by interfering with the legislative monopoly of the Commission – at the EU level.[14]

In the absence of a mechanism for direct and continent-wide popular participation in European government, certain member states have resorted to trying to endow the foundational moments that are treaty negotiations with popular legitimacy through referendum ratification. When a referendum is used, however, the terms of the debate are national as what matters is the acquiescence of that particular country's electorate and the reasons for voting in favour can vary considerably from country to country. This variation between member states in the justification for closer union adds to the problem of identifying a common goal for European construction that has been clearly mandated by a majority of European citizens. What compounds this problem further are the unexpected developments that may follow from the European treaties. The latter, as shown in the previous chapter, are invariably framework documents specifying procedures for taking common decisions rather than detailing the content of these decisions. As a result, a referendum vote is a poor guide to judging citizens' opinion on the legitimacy of certain European policies adopted at a future date[15] or how a national public sphere will react to an ECJ decision affecting domestic political competences. As David Runciman correctly said of the Constitutional Treaty, 'it is not a document that can be put to the people to force the issue of European integration' (Runciman, 2003). This is precisely because it constitutes a compromise amenable to both federalists and intergovernmentalists alike (Jabko, 2007; Magnette, 2007).

Thus popular, pan-European mandates, whether for governing or foundational legitimacy, are not possible in the EU's treaty system as it currently stands. As such, the chances of pursuing supranational integration against the wishes of one or more obstreperous states on the basis that the majority of European citizens are in favour of deeper integration are very slim. This sets the EU very much apart from the US, where the consolidation of the union invariably corresponded to a mobilization of the majority, notably – in Ackerman's periodization of three such 'constitutional moments' – the Founding, Reconstruction and the New Deal (1991; 1998).

Experiments with an alternative to conventional treaty amendment were tried recently as pro-integrationists sought to bypass the stranglehold of the states so as to foster the participation of transnational civil society. Twice now 'conventions' have been assembled, consisting of European and national parliamentarians and other political actors as well as representatives of the member states' governments, to discuss first a charter of fundamental rights and freedoms and later to debate the future of Europe.[16] The results have been underwhelming.[17] Indeed, the convention has fallen well short of its supranational legitimating ambition as the member states continue to reserve the right to oversee the outcome of such proceedings. In the case of the Charter of Fundamental Rights, its legal status remained dependent on treaty revision, which implies member state unanimity, while the draft Constitutional Treaty was picked over by the EU member states in order to conform to their preferences.

Yet for all its highly imperfect ability to mobilize supranational or even national publics in favour of deeper integration, the treaty method is far from devoid of advantages with regard to the maintenance of a dynamic equilibrium. In the EU, the treaty system has so far never been static: it is a dynamic process subject to ongoing speculation, negotiation and revision. Since the Maastricht Treaty, 'there has been, in effect, a semi-permanent revision process, whereby one revision already contained the seeds of the next one' (De Witte, 2003: 213). Given the twin commitments to 'ever closer union' and the preservation of the *acquis*, the ceaseless striving for a renegotiated settlement ensures that these moments are always discussions about how far to move forwards in integration. Treaty amendment in the EU knows of no reverse gear as the member states have never, for instance, claimed back competences[18] or diminished the budget. There is also an inherent pressure to forge ahead with a proposed treaty rather than derail negotiations even when there is a ratification setback. This pressure exists despite the fact that the Vienna Convention on the Law of Treaties stipulates that states cannot be forced to become parties to treaties they have not ratified.[19] Hence the EU's consensus-building politics is capable of making the status quo evolve despite a negative referendum vote. Even the demise of the Constitutional Treaty did not signal the enshrinement of the existing treaty arrangement: Europe's political elite preferred to recycle the document in a new form rather than stick to the clumsy provisions of the Nice Treaty.

The foremost reason for member states' enthusiasm regarding semi-permanent amendment negotiations is the way that these can be used to remedy blockages in consensus-building that threaten the coherence of European government; amended treaties also serve to craft agreement on new projects of integration at times when this prospect seems doubtful (see sections 4.2.2 and 4.2.3). In particular, the process of negotiating deepening alongside widening provides an opportunity for every member to express and defend their interests in order to seek ways of reconciling them with the extension of competences, new rules of decision making or new policy goals. By contrast, territorial expansion in the US reawakened each time tensions over the controversial original compromise about the institution of chattel slavery. Thanks to the three-fifths compromise, whereby a slave counted for the purposes of representation by population as three-fifths of a freeman, federal political institutions bore a permanent over-representation of slave-holding states designed to prevent a questioning of the legal status of slavery by the union. For this reason, as well as for others that are outlined in the next sections, the American union found it increasingly difficult to reinvent a compromise on the subject. This is not true of the process of European integration, in which the original bargain over competences, institutional decision making, the budget and foreign policy has evolved even if the tensions underlying the struggle over the rules of the game have never been settled definitively.

Europe's treaty system for changing the rules of the game of politics, which leaves little room for popular consent, thus negates James Madison's fears about the baneful effect of a frequent revision of the rules organizing a polity. In response to Thomas Jefferson's argument that each generation must give its sanction to the social contract that is the constitution, Madison fretted that 'such a periodical revision [would] engender pernicious factions that might not otherwise come into existence' (Madison, 1962: 19). Nevertheless in the EU compound system, frequent amendment of the treaties has compelled factions (pro and anti-integrationists, free market liberals and partisans of economic intervention, NATO stalwarts and proponents of European defence) deprived of a popular mandate to cooperate with one another. In this way, ambitious projects for a fortified EU have lost out in favour of an incrementalist process of treaty revision. Fundamental compromises have been re-examined but never settled outright, leading to dynamic equilibrium over the rules of the game.

5.4 A project for freedom (the union as a means to an end) v. a project for undefined ever closer union (integration as an end in itself)

Another crucial divergence between the antebellum US and the EU compound systems is, in the latter case, the acute difficulty of articulating a clear idea of what integration is for. Thus popular mobilization of the sort that could dramatically strengthen the power of the EU is doubly impeded. Firstly, by virtue of the institutional problems associated with mobilizing popular participation discussed in the previous section. The second impediment has its origin in the opacity of purpose behind integration beyond peace and economic growth, which hinders the ability to formulate justificatory arguments in favour of deeper integration that will curry popular favour. This section sets out to explain why this opacity exists and how this differs from the comparatively unambiguous political character of the American union.

The American republican founding has limpid ideological origins, notably 'the preservation of political liberty threatened by the apparent corruption of the [English] constitution' (Bailyn, 1971: 19) as a result of maladministration by the British crown. In political theory and practice, as well as in the popular imagination, the constitution is forever associated with the Declaration of Independence. As a result, the great compromise of 1787 was understood less as a blueprint for 'a more perfect union' than as a means for the safeguard and flourishing of 'life, liberty and the pursuit of happiness'. Not only does the integration process in Europe lack a revolutionary founding moment, the treaty system itself makes it harder to understand what the nature of the European political project is.

With the unit of political representation for expressing popular opinion on Europe (either via referendum or through elections) still unquestionably the nation state, the ability to launch a continent-wide debate on the future of European government remains nugatory. Debates over integration are thus fragmented according to different countries' varying preoccupations, if not paranoias. Referendum campaigns on accession or treaty reform are thus permeated by domestic issues and national political narratives, including, invariably, the popularity of the incumbent government. Above all, it is easiest to make the case for deeper integration on the basis of the benefits of expected economic growth and the frightening costs of non-integration: the 1988 Cecchini Report (Cecchini et al., 1988) on the efficiency gains stemming from the completion of the single market anticipated a benefit of 4-7 per cent of combined GDP, an argument greatly in vogue during the French referendum campaign on the Maastricht Treaty. Moreover, even direct democracy is not allowed to obstruct the momentum of treaty reform; these ambiguous, compromise packages are there to be ratified and will merely be voted upon again or rebranded if citizens in certain member states refuse to acquiesce. The net result, as Magnette explains, is that 'under these circumstances, it remains extremely difficult to present European stakes as clear choices between a limited number of collective projects' (Magnette, 2005: 171). It is in this context that supporters of the EU, in the absence of a political programme backed by popular mobilization, fall back on the justification that integration is a goal in its own right.

The significance of the American union's ability to represent a concrete political objective is clear even from a brief examination of the content of nineteenth-century debates over the nature of the antebellum compound polity. During the Senate debate on the controversial tariff legislation that South Carolina threatened to nullify, Daniel Webster repeatedly took to the floor to defend the union. In one of the most remarkable oratorical moments in American history, Webster made a nonsense of the principle and practice of nullification, while also going to great lengths to explain the purpose of the federal union. Claiming – like Jackson before him and as Lincoln would in the future – that the constitution had its origins in the people, the Massachusetts senator went on to remind his audience why the people had seen fit to innovate by creating a new type of union. 'The people brought it into existence, established it, and have hitherto supported it', according to Webster, 'for the very purpose, amongst others, of imposing certain salutary restraints on State sovereignties' (Belz, 2000: 136).

Freedom was thus the keystone of the original American compound polity but its preservation relies on various principles and institutions. Limited government – which the British parliament had egregiously failed to respect – is based on institutional checks and balances at the federal level as well as the federal union's guarantee against potential abuses of liberty carried out by the states. Hence secession or nullification represented in the eyes of Webster and his acolytes a loss of liberty.

Of course, the union did not only place limits on the extent to which the federal government could act and guarantee republican liberty in the states. It also created the possibilities for individual freedom by maintaining peace and overseeing economic prosperity unfettered by arbitrary restrictions on interstate commerce.[20] The dissolution of the union would thus herald the return of European-style interstate rivalry and war, especially as it was easy to imagine the powers of the Old World inveigling themselves into this system. Union was thus a guarantor of peace, a precondition of liberty.

Chief among the reasons why the union was venerated for its contribution to liberty, however, was the fact that by this time the federal government was starting to be defined as an instrument for the representation of the sovereign people, as discussed above. Thus the political institutions of the federal union were defended as the best expression of the will of the people. Webster distanced himself greatly, therefore, from the founding fathers' ambivalence towards democratic majoritarianism, arguing instead that 'the first great principle of all republican liberty ... is that the majority must govern' (Webster, 1833: 33).[21] Thanks to the legislature's bicameralism, the American union functioned with a double majoritarian principle since 'a majority of the representatives of the people must concur, and a majority of the States must concur, in every act of Congress' (ibid., p. 34). South Carolina's obstreperousness in the tariff disputes was thus painted as minority factionalism, which 'denounces the government of majorities, denounces the government of [their] own country, and denounces all free governments' (ibid, p. 35).

Defenders of the antebellum compound republic argued that union was inseparable from the concept of freedom itself since the purpose of the federal constitution was liberty understood both as individual rights and self-government; only with a perpetual and fortified union could this be achieved. Webster railed against 'the delusion and folly' of ranking 'liberty first and Union afterwards'. His final hortative appeal for 'Liberty and Union, now and for ever, one and inseparable' (Belz, 2000: 144) encapsulated the political ideology of American unionism. It was precisely this ideology that Lincoln seized upon, making it his own thanks to his unique and largely self-taught brand of rhetorical magnetism, so that he referred, in 1862, to the 'necessity of proving that popular government is not an absurdity' (quoted in McPherson, 1991: 56). Unsurprisingly, this ideology of federal union as the means for preserving and advancing freedom as both a moral and political goal was the inspiration behind the North's war effort, endowing the bloody struggle with a special sense of mission. In other words, a particular form of political organization – the compound republic – was considered by many to be the crucible that made collective (self-rule by the people) and thus individual freedom a reality.[22]

The ideology of freedom was not the prerogative of the supporters of the union, of course. John Calhoun claimed that a federal government was by definition 'the government of a community of States, and not the government of a single State or nation' (quoted in Forsyth, 1981: 122), meaning that the several states were obliged in the last instance, when subject to injurious federal policy, to protect their own and their citizens' liberty. Political theorists were also not the only ones to dispute whether the union invariably served to promote freedom: 'themes of liberty and republicanism formed the ideological core of the cause for which Civil War soldiers fought, Confederate as well as Union' (McPherson, 1994: 6). What is significant is the fact that in the American case the equation between union and freedom was considered so plausible. Indeed, it was highly convincing to large swathes of the population, notably the young men who enlisted, including those born abroad. McPherson's study of soldiers' letters reveals that 'many Union soldiers voiced with extraordinary passion the conviction that preservation of the *United* States ... was indeed the last, best hope for the survival of republican liberties in the Western world' (ibid., p. 30).

The contrast between this vision of a union as a cause with a distinct political objective, traceable to the revolution of 1776, and the way in which the EU is currently perceived is stark indeed. While the democratic legitimacy of the EU has been subject to manifold stinging criticisms, stimulating a plethora of policy recommendations, Glyn Morgan (2005: 22) rightly points out that 'we know considerably less about the question that really matters: what is the justification for a European polity?' Such an argument is inevitably relative: it must refer back to other forms of polity, in the same way that the American union was justified by invoking the parlous effects of nullification and the spectre of several rival nations in case of secession. Morgan recognizes this point by noting that the European polity 'cannot vindicate its own claims to "political legitimacy" ... without delegitimating its conceptual rivals' (ibid.). Yet in public debate over integration there is a dearth of arguments over the finality of integration, that is, what the EU polity will become and why this is necessary.[23]

There are a number of reasons for this justificatory constipation. These chiefly reflect the way in which the rules of the game of integration have evolved over time. As explained in the previous chapter, the emphasis on compromise, both at times of treaty revision and in the day to day functioning of institutions, has prevented the deliberate and sudden choice between competing visions of integration. By nurturing ambiguity over how EU foreign and security policy relates to NATO or the extent of social policy made possible by the Charter of Fundamental Rights, for example, it is as difficult to understand how far integration has already progressed as it is to discern the goals of integration.

Although economic growth is a perennial justification of the European project – a goal that it sometimes struggles to live up to – European citizens are not moved by the prospect of prosperity alone. Thus another complication arises from the fact that different visions of social justice present in the various nation states do not automatically overlap with arguments in favour of a stronger Europe. For instance, support for a more interventionist model of government per se does not necessarily correspond with a desire to extend EU competences. Nordic countries that favour high social and environmental protection are wary that losing sovereignty over these areas could jeopardize their ability to keep these higher standards. French political debate is even more confused about European construction. Contradictory positions abound, including the desire to insulate *l'exception française* from too much European-induced reform alongside the wish to use the so-called French social model as the basis for European social policy (Glencross, 2009b).

Conversely, laissez-faire models of society correspond with a circumscribed project of integration: free market or neoliberal ideas at the domestic level go hand in hand with a free market model of the EU restricted to promoting a single, ruthlessly efficient market with little political baggage. In other words political debates over the nature and purpose of government within the member states do not link easily with projects for the future of integration in the way that the ideology of liberty, for many, corresponded with the notion of a strong American federal union. Rather, the model that fits easiest, the free market vision, is the one that calls for the most attenuated version of European government.

Finally, the EU's problematic standard of democratic legitimacy also undermines the plausibility of associating integration with the goal of improving the accountability of government and the responsiveness of governors. Sbragia rightly argues that the prior existence of universal political rights at the national level ensures that talk of a democratic EU is 'focused, almost by default, on the mechanisms by which citizens can influence decision-making' (Sbragia, 2005: 168). Yet participation in decision making is Europe's Achilles heel: the locus of authority is blurred, the system of legislation is fiendishly complicated and often the stakes are simply not salient enough to register among voters. Thus concerns over the democratic representation of citizens in the decision-making process, mingled with a desire to ring fence national identity against unwanted erosion, enable the construction, for some member states, of an antinomy between democracy and integration. When outlining its 'red lines' of national competences that could not be breached, the UK government justified this position as a defence of democratic accountability, which would otherwise be in jeopardy were sovereignty pooled to a greater extent (HMG, 2003; cf. Kassim, 2005). The argument that integration needs to be controlled for the sake of democracy is not simply the tool of the most euro-sceptic either. On the contrary, the Lisbon Treaty in effect acknowledged the validity of this critique by incorporating national parliaments into the veto-system for checking the expansion of European governance. Thus unlike in the antebellum US compound system, citizens and politicians alike find it difficult to believe that the future of European democracy lies in a more consolidated polity.

Of the four founding goals of European integration (see section 4.2), therefore, none is a particularly powerful, popular identity-building ideology for the sake of justifying continuing integration. As the above analysis shows, economic growth and the promotion of liberal democracy are both problematic ways of mobilizing support for the EU. The other two foundational goals are hardly more inspiring, thanks ironically to the success of the project itself. A security guarantee against German economic and political resurgence is no longer necessary as fear of this has dwindled. This leaves only perpetual peace as the leitmotiv of integration. Yet while peace between European nations is a clear political objective that explains the need for certain common and binding rules, this argument cannot be used willy-nilly. Regardless of the natural lapse in the power of memory that occurs over time, the peace argument becomes much less plausible as integration is called for in new policy areas. What, after all, does peace between European nations have to do with devising a common foreign and security policy for dealing with humanitarian and crisis-management interventions outside Europe? Similarly, the need to preserve peace is not a convincing argument as to why a common macroeconomic policy for tackling unemployment is required. Hence the success of the EU has in fact undermined the power of the founding vision, a singular weakness that has not been compensated by the emergence of an attractive new vision of the purpose of the project.

Under these circumstances, therefore, it is not surprising that integration has become valued for its own sake. A project that simultaneously envisages being 'united ever more closely' while also 'united in diversity' obviously does not express a single, clear political objective. Faced by the doubly arduous task of both negotiating a new equilibrium during treaty reform and selling this to their citizens, member state governments prefer, above all else, to extol the merits of incremental integration as necessary to maintain the goodwill and trust required to keep integration working. This is how the metaphor of constant pedalling to keep the bicycle that is Europe steady became popular, a metaphor that is doubly apposite as it indicates constant motion but no fixed destination.

Without a justification for a certain type of political project focused on a particular objective and connected to a vision of its future, however, it is almost impossible to see how EU consolidation at the expense of member state competences could become a successful mass political movement. In this section, the analogy with the antebellum US demonstrated how mobilization behind the union when its purpose and powers were called into question depended on a persuasive justification of why this form of government was necessary and what it alone could achieve. Union as the guarantee of republican freedom – itself the legacy of a revolution that needed to be preserved – was the political ideology that justified rallying around the federal republic. Indeed, this spirit has continued well into the twentieth century, for 'it has been the growth of the national government that has enlarged the boundaries of individual liberties' (Abrams, 1996: 18), notably through welfare and civil rights reforms. Fundamental changes in the rules of the game of the American compound polity, therefore, have always relied on justifications – albeit never uncontested – about the nature and purpose of federal union. The remarkable absence of similar justifications advanced to renegotiate the rules of the game in Europe – even after 50 years of integration – is thus another compelling factor for explaining why European integration has resolutely stuck to a scenario of dynamic equilibrium.

5.5 A single fault line v. multiple fault lines

Almost every causal explanation as to why the American compound union proved unworkable has at its heart the existence of slavery.[24] The Philadelphia convention had struck a twofold compromise: it balanced the demands of large and small states through bicameral representation and mollified southern states' fear of federal intervention in matters relating to slavery by guaranteeing them over-representation both in Congress and the Electoral College due to the three-fifths clause (Rakove, 1996; Robertson, 2005). Southerners were interested in maintaining a barbarous system that treated humans as property; they feared the possibility that federal institutions might restrict or abolish the practice. What reignited the debate over the status of slavery was the expansion (peaceful as well as belligerent) of the union, which opened up the question of whether chattel slavery would spread. Adding new states risked upsetting the original institutional compromise. If slavery remained geographically contained, this would diminish the South's over-representation upon which it relied to check federal attempts to intervene in the slavery issue.[25] The situation called for new ways of re-engineering consensus on this most vexing issue. Unable to keep manufacturing compromises over a problem that would not go away owing to continued and expected future expansion, the US no longer remained viable as a compound polity.

The slavery debate in the US centred on containment versus expansion rather than a straightforward antinomy of abolitionists and slave drivers. Containment was considered the most suitable policy by a broad coalition of moral, political and economic opponents of slavery as the assumption was that, if restricted in geographical scope, the institution would eventually wither in political and economic significance. The economic dynamism and social progress of the new free states would become proof of slavery's multiple baneful effects until no redoubt of slave holders could dispute this fact.

The first crisis of containment arose in 1819 over the admission of Missouri as a slave state. The period following the Louisiana Purchase in 1803, which included lands where both French and Spanish colonists had long practised slavery, was one 'without parallel in the territorial expansion of slavery' (Fehrenbacher, 1980: 12). Florida, purchased in 1819 from Spain, added to the list of prospective slave states. Thus containment came to the fore as soon as the new territories were considered ready for admission into the union, thereby threatening to alter the relationship between free and slave-holding states within Congress. The 1819 controversy was sparked off by James Tallmadge's proposed amendment to the enabling bill for Missouri's admission as a state, which would have prohibited 'the further introduction of slavery and provide[d] that slave children born after the date of admission should be free[d] at the age of fifteen' (ibid., pp. 14–5). Containment in this case was explicitly linked to gradual abolition. With the Senate refusing to pass this amendment, which had already passed in the

House, a compromise deal had to be put together. In return for the entry of Maine (hitherto part of Massachusetts) as a free state into the union, no restrictions would be placed on slave-holding in Missouri; however, except for Missouri, in territory acquired from France slavery would be 'forever prohibited' north of latitude 36° 30'.

The manner in which this struggle over the rules of the game of politics affected expectations about the antebellum US compound polity is, in three particular aspects, highly instructive. Firstly, the passing of Tallmadge's amendment in the House of Representatives alerted proponents of slavery to the existence of an antislavery majority in the lower house, which thus 'confirmed the southern need to maintain sectional equality in the Senate' (ibid., p. 21). Northerners and southerners alike realized that the future of slavery hinged on how the entry of new states affected the balance in the Senate, thereby making the question of a territory's policy on slavery vital. Secondly, the amendment controversy opened the door for bitter constitutional dispute about federal powers conferred by the constitution as the anti-slavery movement's claim that Congress had the right to regulate slavery in a new state was acutely disputed by the slave interest. Although the Northwest Ordinance had previously established this right, this had been passed under the Articles of Confederation (Onuf, 1987). If the principle of determining the status of slavery in an acceding territory were accepted, the South began to worry about whether congressional authority could be interpreted by extension as also permitting the regulation of slavery in existing states. The major effect of this new apprehension, as Don Fehrenbacher explains, was that 'after 1820, it became increasingly difficult for a defender of slavery to support the expansion of federal power' (Fehrenbacher, 1980: 22). Thirdly, the compromise that had been brokered showed the limits of flexibility when it came to finding a dynamic equilibrium between both camps. By rejecting 'the possibility of gradual emancipation, even in a part of the country where it would have been neither impractical nor dangerous' (ibid., p. 23). Southern states demonstrated beyond a shadow of a doubt their commitment to the permanence of slave holding.

The second major battle over the containment of slavery occurred as the union expanded through conquest. Following the South's recognition of the need to maintain a pro-slavery balance in the Senate, its political leaders began agitating for expansion in the south-west, whose vast plains seemed particularly propitious for a slave-based plantation economy. Newly independent Mexico, which had abolished slavery in 1829, rebuffed US offers to purchase Texas, which promptly became independent in 1836 after a revolt of American settlers. The annexation of Texas in 1845 – which had been one of the central themes of the 1844 Presidential election – was promoted by the slave interest as a way of further strengthening the permanence of slavery in the US.[26] Annexation itself sparked off considerable animosity between the two sectional interests; at first opponents of slavery managed to prevent a policy of annexation, leaving Texas an independent, slave-holding republic from 1836 to 1845 (Winders, 2002). America's Texas policy antagonized Mexico, itself in a state of post-colonial turmoil, which combined with the lure of further territorial gains for the slave interest to ignite a conflict with the union's enormous southern neighbour in 1846.

At this point the anti-slavery section had an epiphany: they realized the extent to which they had lost control of the agenda of the federal government. A quarter of a century had elapsed since the Missouri Compromise and in the meantime three slave states (Arkansas, Florida and Texas) had entered compared to but one free state (Michigan). Although well outnumbered in the House of Representatives as population growth was much greater in the free states, the South had kept control of the Presidency thanks to its dominance of the Democratic party that linked both sections – a point that will be developed in the next section on the importance of party politics. Paradoxically then, the South was dominant in American political life at a time when 'in population, wealth, and industrial capacity, the South had fallen far behind the North and was much more conscious of its minority status than it had been before' (Fehrenbacher, 1980: 29). Thus it was a Virginia plantation owner, John Tyler, who annexed Texas in the last days of his presidency on the basis that the 1844 presidential election gave a mandate for doing so. His successor and fellow slave owner, who had campaigned successfully for annexation, James K. Polk, set his ambitions on purchasing Mexican territory and sent federal troops into the disputed Mexico-Texas border, an action that eventually led to out and out conflict.[27]

Provoked by their evident failure to control the agenda of the federal government, at the outset of war with Mexico in 1846 the North sought to reimpose its vision of contained slavery by preventing the expansion of slavery in territories that might be acquired from America's southern neighbour. Named the Wilmot Proviso after its congressional sponsor, the proposal to ban slavery in former Mexican lands easily passed the House, proving once again the importance of controlling the Senate. It was at this moment that the slavery issue 'took on a life of its own' for once it had 'entered the political arena, it proved impossible to get out' (Gienapp, 1996: 83). With the massive territory acquired by the

Treaty of Guadalupe Hidalgo (1848), which practically doubled the size of the US republic, the West held the key to the future of slavery. If constituted as free states, then the South would lose its Senate majority, potentially enabling the anti-slavery side to reach the two-thirds voting threshold in Congress necessary for amending the constitution to curtail slavery; if constituted as slave states, this majority hostile to slavery would never exist and the institution would be more firmly established than ever before.

A complex settlement (1850), orchestrated by Henry Clay, usually known as 'Clay's Compromise', just about managed to preserve a dynamic equilibrium between both sectional interests. This compromise represented a 'last desperate attempt to save the Union without dealing firmly and finally with the one thing which chiefly threatened it, namely slavery' (Butler, 1939: 226). In return for California's admission as a free state (for the sake of sectional balance, initially one pro- and one anti-slavery senator were sent to Congress) and the abolition of the slave trade in the District of Columbia, the New Mexico and Utah territories were organized with no prohibition on slavery. The South was further mollified by the adoption of more stringent federal laws on fugitive slaves.[28] But the compromise unravelled quickly as southern fears of containment leading to an insidious pressure for extinction were not allayed. Equally important, Northern politics by this stage was becoming principally exercised by the question of slavery and whether it was compatible with the nature and purpose of the union.

It was during the Wilmot Proviso clash that the prospect of disunion became a reality, since the 'Unionism that had triumphed in the Lower South and Middle South was predominantly "conditional" Unionism – which is to say, conditional *dis*unionism' (Fehrenbacher, 1980: 44). The only remaining mechanism that could hold the union together was the party system. In other words, in the 60 years following the creation of the republic, political strife in all its various manifestations (interpreting the constitution, relations between states and the federal government, party politics, foreign policy) increasingly revolved around the central cleavage of slavery. Indeed, it became the sole cleavage in the compound republic. This sectional crisis reached a paroxysm in the 1850s as both sides developed 'conflicting sectional ideologies, each viewing its own society as fundamentally well-ordered and the other as both a negation of its most cherished values and a threat to its existence' (Foner, 1995: 9). As the ideological antagonism grew more bitter, and the values of the other side became more of an anathema, compromise and thus the chances of maintaining a dynamic equilibrium dwindled.

What fuelled this struggle was the notion, as shown in the previous section, that the union was instrumental to the pursuit and realization of certain values – a vision of what the polity was for. Both sides claimed to be defending the true version of what founders and citizens alike wanted, a clash that has been deemed a contest between 'two distinctive democracies'. 'The southern democracy', Wilentz explains, 'enshrined slavery as the basis for white men's political equality', while northerners 'thought slavery a moral abomination that denied the basic humanity of blacks and whose expansion threatened white men's political equality' (2005: 791). Thus southerners argued for state sovereignty in the name of liberty, the freedom to keep the economic and social institution upon which their existence was founded; the union existed to respect this principle or otherwise (white) people in the southern states could not continue to be a party to it. Northerners had an altogether different concept of American freedom for which the revolution had been fought and which was the guiding spirit of the constitution. As Foner argues, 'the integrity of the Union, important as an end in itself, was also a prerequisite to the national greatness Republicans felt the United States was destined to achieve' (1995: 316). It was this intoxicating, hubristic understanding of freedom that Lincoln captured in his view that 'the American nation had a special place in the world, and responsibility to prove that democratic institutions were self-sustaining' (ibid.). By linking the union to this concept of democratic freedom it was possible for a single socio-economic cleavage to evolve into a devastating and all-encompassing economic, moral and political argument against slavery. A vast camp of citizens could be mobilized for various interrelated reasons: ethical opponents of slavery, pioneer farmers attracted by land in the West and the corresponding promise of social mobility, unionists who objected to the South's quasi-aristocratic social hierarchy as a violation of liberty, northerners resentful of southern political power, industrialists who thought the expansion of inefficient slavery ruined commercial opportunities and northern workers who thought slavery depressed wages. In this way, Republicans 'hammered the slavery issue home to the northern public far more emphatically than an appeal to morality alone could ever have done' (ibid., p. 309).

Eventually the escalating mutual antagonism led to a zero-sum game because 'the struggle for the West represented a contest between two expansive societies, only one of whose aspirations could prevail' (ibid., p. 312). Given the neat geographical divide between both sides, the cleavage was directly transferred into the system of political representation. In the institutions taking into account population – the House of

Representatives and the Electoral College – it was now clear that one side was in the majority, meaning that in a polity increasingly moving towards a majoritarian system of popular sovereignty the territorial minority would inevitably lose out if the party system realigned on sectional cleavages. Once the intraparty mechanisms for depoliticizing the slavery issue failed (see section 5.6), the principle of the extended republic, supposed to prevent rule by faction in a compound polity, was not enough to prevent polarization on a cleavage with a geographically differentiated majority and minority.

A similar breakdown in the conditions that favour a dynamic equilibrium seems much less likely in the EU compound polity precisely because it has neither a fixed majority/minority nor a comparable zero-sum socio-economic struggle. Firstly, the struggle over the rules of the game of the integration process has been riven by multiple and overlapping cleavages. For instance, as already mentioned, countries with high social and environmental protection do not necessarily want to see the EU legislate in these areas, out of a fear that their own high national standards may be diluted. Thus, as Neil Nugent explains, these sectional disputes have not 'rotated around fixed internal majority or minority power blocs or coalitions, but rather around viewpoints, alliances and coalitions that have shifted according to issues' (2004: 12). Given this fact, the EU is thus closer than the antebellum US to the model of the extended republic with diluted and fluctuating factions that Publius thought necessary for preserving a compound system incorporating the legal authority of the centre with a certain autonomy for the units. It is precisely these overlapping and evolving interests and preferences that make package deals for internal reform possible.

A second reason why dynamic equilibrium has not been threatened is the EU member states' ability to retain control of the agenda and process of integration. Thanks to the conferred basis of competences, member states do not need to fear that the EU will become competent in an area that they have not all acquiesced to either through the consent of the government (and parliament) or by referendum. Even where the EU is competent to act through QMV, the institutional pressure for consensus described in section 5.2 promotes compromise to mollify acute opposition.[29] This explains why perhaps the biggest concern among recalcitrant member states is that the ECJ will, in the absence of EU legislation, use its powers of treaty interpretation to establish individual rights, notably in the field of social policy, which would never be accepted by the Council. Hence the UK fought tooth and nail to restrict the Court's ability to interpret freely the provisions of the Charter of

Fundamental Rights, culminating, ultimately, in the negotiation during the Lisbon Treaty of a complete opt-out from the application of the Charter for the ever-obstreperous UK. Finally, a similar kind of polarization between two antithetical visions of what integration is for is highly unlikely since the EU is far more robustly anti-majoritarian. Section 5.2 demonstrated how it is in the nature of the unanimous treaty system, including the occasional but growing use of national referendums, to hamper collective expressions of what citizens want the purpose of the EU to be. In other words, a fundamental part of the rules of the game, the basic unit of political representation in European politics, has not changed: it remains the nation state rather than European citizens in the aggregate.

Regardless of the proven pitfalls of popular mobilization in the EU, there is a more fundamental reason as to why even the two most opposed visions of integration – free market Europe versus social Europe – cannot polarize the European public in a way that renders the process of dynamic equilibrium untenable. Although supporters of either political project may see the rival vision as contrary to their own economic interests or indeed moral values, neither competing vision, let alone both, has by definition to regard the existence of the other as inimical to the survival of their favoured model. A compromise that allows both to coexist is possible. This can be seen in the maintenance of higher national standards and especially in the possibility for 'enhanced cooperation': a recognition that a minority of states pooling sovereignty to a much greater degree among themselves is not incompatible with the preferences of the majority. Ideological rivalry in the US, based largely on despondent expectations of what would happen if one side expanded its socio-economic model, made exactly such a compromise impossible; the minority was the problem of the majority and vice versa. Consequently, it is of primordial importance to understand the functioning of the antebellum party system and contrast it with the way in which the politics of treaty reform and member state power in the Council of Ministers structure the renegotiation of the rules of the game in the EU.

5.6 A party system and Supreme Court arbitrator v. politics of treaty reform and Council arbitration

The US party system was very much unwanted and arose originally only as an unintended consequence of the struggle among the political elite to define the proper extent of federal competences. Such was the nature of the first party system, which pitted Federalists, typified by Alexander Hamilton, against Republicans, among whom Thomas Jefferson was pre-eminent: a conflict between proponents of a strong federal state and defenders of state autonomy respectively. Thereafter, the story of antebellum politics is one in which disputes over the rules of the game were conducted largely outside the remit of the Supreme Court, and without recourse to amendment, leaving parties and party systems to try and resolve fractious issues by appealing to the public. Prior to the Civil War, therefore, political parties attempted to mobilize a wider and wider public over the politics of the union at the same time as sectional antagonism grew in intensity, fuelled by territorial expansion (Wilentz, 2005). Owing to a series of changes in democratic practices in the first decades of the nineteenth century, the politics of the republic tended increasingly towards majoritarianism at the level of the union. The basis of political representation thus shifted away from the individual states as political debate gravitated around the union, while the existence of a deep-rooted and fundamental minority/majority cleavage that re-emerged with each period of territorial expansion made it harder to reconcile both antagonists.

Before detailing how the party system responded to the challenge of the slavery cleavage, it is necessary to highlight some of the significant developments in the democratic practices of the early American republic. These were notable for breaking up the aristocratic elite's monopoly on office holding and for transforming the contest for the executive into a competition for the popular vote more than an indirect election of the most suitable candidate by those who should know best. Popular sovereignty became the leitmotiv of the union via the expansion of the franchise – states determined who could vote and in the first two decades of the new century 'the American electorate underwent sweeping change' (Swift, 1996: 99) thanks to the reduction and removal of property requirements – and through a change in the method for selecting Electoral College voters.[30]

In 1804 eight of the 17 states provided for the direct election of presidential electors; by 1824 only six out of a total of 24 did not allow for direct election (Aldrich, 1995: 106). Only Delaware and South Carolina had not followed suit by 1828.[31] In this way the state legislatures lost control over the selection of Presidential electors, enabling politics to become both more populist and cross-unit. The demise of the congressional nominating caucus for selecting party candidates – under fire for being prone to 'aristocratic intrigue, cabal and management' (Wilentz, 2005: 246) and which was buried after the 1824 election[32] – further helped transform the presidential election into a popular vote. From this moment, nominations would be at the discretion of the party outside Congress, making them more susceptible to popular influence.

The development of the second party system (from 1824 to the early 1850s) and its mobilization of millions of voters was largely the creation of President Andrew Jackson – a former general with a glorious reputation won through battles with the British and during the Indian Wars – and his followers. They sought to take advantage of Jackson's election in 1828 to reduce the dominance of the Virginia dynasty that had formed an oligarchical political grouping whose influence on federal institutions was still great. Jackson had famously been a victim of their powerful hold on politics. In the 1824 election he won the popular vote and a plurality of Electoral College votes yet the lack of an absolute majority forced the vote to be decided by the House of Representatives (voting by state), which chose John Quincy Adams. Unsurprisingly, after the 1828 victory, as Shefter explains, there was a deliberate attempt to purge the influence of the notables:

> By removing the bureaucrats appointed by their predecessors, the Jacksonians sought to sever the ties between the bureaucracy and these [oligarchic] social structures; and by reorganizing the bureaucracy, they sought to subject it to the control of the officeholders whom they had elected, the institutions (especially the party organizations) they commanded and the social groups for whom they spoke.
>
> (1994: 68)

Furthermore, as the parties in the post-Jacksonian era organized to mobilize political support they turned the election of presidential electors from one based on congressional districts to a winner-take-all principle so that the winning candidate received all the Electoral College votes (Gienapp, 1996: 87). This made it much easier for a candidate to win a landslide of states' Electoral College votes with only a relatively small percentage of the popular vote – in 1860 'Lincoln received 98 per cent of the North's electoral votes although he won only 54 per cent of the popular vote in the free states' (ibid.). In addition, voter turnout was very high in the last two decades before the Civil War: 'over 70 per cent of the eligible voters regularly cast ballots in presidential elections' (ibid., p. 91).

With these democratic developments the Presidential office therefore became the scene of hotly contested elections pitting rival parties and candidates against one another in the race for winning enough Electoral College votes across the union. The presidency – which some had originally considered quasi-monarchical, especially in comparison to the collegiate executive of the Articles of Confederation – was greatly enhanced in legitimacy and prestige as a consequence of these democratic changes. Under these new conditions, the leadership, platforms and organization of the parties became crucial to the challenge of winning votes on a national basis. Given the size of the southern minority, in the second party system that emerged in the wake of Jacksonian democracy politicians and party leaders realized that the simplest way to win the vote meant finding a figurehead and a fluid platform that could transcend the divide between free and slave states. This can be seen from the actions of Martin Van Buren, the New York politician most credited with crafting a new party organization – the Democratic Party – for the express purpose of winning the presidency.

Van Buren was very deliberate in his choice of party principle and its appeal to potential electors. The Democratic electoral equation he envisaged was a party linking 'the planter of the south with plains republicans of the north' (quoted in Aldrich, 1995: 108). This intersectional alliance was intended by Van Buren to counteract the political representation of sectional interests by reviving the principle of party distinctions, notably the old debate on the proper role and extent of the federal government for 'if the old [distinctions] are suppressed, geographical divisions founded on local interests, or what is worse prejudices between free and slave holding states will inevitably take their place' (ibid., p. 108). With the war hero General Andrew Jackson installed as the charismatic leader of this new party, Van Buren's project met with success since, in addition to his personal fame, Jackson cultivated an amorphous policy stance that built up a broad church of support.[33] This deliberate ambiguity by the party's figurehead allowed for a great cross-unit mobilization as this 'made it possible for those in the new party to run on whatever platform they wanted to, perhaps taking the opposite position from those running in the same party elsewhere in the nation' (ibid., p. 109).

Van Buren's idea was a triumph. Jackson won two terms of office and Van Buren himself was elected in 1836. The success of the system was based on the fact that the Democratic party did not require a coherent national platform in order to gain election: state and local organization and leadership were largely autonomous. Under the banner of a single party different policy positions could coexist as long as no one faction dominated and provided that 'controls to keep [the] "peculiar institution" of slavery off the national agenda' (ibid., p. 125) worked. So successful was this strategy that it was emulated by Jackson's opponents – who increased considerably in number following the vetoing of the rechartering of the national bank in 1832. The paradox of the second party system, as pinpointed by Richard McCormick, is that 'highly sectional responses in a series of presidential elections resulted in the formation of non-sectional parties' (McCormick, 1975: 112). For when the New Yorker Van Buren ran in 1836 'the South and the West ceased to be politically monolithic, as anti-Van Buren parties quickly mobilized' (ibid.). By 1840 these anti-Jacksonians and anti-Van Burens had constituted themselves as the Whigs and won the Presidency by running a war hero candidate – General Winfield Scott, veteran of the Black Hawk War – with a suitably flimsy platform to appeal across the union.

Thus the second party system (Whigs v. Democrats) represented a common endeavour to win the presidency on an intersectional alliance that would keep slavery off the political agenda of the federal government. Balanced party tickets, where a northerner and southerner would share the presidential and vice presidential nomination, were the most evident manifestation of this tactic. The Democrats had one in every election between 1836 and 1860 (except in 1840); the Whigs balanced their tickets in the three elections of the 1840s. In fact, the Democrats went even further in their attempts to lock the South into this political alliance thereby guaranteeing that the party would not work against slave interests. To this end the party established a national convention for electing the party ticket. Nomination was based on a two-thirds majority vote at the convention, where state delegates were proportional to each state's electoral votes – thereby over-representing the South given the Constitution's three-fifths rule. Thanks to this supramajoritarian procedure, as Aldrich explains, southern votes held the balance of power over nomination and thus 'made certain that no extremist, whether pro- or anti-slave, could be nominated', which 'helped produce balanced tickets and effectively attained and maintained the intersectional alliance in the Jacksonian Democratic party' (1995: 132).

For their part the Whigs relied on 'the personal commitment and leadership of moderates, most of all Clay' (ibid., p. 135; cf. Holt, 1999) to maintain the intersectional alliance in union politics. Thus 'it was no coincidence that the Whig party was torn apart and effectively collapsed the same year Henry Clay died' (Aldrich, 1995: 135). The mechanism of party organization under the second system was, therefore, as McCormick explains, 'better designed for achieving agreement on nominations than for formulating policies' (1975: 106). What mattered most was a palatable nomination rather than a pellucid platform as the first could unite sections in a way that the latter could only divide. Thus in the era of the second party system, political leaders did 'everything they could to contain and deflate the slavery issue, correctly perceiving its sectional character as the single greatest threat to the constitution' (Altschuler and Blumin, 2000: 154).

Another fundamental reason for the importance of establishing party control over electoral politics and the federal government was the difficulty states had in reining in their own representatives in the Senate. An upper house based on equal state representation was supposed to be, according to Federalist 62, 'a constitutional recognition of the portion of sovereignty remaining in the individual States and an instrument for preserving that residuary sovereignty' (Hamilton et al., 2003: 301). But as William Riker has shown, state legislatures, the body originally responsible for electing senators, lacked the ability to instruct their own representatives. Whereas the Articles of Confederation allowed states to recall their delegates, meaning that instructions could be backed by effective sanction, the Constitution did not provide such a mechanism. In fact, the first Congress 'refused by a large majority to add "the right to instruct" to the First Amendment, apparently because it seemed "too democratic" for the representative system and smacked too much of the localism of the Articles' (Riker, 1955: 456).

Naturally, state legislatures – especially those in the South – sought substitute sanctions against disobeying senators. The only successful alternative was forced resignation, which the states could hope to achieve by creating a furore if their senator voted against their perceived interests. Yet the divergent terms of office made such a method ineffective because 'resignations were not easily forced when senators sat for six years, state legislators for one or two' (ibid., p. 460). Love of office generally prevailed over pride as senators could cling on to office and await re-election knowing the composition of the legislature would have changed by then. Furthermore, in the age of Jacksonian democracy, senators began canvassing voters directly rather than state legislators for support even though only the latter could elect representatives to the Senate. In effect, would-be senators were urging voters to elect state legislators who in turn backed the former in the senatorial race. This canvassing complicated the power relationship as it meant that 'each state legislator then owed his office less to his own merit and more to the merit of the candidate for the Senate with which he was aligned. As a result, senators earned gratitude as much as they owed it' (ibid., p. 463). Thus without direct state control over the votes of senators, the centrifugal institution that was the Senate became susceptible to a centripetal tendency courtesy of party organization. This was especially true since Whigs and Democrats were both intersectional alliances that promised to respect and maintain intact slavery and so when it came to protecting states' interests party discipline became a substitute for state instruction.

At this point it is important to reflect on the extent of voluntary centralization that had occurred in the American compound republic by mid-century. It was not the powers of the US federal government that had changed dramatically, although its prestige and authority were greatly consolidated. What had been centralized was the political life of the union itself via a change in democratic practices. Under the impulse of democratic reforms – in keeping with the notion of freedom enshrined in the republic's foundational moment – election campaigns, political actors and, most importantly, policy issues, were gradually centralized around the federal capital. Institutions like the Electoral College, as well as the Senate, had originally been intended to preserve the states as the dominant actors in an American political sphere inhabited by notables. Democratic populism broke the stranglehold of both the notables and the states. In doing so, the states were stripped of their control over agenda-setting and their ability to veto or frustrate legislation was greatly diminished. Thus the rules of the game changed not in terms of federal competences and understanding of the nature of the union or the location of *Kompetenz-Kompetenz* but thanks to a change in the procedures of political decision making and participation, which in turn affected the basis of representation. The basis of representation both for mobilization of the electorate and political debate became the union as a whole rather than its separate political units.

Paradoxically, this process of centralization through democracy and political parties was motivated, during the second party system, by the desire to maintain a dynamic equilibrium on the slavery problem. This was a very volatile admixture, however, as centralization was resisted by violence when the party system failed to maintain the dynamic component and there appeared no prospect of resurrecting it. Given the importance of nomination over platform or principle, the party system was brought to its knees not as a result of competition between the two parties but from internal weaknesses that spelt the end of prevarication over the slavery cleavage. This internal flaw was a function of the parties' attempt to reach out across the sections while also repressing sectional interests. Hence, as McCormick has shown, 'intra-party tensions were greater than the tensions between the two parties ... the inability of any national party agency to exercise firm discipline made it all but impossible to restrain the intra-party tensions' (1975: 112).

The Whigs were the first to be convulsed by the inability to keep repressing the slavery issue as the union kept expanding and the status of slavery in prospective states had to be addressed.[34] Presidential elections were once again decisive for political realignment. In the aftermath of the resurgent antagonism that followed the 1850 Compromise, the comprehensive defeat of another military hero, Whig candidate Winfield Scott in 1852, revealed the limitations of the contrived strategy of keeping an intersectional alliance at the cost of a credible platform. As soon as this strategy failed, the South began to fret that Whiggism would not safeguard the slave interest and thus it became difficult for 'southern Whigs to remain within a party dominated by antislavery northerners' (Fehrenbacher, 1980: 48) thereby making the Democrats a more credible guarantee for slavery. Shortly afterwards, however, the Democrat party was torn apart by the passage of the Kansas-Nebraska bill (1854) that ironically, as Fehrenbacher argues, 'could never have been accomplished if the Democrats had not held such large majorities in both houses of Congress' (1980: 49).

The Kansas-Nebraska bill transferred the decision over the status of slavery in these two territories to their inhabitants and was the Democrats' attempt to make good on their 'credible commitment to attempt to reinstate balance at the first available opportunity' (Weingast, 1998: 158) following the 1850 Compromise. However, this principle of 'popular sovereignty' ran counter to the established and expected practice dating back to the Northwest Ordinance, which granted Congress alone the power to decide on the status of slavery when organizing a territory prior to statehood. Many northern Democrats baulked at this measure, which by also deliberately repealing the 36° 30' restriction of the Missouri Compromise (both Kansas and Nebraska lie above the famous line of demarcation) clearly spelt the end of the policy of containing slavery in an expanding union. Thus the method chosen by the Democrats to restore their intersectional credibility in the eyes of the South resulted in the Democrats losing so much ground in the North that they 'lost the ability to reinstate the sectional balance' (ibid.).

Northern opponents of the Kansas-Nebraska Compromise felt compelled finally to organize the first major party founded on antislavery principles, the Republican party.[35] Although inauspiciously weak at its origins in 1854, the Republicans found succour in the bloody confrontations in Kansas, where pro- and anti-slavery factions established rival governments and fought pitched battles, and adopted some of nativism's rhetoric of anti-Catholicism (Foner, 1995: 226-37).[36] Republican success was striking, in 1856 they carried 'all but five free states and finished second in the national totals' (Gienapp, 1996: 102), thereby hammering the final nail in the coffin of the second party system.

It was at this point that the other institution for settling scores between the states and the union, the Supreme Court, also revealed its limitations for promoting a dynamic equilibrium despite its supposed insulation from parties or popular passions. Seized by the slave Dred Scott, who had been taken by his master to a free state, the Court had to determine, besides whether Scott was in fact a citizen,[37] whether 'the Missouri Compromise [was] constitutionally valid in prohibiting slavery north of 36° 30' and whether 'the Scotts' [his wife was also a litigant] prolonged residence in a free state and a free territory earned them their freedom' (Wilentz, 2005: 710-11). By this stage of the struggle to re-establish a compromise over slavery, the justices 'were determined to pronounce a sweeping statement concerning slavery and its extension. They hoped thereby to take the subject out of politics forever' (McDonald, 2000: 178). With five southern justices out of a total of nine,[38] the South already had a majority in the Supreme Court and only needed 'one northern Democrat to sign on in order to give the comprehensive ruling some bisectional protective coloration' (Wilentz, 2005: 711).

Not surprisingly, the Court ruled in favour of the slave interest. Indeed, it went so far as to deny Congress the authority to rule on the status of slavery in territories, suggesting the Missouri Compromise was unconstitutional from the start. More egregiously still, the ruling stated that since the Fifth Amendment constituted an absolute protection for property, slavery was thus lawful throughout the US. With this far-reaching verdict the Supreme Court had failed utterly in managing its political role in the compound republic. It had overruled the legal basis of existing compromises over slavery and left only a vacuum of uncertainty. Additionally, the justices had alienated most of the northerner population, thereby making it imperative to succeed in efforts to win control of the executive in order to reverse the pernicious dominance of the slave interest.

By 1860 the sectional struggle degenerated as the Republican Party mobilized to defeat the slave power. This defeat was made possible by the schism of the Democrats as northern and southern factions could not unite over the principle of leaving popular sovereignty at the state level to determine the status of slavery in acceding states.[39] Lincoln won an easy victory, carrying a clear majority in the Electoral College with only 39.9 per cent of the popular vote. At this point southerners assumed that the game of contesting the status of slavery according to the rules and institutions of the US constitution was up. Even before Lincoln's inauguration, seven states of the Deep South had seceded. The fact that secession occurred as a result of expectations that Lincoln and southern slavery would be incompatible shows that by this point in time the antebellum compound polity was no longer viable. It could no longer find a dynamic equilibrium over the rules of the game to reconcile the interests of northerners and southerners alike. The transformation of the contest over the rules of the game of politics into violent conflict is the natural point to close the analysis of the viability of the US compound system. Coercion was needed to maintain the federal union. Moreover, a transitional period, known as Reconstruction (see section 3.2), gave rise to the recalibration of the rules of the game, thereby acknowledging the fundamental transformation in the compound system that had resulted from the demise of antebellum attempts to find a dynamic equilibrium.

The struggle over the rules of the game in the EU has already been discussed in great detail in the previous chapter. Hence it is sufficient here to make a few broad remarks pertinent to the contrast with the US party system. Despite the ongoing process of European integration, party systems aggregating European citizens on the basis of Eurocentric political debates have not emerged to negotiate struggles over the rules of the game of the EU. However, much the disparate national political parties constitute themselves into groups in the European Parliament, the peripheral nature of this institution – particularly when it comes to deciding the finality of the integration project – greatly limits its effect on the politics of treaty reform. By contrast with the development of the US party system, therefore, the EU's member states have retained a firm grip on the agenda of integration, notably when it comes to the attribution of competences and the definition of the purpose of integration. This holds true both during negotiations over treaty reform and in the day-to-day exercise of power. In the latter, the Council of Ministers has also been vigilant not to lose its grip over the contestation of the rules of the game, either by retaining the veto in the most sensitive policy areas or else thanks to the consensus-building pressure introduced into the institutional design of co-decision. This can be seen *a negativo* by the absence of disputes like nullification or secession, which in the US case signalled the frustration born of the impotence of states that felt they could not otherwise influence the rules of the game of politics.

The area where the dynamic equilibrium over the rules of the game in the EU has proved most difficult to maintain is the issue of competency over competences as a result of the actions of the ECJ.

In the EU compound polity, the judicial power poses a serious challenge to consensus over the rules of the game – notably competency over competences – outside treaty reform and arbitration by the Council of Ministers. However, this is not merely a consequence of the generally sympathetic attitude the court has towards integration: it is also a reflection of the logic of delegation governing the functioning of the Court.

Understood as a fiduciary or trustee institution (Majone, 2001) rather than an agent with the same preferences as the 'principal' that delegates authority, in this case the member states, the ECJ is expected to 'make decisions based on [its] best professional judgment ... and on behalf of a beneficiary' (Alter, 2008: 35). In doing so, the Court 'increases the likelihood that states will comply with their obligations in situations where compliance generates short-term political losses but long-term political gains' (Helfer and Slaughter, 2005: 35). This logic of enhancing the credibility of treaty commitments by delegation to a fiduciary oversight mechanism (the Commission and the Court) explains the paradox of why a diffident integrationist country like the UK nevertheless favours the existence of the Court. Yet the practical result of this delegation of authority is that the Court sometimes has to rule in cases where the policy implications of its jurisprudence go beyond the realm of conferred EU competences. This gives rise to disputes concerning competency over competences that are very difficult to resolve.

A telling illustration of how jurisprudence affects policymaking in areas beyond the realm of EU legislative competences can be found in the 2005 case *Commission* v. *Austria*,[40] concerning the Austrian government's decision to impose quota restrictions on the admission of students in dental and medical faculties. This recent conflict between the Commission and Austria was sparked off by the influx of German students taking advantage of the fact that, unlike Germany, Austria does not use a *numerus clausus* entry system[41] to restrict admission in dentistry and medicine. In response, the Austrian government sought to restrict the number of EU students in these courses to 20 per cent of total admissions by reserving 75 per cent of places for students with a secondary education diploma obtained in Austria.[42] In its ruling on the case, the ECJ invoked treaty provisions on the freedom of movement of students to find in favour of the Commission. In its opinion:

> [B]y failing to take the necessary measures to ensure that holders of secondary education diplomas awarded in other Member States can

gain access to higher and university education organized by it under the same conditions as holders of secondary education diplomas awarded in Austria, the Republic of Austria has failed to fulfil its obligations under Articles 12 EC, 149 EC and 150 EC.
(*Commission* v. *Austria*, 2005)

Consequently, the ECJ has transformed a question of education policy into something other than a purely domestic affair. Of course, the irony here is that education policy is not part of the shared competences of the EU where European legislation could trump domestic legislation. Instead, according to EC article 149, the powers in the area of education policy conferred by the member states are restricted to 'incentive measures, excluding any harmonization of the laws and regulations of the Member States'. In other words, ECJ jurisprudence can have immense implications for national policymaking in areas where member states have tried to retain their autonomy. The Austrian higher education dispute was in fact only resolved, at least temporarily, as part of the negotiations for the Lisbon Treaty: the Commission agreed to a five-year moratorium (also covering Belgium) on infringement proceedings, permitting the Austrian government to supply further justifications for its restrictions on the free entry of EU students.

Thus in the EU compound polity the ECJ poses a constant challenge to the negotiation of the rules of the game according to a logic of dynamic equilibrium. Unsurprisingly, therefore, one of the thorniest questions in the nearly decade-long attempt to find a replacement for the Nice Treaty concerns the legal status of the Charter of Fundamental Rights. With member states fearful that it could open up a Pandora box's of new justiciable socio-economic rights for EU citizens, it has only been granted treaty-like legal status after the insertion of a declaration in the Lisbon Treaty specifying that 'the Charter does not extend the field of application of Union law beyond the powers of the Union or establish any new power or task for the Union, or modify powers and tasks as defined by the Treaties'. Yet even this proviso was insufficient to allay the United Kingdom's fear of relinquishing control over competency over competences; it preferred a complete opt-out instead. This is a sure sign that in the absence of a pan-European party system for mobilizing citizens, it is the ECJ that is considered most likely to disrupt the dynamic equilibrium over the rules of the game that member states have until now managed to maintain.

5.7 Conclusion: Recognizing what makes the EU viable

The antebellum compound polity failed despite the fact that the contest over the rules of the game became more centralized as the agenda and practices of political life migrated from the states to cross-unit, mass parties. Individual states and their citizens could not veto policies and found it nearly impossible to set the agenda of union politics. Hence there was a great incentive to aggregate, which also fitted neatly with the American creed of republican popular sovereignty. Yet the party system could not maintain a dynamic equilibrium over the single cleavage – which polarized the compound republic into a clear majority and minority – that divided the member states geographically and was therefore translated into political representation at the union level.[43] Conversely, the EU appears to have remained viable as a compound polity capable of evolving according to a logic of dynamic equilibrium precisely because it has avoided practically all centralization of the contest over the rules of the game by remaining resolutely anti-majoritarian. In this context, the biggest threat to this dynamic equilibrium appears to stem from ECJ jurisprudence, which the member states seriously struggle to control *ex ante*.

Tocqueville once predicted that the American federal government's legitimacy would be a by-product of its ability to uphold the constitutional order outlined in the founding document of the union. The 'idea' that Tocqueville saw behind the union, as Donald Maletz explains, was a 'moral force' derived from the federal government's constitutional objectives of liberty and justice; it was this force, and not physical might, that was supposed to unify the 'diverse democracies of the past into a larger union' (1998: 610). According to Tocqueville, the supremacy of the union could only be maintained if the national courts 'defend the union by using the formalities of the judicial process' (ibid., p. 611). The strength of the union lay, therefore, in its legal order – the embodiment of the principles enshrined in the constitution – rather than in its ability to mobilize political support throughout the population of the various states. Yet as this chapter has shown, the US remained a viable polity thanks to the party system's efforts to maintain a minimal consensus over the slavery question as much as a result of its constitutional and legal order. Ultimately, the union prevailed because Lincoln drew on the promise of freedom inherited from the Revolution in order to mobilize popular support for his government and its campaign against secession (McPherson, 1991; Greenstone, 1993).

The analogy with the EU suggests that the strength of the European compound polity does not necessarily lie in its courts or constitutional order, as many suppose. Faced by multiple interest and identity cleavages, it is hard to see how the ECJ could function as the arbiter to solve these disputes in a way that would be accepted by all parties. Indeed, as pointed out in Chapter 4, it has consistently forborne to address the political questions raised by the introduction of the principle of subsidiarity. The antebellum Dred Scott case demonstrates well the inherent risk in using courts to settle political issues in a compound polity. Thus it is the intergovernmental system of bargaining and treaty negotiation that has played the determining role in maintaining the dynamic equilibrium upon which EU viability depends. Furthermore, the analogy also suggests it is important to query the nostrum that a pan-European party system is a natural cure to Europe's integration ills. The US example shows that partisan politics was far from an ideal way of finding a settlement to disputes over the rules of the game in a compound system.

This implies that European integration ought to be circumspect about pursuing a strategy of finding proxies to shift politics away from the domestic level to a supposedly more democratic pan-European one. The antebellum case shows that mass party mobilization of citizens to determine the contest over the rules of the game is liable to undermine the ability to find the dynamic equilibrium necessary when faced by an important ideological or interest cleavage. The following chapter examines in more detail the consequences this analysis has for understanding how the EU can best remain viable. It does so by exploring what a radical reconfiguration of political representation, allowing a majority of EU citizens to determine future rules of the game, would entail and how such a dramatic change – tantamount to voluntary centralization – could be managed successfully.

6
The Future Evolution of the EU Compound Polity: The Obstacles to Voluntary Centralization

> *Any federal arrangement likely to have long-term survival prospects is predicated on representation as a necessary condition.*
>
> Heinz Eulau (1974: 154)

6.1 Introduction

This penultimate chapter has three aims. Firstly, it questions whether the hitherto successful maintenance of a dynamic equilibrium is self-reinforcing or liable to potential future disruption. In particular, this necessitates an examination of what might threaten the ability to maintain a compromise between supranational and intergovernmental visions of integration. Here the obvious threat is the exacerbation of the two longest-standing cleavages between member states: the face-off between partisans of a free market Europe and advocates of a 'social Europe', based on market regulation, and the conflict between backers of NATO and Europeanists calling for security and foreign policy independence.

In fact, the continual blockage over these two divisive issues has led many to call for a change in Europe's system of democratic representation in order to produce the possibility of greater integration mandated by a supranational expression of democratic will, on the assumption that this will is currently fettered by intergovernmental constraints. Thus the chapter's second aim is to show that reconfiguring the nature of political representation in Europe is not necessarily a better way of managing long-standing tensions over the other three rules of the game. To do so, the analysis revisits the example of the voluntary centralization of political representation in the US prior to the Civil War. The antebellum experience clearly demonstrates the limitations of creeping majoritarian democracy when it comes to defusing crises over the rules of the game. The democratized compound polity representing individual citizens rather than states, without new features to safeguard the prerogatives of the units, proved unable to find a viable dynamic equilibrium over the rules of the game of politics.

Thirdly, in the light of the analysis of transformations in the antebellum US compound polity, the chapter asks how the voluntary centralization of European politics promoting the representation of individuals directly rather than via states – democratization in other words – could be managed to help maintain the viability of the EU polity. As Fabbrini has recently remarked, it is now commonly assumed by pro-integrationist critics of the democratic deficit 'that the parliamentary model is the only viable solution to the question of the democratization of the EU' (2005c: 188). I argue that it is too simplistic to expect that such a move, or other attempts to enhance the supranational element of representation, will inevitably have positive consequences for the EU compound polity. Trying to overcome the current intergovernmental impasse between federalist-minded member states and euro-sceptic ones by virtue of supranational democracy, whether by strengthening the role of the parliament, holding a pan-European referendum on treaty reform or turning the Council into an upper chamber, goes against the anti-majoritarian tendency that has contributed greatly to EU viability.

This study of EU viability has not relied on the assumption that the development of some form of cross-unit democratic majority is sufficient to settle the contest between competing visions of integration. Instead, an analogy with the antebellum US has been used to provide crucial insights into understanding how such a change in the nature of representation could be managed. In particular, the American example suggests that any significant strengthening of supranational representation would require the introduction of certain new modes of *ex post facto* intergovernmental – rather than judicial – control that currently do not exist. It is in this context that certain innovations – in particular Calhoun's nullification mechanism – proposed in the antebellum US, when the nature of representation changed significantly, might prove valuable for sustaining the viability of the EU compound polity.

Ultimately, however, such a rebalancing of the principle of representation in the EU away from the representation of the units and towards the cross-unit representation of individuals *qua* citizens of the union will only be possible under strictly limited conditions. The US example offers *ex negativo* proof of this conclusion because the American compound polity unravelled as the federal government attempted to address a policy question it was not originally designed to tackle: the legal status of slavery. Hence the analogy suggests that any significant change in the nature of political representation in the EU would have to be preceded by a redefinition of the purposes of integration. In this way, altering the element of representation in the rules of the game of EU politics would have to be a derivative of a change in the expectations about the purposes of integration. Such a fundamental departure is most likely to succeed if anchored in national democratic representation, especially, it is argued, through the use of referendums on EU treaty reform. Yet the ability to articulate a justification for changes in the rules of the game from within national systems of democratic representation – even when resorting to referendums – is shown to be an extremely difficult exercise given the chronic problem of establishing a meaningful debate between domestic elites and a mass public about what Europe is for. Nonetheless ambitions for a viable more supranational EU depend on generating this debate.

6.2 Dynamic equilibrium: A self-reinforcing process?

The intention of this study has never been to portray the EU as inexorably destined to sustain a dynamic equilibrium, although European integration has hitherto succeeded in managing this feat in the face of considerable odds. The logic of dynamic equilibrium in a compound polity implies that an alternative can be found between a voluntary centralization of the rules of the game or leaving the status quo unchanged. The EU's current straits, however, are sufficiently difficult to prompt the question of whether this process of dynamic equilibrium is likely to continue as before. This is precisely because there are certain issues where it is difficult to discern a middle path between voluntary centralization and the retention of the existing rules of the game.

On the horizon there appear to be looming complications concerning future enlargement given the level of antipathy in some member states towards the potential accession of Turkey, which was already a factor in both the Dutch and French referendums on the Constitutional Treaty (Stefanova, 2006). Yet the enlargement process can still experiment with alternatives – albeit untried – to full EU membership, meaning there is a potential middle ground between opposition and support for the continued widening of Europe. The fact that the momentum for enlargement is vanishing may adversely affect the maintenance of a dynamic equilibrium over the rules of the game. This is because expansion is typically, as amply demonstrated in Chapter 4, an opportunity for persuading member states to renegotiate those rules via treaty reform. The rejection of the Constitutional Treaty, which was supposed to ensure efficient decision making in an EU of over 25 member states, is in this sense a bad omen as it demonstrates the increasing difficulty the EU faces in connecting enlargement to a process of treaty revision. Furthermore, the desperation with which Europe's elites have sought to avoid holding referendums on the constitution's successor, the Lisbon Treaty, bodes ill for the already tense relationship between political elites and citizens over the progress of European integration.

However, the greatest challenge to the process of dynamic equilibrium that has so far ensured the viability of the EU compound polity relates to social policy, the area where the underlying and long-standing tension between supranationalism and intergovernmentalism is most likely to be put under particular strain. This is true even in comparison with that other great EU policy fudge: the Common Foreign and Security Policy (CFSP). Despite the early setback with the EDC (see section 4.2.1), the development of a European foreign and security policy has always been a long-term objective of partisans of integration. So far a dynamic equilibrium has been achieved by balancing, on the one hand, the establishment of foreign policy 'joint actions' and 'common positions', while, on the other, providing safeguards by opt-outs (notably for Denmark) and unanimity requirements, while ensuring the overall compatibility of CFSP with NATO objectives (Nugent, 2003: 407–41).

Yet there are good reasons for believing that a more consolidated CFSP, one based on QMV for instance, could stay faithful to the logic of dynamic equilibrium by preserving a mixture of intergovernmentalism and supranationalism and maintaining a compromise over NATO commitments. This is because a QMV-organized CFSP would not overturn Europe's joint federal architecture and its concomitant pressure for consensus building. Joint federalism means that the EU relies on the resources of its members to put into effect its policies (see section 5.2). In CFSP this entails using the self-financed military capacity of the member states, which not only suggests that, ultimately, a state could choose to defy QMV and withhold its cooperation but also that, for the sake of credibility, the EU is always obliged to find a line that curries favour with a plurality of big-hitters, constituting a *de facto* mechanism for consensus.

Equally important, the extent of the overlap between CFSP objectives and NATO's novel post-Cold War priorities such as crisis management, fighting the spread of weapons of mass destruction and combating terrorism, implies that NATO stalwarts would, in principle, find little objectionable about changing the decision-making rules of CFSP based on its current agenda. This is demonstrated in practice by the United Kingdom's lead since the late 1990s in promoting EU defence cooperation, notably the creation of a rapid reaction force. The compatibility between the respective objectives of NATO and CFSP, as also shown by German and French participation in NATO's Afghanistan mission, means that a move towards a more supranational CFSP need not produce an antagonism between Atlantic alliance and European integration. Conversely, truly beyond the pale would be the attempt to transform the EU into a collective security community replacing NATO or a proposal to obtain a UN Security Council permanent member seat at the expense of the UK and France's individual seats.

Thus as far as CFSP is concerned, there is an alternative between voluntary centralization and leaving the status quo unchanged. Leeway still exists for continued dynamic equilibrium by introducing a supranational dimension into decision making. By contrast, the issue of incorporating social policy into the integration project poses a greater risk of destabilizing the process of finding a dynamic equilibrium over the rules of the game. This is because social policy, a broad field taken to include the regulation of taxation and social transfers,[1] poses a starker problem when it comes to reconciling the competing principles of supranationalism and intergovernmentalism.

Social policy is a favourite topic for the growing literature in transatlantic comparisons, which commonly point out the tardy and incomplete establishment of a federal welfare state in the US by contrast with European nation states. This phenomenon is usually explained in terms of a different trajectory of state-building (Fabbrini, 2005b) and, in the US, an ideological consensus over the benefits of a laissez-faire approach to government intervention in the economy.[2] Whatever the precise explanation – they are in any case mostly complementary arguments – the result is that the paucity of federal welfare programmes 'does not question the legitimacy of the American federal state' (ibid., p. 130). The same cannot be said of the EU's member states, whose national welfare systems, sometimes dubbed 'social models', are an intrinsic component of the legitimacy of their political institutions given that the twentieth-century European state 'incorporat[ed] social rights in the status of citizenship' (Marshall, 1992: 28).

The crucial role these welfare systems play in undergirding political legitimacy can be gauged from the increasingly frantic calls by the centre-left for greater EU intervention in the market economy to secure citizens' social rights (Habermas, 2000). At its most extreme, the argument is that integration can only become legitimate in the eyes of its citizens if it delivers substantively on social policy issues: whence the call to complement negative integration (market making) with positive integration (market correcting).[3] This supposed urgency is taken to be the result of the dwindling possibility of providing a certain level of social protection in national isolation; EU legislation – not least the Stability and Growth Pact – and the pressures of global economic competition sap states' room for autonomy (Scharpf, 2000). Thus it is no coincidence that the majority of the European left, which was originally quite hostile to integration, has now converted to the Euro-cause. Their ambition is to transform the EU into a social-democratic project, a *Sozialstaat*, now that the safeguarding of the welfare state at the national level seems less and less feasible. 'The left', as David Marquand has neatly put it, 'is now condemned to be European in a sense which does not apply to the right' (1997: 121).

Thanks to the legacy of the welfare state, therefore, it is fair to say that European citizens expect more from government in terms of social policy than has historically been the case of their US counterparts. So much so, in fact, that Majone argues that 'only a withering away of the European welfare state ... could facilitate the popular acceptance of a European federal state by drastically reducing the difference between what can legitimately be done at the national and at the European level' (Majone, 2006: 622). Yet it is precisely because this rolling back of Europe's welfare states, leaving only a level of social protection equivalent to that in the US, has not occurred that there is such a cleavage over social policy among the member states of the EU. Whether the EU will continue to be able to negotiate a dynamic equilibrium over the rules of the game, one that finds a new way of mixing intergovernmentalism and supranationalism, depends on the interaction between integration and the domestic politics of social policy.

In fact, there are three facets to the dispute over the legitimate role of the EU in promoting social justice through intervention to regulate the market. Firstly, there are those member states, the exemplar being France, where citizens are increasingly concerned about the consequences of negative integration – the opening up of domestic markets to European flows of capital, goods, services and workers. In this case, integration is associated with both commercial predation whereby foreign mergers and takeovers result in redundancies and job relocation, where employment shifts to member states whose lack of redistributive social policies gives them a supposedly unfair competitive advantage in labour costs. Hence the proposed solution to these adverse externalities of integration is to harmonize upwards levels of social protection so as to ensure a level playing field, which would require a radical change in the rules of the game as the current EU is neither expected nor competent to play this interventionist role.

The antinomy of this position is the neoliberal perspective, best represented by the UK, which supports further negative integration and is hostile to any change in the rules of the game concerning the area of social policy. Given that unanimous agreement is necessary to effect a meaningful change in the rules of the game in this area, the fear exists that – as demonstrated by the UK's preference to opt out of the Charter of Fundamental Rights – despite the lack of relevant EU competences, such regulation will be introduced by the back door through the jurisprudence of the ECJ. This fear harks back to the infamous 1990 Barber decision,[4] which unexpectedly outlawed gender differences in pensionable age, provoking a hasty upward realignment of the state pension age for women in the UK.[5]

The dispute over the scope of EU social policy is further complicated by the position of Nordic countries, which seek to retain high levels of welfare provision without the concomitant wish to export this model to the EU-level. Their primary concern, therefore, is the compatibility between negative integration and their own systems of social justice. Above all, they are alarmed by putative ECJ interpretations of the four fundamental freedoms necessary for the internal market that might unravel key elements of their national systems of social welfare, such as collective bargaining arrangements over wages.[6]

Hence integration is faced with a trilemma since there are three contrasting visions of the legitimate place of social policy within the integration project. At the same time as there is a demand for social justice to become a supranational concern, certain member states seek to prevent this ever happening, while another set of member states wish to insulate their successful and generous welfare systems from the possible negative impact of integration. Satisfying all three demands simultaneously is evidently an immensely difficult balancing act. In fact, it is the current arrangement that perhaps comes closest to squaring this circle. This is because the rules of the game, as contained in the Lisbon Treaty, have been renegotiated to give treaty status to the Charter of Fundamental Rights – a satisfactory supranational innovation for some – while the maintenance of higher Nordic welfare standards continues alongside a total opt-out from the Charter for the UK.

Yet all three elements underpinning this current compromise might still unravel. Firstly, the robustness of the UK opt-out is yet to be tested by the ECJ, which means its effectiveness in shielding the UK from what its government considers the unwanted consequences of the Charter is unproven. Secondly, the ability to maintain generous welfare states, if based on the restriction of EU internal market principles, may also fall foul of ECJ jurisprudence. This tension was reflected in a recent case, *Laval v. Svenska Byggnadsarbetareförbundet* (2007), where the EU's top judges had to rule on whether Swedish trade unions acted within their rights by taking collective action against the subsidiary of a Latvian construction company – forcing it out of business – that was not party to Swedish collective bargaining agreements on pay. In this instance, the Court judged the strike action an unlawful prohibition on economic freedoms within the EU. Finally, the granting of treaty status to the Charter might nonetheless prove underwhelming for proponents of greater integration in the field of social policy who expect more to be done. Thus the factors affecting the ability to find a dynamic equilibrium over the rules of the game that determine social justice are the self-restraint of the ECJ justices and the politicization of social policy as an issue that might be addressed by the EU.

Of course, the ECJ has not always sought to promote supranationalism at any cost,[7] while there are many obstacles that make it difficult for a domestic policy debate to mould EU policy directly, most notably the absence of a pan-European party system and the unlikelihood of having a majority of both member state governments and of MEPs belonging to the same political family. Nonetheless if the current consensus over the rules of the game breaks down because of contrasting visions of social policy, it is difficult to imagine what kind of dynamic equilibrium could be renegotiated. The remaining untried alternative would be the launch of an initiative of 'enhanced cooperation' in this area among advocates of greater supranationalism, but this partial measure is hardly likely to address the problem of establishing a level playing field for economic competition between EU member states. Should the rules of the game not be able to accommodate different preferences over social policy, the likely result is a stalemate between supranational and intergovernmental visions of integration in this area as there is a dearth of other options for re-establishing a dynamic equilibrium. Needless to say, such an impasse will be more satisfactory for opponents of supranationalism; pro-integrationists are unlikely to acquiesce to any new understanding of the rules of the game that would entail abandoning the aspiration of an EU-wide social policy.

Yet the saving grace for the EU compound polity might well prove to be the fallout from the recent, nearly decade-long process of renegotiating the rules of the game, from the Nice Treaty of 2001 to the protracted ratification of the Lisbon Treaty at the end of that same decade. Given the tremendous unexpected difficulties European elites encountered during this process, it is unlikely they will be willing to begin it all again in the near future. Therefore, Europe's elites are unlikely to provoke a zero-sum stand-off that would undermine the viability of the EU compound system. At the same time though, the viability of the existing arrangement will also depend on the acquiescence of citizens to the absence of a robust redistributive EU social policy as well as the rulings emanating from the ECJ, whose role is set to become all the trickier if elites retreat from tackling this particular issue.

The pusillanimity which the EU has so far shown towards the issue of social justice under the current system of unanimity has led to a growing clamour for changing the system of democratic representation and decision making. To free the EU from the fetters of intergovernmental constraint, thereby enabling it to respond better to the policy priorities of citizens, it is thought necessary to reconstitute the EU on the basis of greater supranational representation (Schmitter, 2000; Hix and Follesdal, 2005; Hix, 2006, 2008). Hence the desire to shift the debate over what policies the EU should pursue from the Intergovernmental Conference (IGC), European Council or Council of Ministers level, where national vetoes prevail, to an alternative European level of representation based on an aggregation of individual citizens. This is the common theme that runs through calls to increase the European Parliament's competences (Andersen and Eliassen, 1996), to replace IGCs with the convention method of treaty reform (Pollak and Slominski, 2004), to encourage European political parties (Sarkozy, 2006), to introduce Europe-wide referendums for treaty amendment (Weiler, 1997) or waive the unanimity requirement for tinkering with the treaties (Trechsel, 2005). These recommendations also probably reflect a fear that only democracy – not intergovernmental diplomacy – can rescue the EU if, in the worst-case scenario, consensus over the existing rules of the game breaks down completely.

As representation is a key component of the rules of the game, it is necessary to understand how changes in the balance between supranational and intergovernmental principles of representation are liable to affect viability in a compound system that has hitherto been able to maintain a dynamic equilibrium. To this effect, the next section revisits the analogy with the antebellum US to examine how changes in the system of representation were contested and what this entailed for the viability of the US compound polity. More precisely, the analysis shows that changes in the compound system of dual representation (of states as well as of individuals) that led to a more majoritarian polity did not facilitate the resolution of the major cleavage issue the polity was not originally designed to solve.

6.3 Compound polities and the problem of representing both states and individuals

This section explores the significance of the EU's dual system of political representation within the context of the struggle to establish the rules of the game of politics in a compound polity. To show the relationship between viability and representation it is necessary to investigate what impact a move away from the representation of states to one based more on an aggregation of individual citizens *unaccompanied by any explicit and unanimously accepted transformation in the objectives of the union* has on viability. To do this, it is important to re-examine the evolution of the US system of democratic political representation in the antebellum and the struggles that ensued over the rules of the game. Following the Jacksonian era, there was a reduction in both the decision-making influence of individual states and an attenuation of the anti-majoritarian safeguards of the constitutional system. Crucially, this constitutive change in representation was not accompanied by any new agreement or expectation that the US now had to settle the slavery issue once and for all. As the rules of the game evolved in this way, the threat of withdrawal was first voiced, accompanied by an ideological affirmation of the constitution's original anti-majoritarianism as well as proposals for new mechanisms to safeguard the independence of the units. Thus although the states initially agreed to abide by the changed rules, it soon became obvious that there were inherent limits to their commitment to allow their autonomy to be overruled by a popular majority.

The tension produced by the change in representation as states proved unable to control their senators – who also became linked to national parties – and as the presidency became a cross-unit vote of popularity, can be characterized as the clash between Daniel Webster and John C. Calhoun.[8] Whereas the first welcomed the advent of greater majoritarianism, holding democracy to be the cardinal virtue of US republicanism, the second denounced this as a betrayal of the federal principle of the republic. Political theory, however, was not the alpha and omega of this debate since opponents of the slide towards a 'merge[r] into one great community or nation' (Calhoun, 1992: 102) proposed practical measures to attenuate the implications of democratization at the union level.

The great nullification controversy over the 1832 protectionist tariff, which manufacturing-poor South Carolina thought unfairly targeted plantation states, is often noted as a harbinger of that state's central role in the eventual dissolution of the union. More important, though, is the fact that the doctrine of nullification it espoused – which the Hartford convention of north-eastern states had earlier raised in the context of conscription during the 1812–14 war with Britain (DiLorenzo, 1998) – was explicitly linked to the threat of secession. Under the terms of its Ordinance of Nullification (1832), South Carolina promised that if the union attempted to use coercion to make the state toe the line, it would 'forthwith proceed to organize a separate government, and do all other acts and things which sovereign and independent states may of right do' (Rabun, 1956: 88). Thus a recalcitrant state not only claimed the right to refrain from obeying federal law, it also proclaimed the right of unilateral exit. Hence secession only entered the contest over the rules of the game in reaction to a policy decision stemming from a democratic majority even though 'there was no ambiguity about the tariff's constitutional correctness' (Wilentz, 2005: 380).

This threat of secession re-emerged less than two decades later as the introduction of the Wilmot Proviso (see section 5.5), which would have outlawed slavery in lands conceded by Mexico, led to the establishment of the Nashville Convention to discuss southern rights.[9] Whereas the Kentucky and Virginia Resolutions of 1798 merely claimed that states had the residual right to interpret the constitutionality of federal law, the second meeting at Nashville proclaimed a general right of withdrawal as a form of self-help in the case of injurious federal legislation. Although the convention met after Congress had approved the acts constituting the 1850 Compromise, the delegates declared that 'we have a right, as states, there being no common arbiter, to secede' (Cole, 1914: 385). State conventions meeting in Mississippi and South Carolina in 1851 explicitly reiterated this right. At this point the nature of the constitution itself rather than the constitutionality of federal legislation – as with the Alien and Sedition Acts, the conscription bill of 1812 and the tariff controversy – became the fundamental focus of political debate. Given the centralization and democratization of federal politics that had taken place during the Jacksonian period it was a matter of crucial importance as to whether the constitution had been enacted by a united and indissoluble people or else by independent states. The first interpretation implied acquiescence to a majoritarian solution to the problem of slavery. The second indicated that even if the South lost its veto power in the Senate and was deprived of its ability via the party system to designate a poodle president there remained other means for resisting an attack on slavery.

Thus Calhoun and Webster alike, as well as their acolytes, recognized that, following important developments in the nature of democratic political representation (discussed in section 5.6), the rules of the game needed to adapt in order to reconcile the slavery compromise with the changed system of representation. Expectations as well as institutional rules had to be renegotiated, which entailed a re-examination of founding intentions. Webster's side insisted that – despite the elitist leanings of the founders and attempts to prevent rule by majority faction – from the outset the constitution, as the work of a single community, could not be undone and that federalism was therefore compatible with majoritarianism.[10] Indeed, the very maxim that the majority is to govern has been described as 'the first principle of Jacksonian Democracy' (Remini, 2001: 304).

Webster's opponents spoke of the right to secede, leaving open the possibility of future withdrawal if a minority of states (or even a single state) could not accept what the representatives of the majority deemed constitutional. It was precisely this need for compromise – over a cleavage that the compound system was not designed to resolve – that Calhoun placed at the centre of his discussion of the nature of the US Constitution. His analysis revealed that Publius' design to impede the emergence of a ruling faction by extending the republic to 'make it less probable that a majority of the whole will have a common motive to invade the rights of other citizens' (Hamilton et al., 2003: 45) was a failure. As well as delivering the definitive compact interpretation of the constitution, he developed a theory of 'concurrent majorities' as the cornerstone of federalism and set forth anti-majoritarian proposals to counterbalance the development of a system of representation more centralized and majoritarian than at its origin.[11]

As the central protagonist in the 1832 South Carolina nullification crisis, Calhoun was well placed to articulate a cogent defence of the role of a state's veto in the federal constitution. This was not merely an attempt to justify the actions of his native state. In the light of the centripetal development of American politics, Calhoun fundamentally 'thought that it was essential to revise republican theory and constitutional arrangements to fit these new circumstances' (Ford, 1994: 45). The American union had to adapt to a novel situation in which, despite the size of the republic and the founders' elitist constitutional devices, the federal government was now potentially the instrument of a partisan majority. According to Calhoun, nullification served not merely to protect the autonomy of a particular state; it also played a positive and mediating role in negotiating the relationship between the states and the union.

Hence nullification was more than just a residual prerogative of state sovereignty. A state veto was an essential part of the rules of the game because Calhoun associated it with an amendment procedure in reverse to determine questions of constitutionality. Instead of amending the constitution to limit or expand federal competences thereafter, Calhoun envisaged that nullification of an existing law would stand 'unless and until three-fourths of the states, acting in sovereign convention, overrode the veto of the nullifying state and established beyond dispute the constitutionality of the law in question' (ibid., p. 48). The constitutional principle at work here was what Calhoun termed concurrent majority, whereby the federal government was based on the accumulated acquiescence of majorities in the individual units rather than a numerical majority of American citizens as a whole. In other words, he advocated the preservation of the representation of states in reaction to changes in representation that promoted the aggregate representation of individual American citizens. This system of concurrent support from the states was necessary, he argued, to halt the unwanted accretion of power that would occur if the federal government was left to judge the extent of its own authority. It was not simply the legislature that could not be relied upon because, as Ford explains, 'neither the Supreme Court through judicial review nor the president through his veto could be trusted to determine the extent of federal power since they were themselves branches of the federal government' (ibid., p. 49).

Thus the compact reading of the constitution, which asserted that 'the constitution was ordained and established *by* the several States, as *distinct, sovereign communities*' (Calhoun, 1992: 94, emphasis in original), was not simply a paean to state sovereignty to be used at their whim. Nullification and its concomitant of concurrent majorities was a political instrument essential for preserving the unique compound American republic. Faced by the spectre of a national majority that could decide the powers of the federal branch – that is, exercise competency over competences – it was necessary to invent a remedy because 'the duration and stability of our system depends on maintaining the equilibrium between the States and the General Government – the reserved and delegated powers' (Calhoun, 1978: 635).

Originally, the Constitution had enshrined a principle of concurrent majorities when it came to the election of the president and his deputy, at least so thought Calhoun. This was how he understood the Electoral College's rule whereby each elector proposed two candidates, without specifying for which position, and where the House of Representatives, voting by state, would select the candidates for office in the case of a tie or when none had an absolute majority.[12] Yet this practice had been dismantled by the democratic presidential election circus pioneered by Van Buren and Jackson, which left the electors tied to popular votes and party tickets (see section 5.6). In this way, Calhoun explained, the balance between the representation of states and individuals, designed to complement each other by nurturing a concurrent majority, was disrupted:

> Had these provisions been left unaltered, and not superseded, in practice, by caucuses and party conventions, their effect would have been to give to the majority of the people of the several States, the right of nominating five candidates; and to the majority of the States, acting in their corporate character, the right of choosing from them, which should be President, and which Vice-President. The President and Vice-President would, virtually, have been elected by the concurrent majority of the several States, and of their population.
> (Calhoun, 1992: 128)

Calhoun's fear for the viability of the compound polity as majoritarian party politics became a permanent feature heightened as the sectional crisis erupted in 1850. As it became obvious that northerners would eventually become the dominant majority, which could then constitute a party based around their interests, Calhoun proposed a dual presidency. North and South would elect a president (one for foreign relations the other for domestic policy) with both required to approve the legislative acts of Congress. This veto system was designed to constitute a guarantee of concurrent majority in a federal union heading towards centripetal democratic majority. If implemented a dual executive would mean that:

> [A]s no act of Congress could become a law without the assent of the chief magistrates representing both sections, each, in the elections, would choose the candidate, who, in addition to being faithful to

its interests, would best command the esteem and confidence of the other section. And thus, the presidential election, instead of dividing the Union into hostile geographical parties, the stronger struggling to enlarge its powers, and the weaker to defend its rights – as is now the case – would become the means of restoring harmony and concord to the country and the government.

(ibid., p. 277)

Calhoun's theory of concurrent majorities can be illuminated further by turning to the theory of political representation. Hannah Pitkin classically argued that 'the substance of the activity of representing seems to consist in promoting the interests of the represented, in a context where the latter is conceived as capable of action and judgment, but in such a way that he does not object to what is done in his name' (Pitkin, 1972: 155). This 'non-objection criterion', as David Runciman calls it, is necessary to escape from the independence/mandate controversy that has tended to dominate theoretical discussions of representation.[13] Thus representative democracy is based on allowing groups and individuals to judge the actions (and perhaps even the private lives) of those who claim to speak and act on their behalf. 'Political representation is best understood', Runciman argues, 'not in the language of veto but of competition. Objections to the actions of representatives can prove decisive when they constitute a plausibly competing claim to speak in the name of the person or thing being represented' (2006: 22).

In a compound system (i.e. a union of both states and citizens), however, matters are fundamentally more complicated given the existence of territorial units with the right to object in their own name and not merely as a part of a wider aggregation that must be mobilized. Calhoun's insistence on understanding the antebellum US republic as based on concurrent majorities and compromise can thus be explained as an attempt to safeguard the possibility of state objection in a system of dual representation of states and individuals. In theory, this compound mixture does not preclude any action in the name of the aggregation of individual citizens but this has to be balanced against the need to take seriously objections from the units and their citizens. It is thus not surprising to find that several commentators have described the EU's consensual model of decision making in terms of concurrent majorities (Katz, 2000; Moravcsik, 2002: 620).

Although the antebellum compound system succeeded for over 60 years in maintaining a dynamic equilibrium when renegotiating the rules of the game, there was no guarantee that an enduring consensus of this nature could be maintained. By the time of the breakdown of the second party system in the 1850s, not only was the union trying to resolve a policy problem it had originally sought to elide but the means of doing so went against the grain of the original principle of representation. No less an authority than James Madison makes this latter point clear. In 1787 he explained that it was incorrect to consider the US 'as analogous to the social compact of individuals: for if it were so, a Majority would have a right to bind the rest, and even to form a new Constitution for the whole' (Koch, 1969: 141). Hence the nineteenth-century – albeit limited (R. Smith, 1993) – democratization of the American compound republic, which transformed its representative institutions, was eventually accompanied by an unprecedented new contestation of the rules of the game. The unexpected development of party democracy on a federal level did not at first disrupt the constitutional system. However, as soon as the nascent system of mass, cross-unit party politics appeared to want to settle the slavery question there was an immediate backlash. The antebellum compound republic, therefore, remained viable despite a radical departure from its original model of representation until, that is, partisan democratic politics was used to try to solve a problem the compound system was designed to avoid.

Returning to the EU, it is important to reiterate the significance of both the original objectives behind the integration project and its unambiguous character as a voluntary association. Integration is a solution to a set of problems but from the outset there were others that were deliberately set aside.[14] The four founding objectives of integration were: peace, security against German resurgence, economic growth and the strengthening of domestic liberal democracy (see section 4.2). Hence 'ever closer union', as a result of the failure of EDC, did not include the expectation that its members would have to choose between Atlantic security and European independence. Moreover, the hybrid intergovernmental and supranational structure of government was testimony to the fact that while no *finalité politique* was excluded, integration promised only a potential for voluntary centralization. Member states have thus from the outset been engaged in a process that tries to combine both principles of intergovernmentalism and supranationalism rather than eliminate one of them. Likewise, integration is supposed to reconcile a growth-oriented free market[15] with social protection rather than engender a competition and eventual winner between competing visions of negative (boundary-removing) and interventionist (boundary-building) integration in the economic sphere.

Furthermore, as members of a voluntary association, EU member states are free 'in that they can choose to associate or not depending upon approval of the substantive purpose imposed' (Boucher, 2005: 104). This approval is the rigorously anti-majoritarian criterion against which mandates for policy change stemming from the supranational representation of the aggregate of individuals have to be balanced. Whatever the claims made by those speaking in the name of European citizens, the representative function of objection or non-objection is institutionally safeguarded (especially through the veto and unanimous treaty amendment) to remain with the member states and their own citizens *qua* national citizens. It was precisely this possibility of objection via withdrawal or non-participation that was denied to the recalcitrant southern US states even though, and unlike the Articles of Confederation, the Constitution made no mention of perpetuity while secession could also be implied from the reserved powers granted by the Tenth Amendment.

Thus EU viability, when understood in the context of these founding purposes and expectations, is not simply a matter of causal preconditions for consolidation or pious pleas for legitimacy through 'democratization' as the dominant binary paradigm suggests. Instead, continued viability consists in the ability to successfully renegotiate the rules of the game, in a way that is either faithful to these purposes and expectations (dynamic equilibrium) or else in a manner that establishes clearcut acquiescence to new expectations and objectives for integration (voluntary centralization). Previous chapters have explained in some detail how the EU's viability has until now been linked to its ability to maintain a dynamic equilibrium. The current section complemented this analysis by showing that a constitutive change in political representation that reduces the influence of the territorial units, *when used as a proxy to redefine the political objectives of the compound polity*, is likely to run foul of the units and their citizens. Hence the scenario of possible voluntary centralization in the EU is likely to require new safeguards for member state autonomy in order to respect the compound nature of a union that represents both individuals in the aggregate and member states. Since the EU already contains a strong pluralist model of concurrent majorities, the following section, drawing once again on the US analogy, argues that the necessary safeguard will probably have to take the form of nullification rather than a recalibration of concurrent majorities as recently suggested by Philippe Schmitter (2000: 84–106).

6.4 How to manage the voluntary centralization of representation

The EU compound system is characterized by far stronger anti-majoritarian institutions than was the case in the antebellum US republic. These are recognized in both this study and others as playing a crucial role in making integration politically palatable (Dehousse, 1995; Schmitt and Thomassen, 1999). Democratizing the EU is synonymous with increasing the importance of supranational representation, broadly conceived, at the expense of intergovernmentalism. The expansive version of this argument is Philippe Schmitter's proposal for institutional change of a radical nature. This contrasts with a more attenuated version, labelled 'limited democratic politics' by its chief advocate Simon Hix, which claims this goal is possible within the existing institutional architecture.[16] Schmitter's ambitious project of EU democratization seeks both to bolster existing mechanisms of supranational representation and to encourage the emergence of new forms of supranationalism. This entails beefing up the powers of the European Parliament, with the ultimate ambition being to transform it into a full and equal co-legislator alongside the Council of Ministers. Additionally, this type of democratization supposes a corresponding reduction of the preponderance of the intergovernmental legislature, the Council of Ministers, so as to transform it into an upper house of parliament akin to the US Senate, with the task of checking and balancing power.

In terms of institutional innovation, democratization as proposed by Schmitter consists of two new elements of supranationalism. The first is in fact loosely drawn from the Calhounian theory of concurrent majorities and would involve redrawing from scratch the EU voting system used in the Council of Ministers. According to Schmitter (2000: 84–106), member states would be classed according to population size into three *colegii* [sic] (small, medium and large states). A weighted majority in two or, for legislation dealing with more fundamental constitutional matters, three, *colegii* [sic] would be required for decision making, national vetoes thus disappear from the system. However, this would allow one group of states a veto power in constitutional affairs, while necessitating concurrent majorities in two groups of states for ordinary legislation. Moreover, this same principle of concurrent majorities could be used to designate both the president of the Commission and the college of Commissioners as well as for electing the presidency of the Council of Ministers. Schmitter's second supranational novelty 'is to democratize [the EU's] multiple channels of representation' (ibid., p. 54). The argument starts from the empirically well-established premise that business and professional interests have far greater influence in the legislative process at the EU level than civil society. Consequently, he calls for the European Parliament to issue citizen vouchers to finance transnational interest associations and social movements that would diversify the interests and values influencing EU politics (ibid., pp. 59–64).

Hence the basic objective behind democratization is the abandonment of the national veto in decision making and the nurturing of supranational representation. Yet the American analogy suggests that it would be naive to think that enhanced supranational decision making and the creation of transnational political representation would be possible without offering the member states at least some new safeguard to control the course of integration. The replacement of the veto system with a fully fledged system of concurrent majorities assumes that member states will be placated purely by this kind of *ex ante* mechanism for consensual decision making. Such reasoning rests on a partial reading of Calhoun since as a theorist of nullification, as explained above, he was also fundamentally concerned with the ability of units in a federal union to open up constitutional and policy dialogue by individually signalling *ex post facto* opposition to federal legislation. From an EU perspective, where member states have often been confronted with the unexpected consequences of integration, it seems particularly important not to overlook this aspect of Calhoun's theory. Indeed, Calhoun's constitutional thought provides a valuable insight into the kind of device necessary for managing a fundamental reconfiguration of political representation in the EU.

Calhoun argued that creeping majoritarian representation had to be counterbalanced by an *ex post facto* anti-majoritarian safeguard. The doctrine of nullification was intended, therefore, as a way of fundamentally reforming the US political system to bring it back into line with the constitutional tenets of the founding fathers; it was a positive political principle in comparison with the option of last resort: secession. In particular, the fact that Calhoun envisaged that nullification would automatically trigger a convention of all the states to settle, by a three-quarters majority, whether a disputed law was constitutional made this a potent yet politically savvy means of balancing the dynamic relationship between the states and the union. Savvy because it bypassed the use of the Supreme Court – deemed biased towards federal self-aggrandizement – to resolve issues of constitutional authority and denied the federal government the right to interpret the limits of its own authority.

This point highlights one of the fundamental complications concerning judicial politics in a compound system. As John Kincaid points out, 'the acceptance and legitimacy of an independent judiciary in democratic nation states is premised on the existence of a constitution or fundamental law grounded in popular sovereignty' (1999: 51). Yet in the EU this link between judicial independence – crucial when judges are to rule on sovereignty or competence issues – and popular sovereignty is entirely indirect. EU treaties are ratified by the representatives (and sometimes the people) of each member state while day-to-day decision making undertaken in accordance with treaty powers requires complex consensual negotiation between different institutions with different principles of political representation. As a result, the ability to respond politically to judicial judgments is trifling, a fact well recognized by the member states which, as described in section 4.4, have increasingly resorted to pre-empting ECJ activism by circumscribing the scope of their potential verdicts through the use of anti-harmonization clauses, the pillar system, treaty protocols and opt-outs.[17] In the antebellum US, when consensus over the rules of the game broke down, nullification was proposed as a way of accepting a stronger representation of citizens in the aggregate. The transformed nature of political representation in the compound polity would thus be counterbalanced by a novel form of political oversight for the units and their citizens, not least because Calhoun envisaged that a nullification decision would only be taken by a specially elected state convention. In this way, the principle was directly tied to the exercise of popular sovereignty at the unit level.[18] Furthermore, instead of being simply a unit veto, nullification was a means to engender constitutional debate about competences between, on the one hand, states and their citizens and, on the other, the federal level – a dialogue not otherwise possible.

Certainly this solution to the problem of clashing constitutional authority resulting from changes in the system of political representation appears far more appropriate than the stillborn mechanism of *ex post facto* control over the accretion of EU competences. The 'subsidiarity' principle announced with fanfare in 1992, albeit as a concession to sceptics, was supposed to introduce a judicially enforceable efficiency criterion to uphold democracy by ensuring that according to the pompous preamble of the Maastricht Treaty, policy decisions 'are taken as closely as possible to the citizen'. The difficulty with the subsidiarity principle is precisely that it does not establish a division of competences for the present and even less for the future, given its insistence on efficiency (see section 4.3.1). Moreover, the special constitutional protection afforded the *acquis communautaire* also prevents the clawing back of competences to the domestic level even if this were proved to be more efficient at some later time (Wind, 2001: 176). Not surprisingly, therefore, this lack of an effective principle of limited government, leaving open competence accretion, has caused consternation (Bartolini, 2005: 132-6) and has done virtually nothing to settle either the question of the division of powers (Magnette, 2005: 53) or competency over competences, as shown by the dispute over the autonomy of national higher education policy discussed in section 5.6. These drawbacks notwithstanding, subsidiarity continues to play a key rhetorical role in the treaty definition of the exercise of political authority by the EU. In fact, a new explanation of subsidiarity, which allows a third of national parliaments to object to a proposed legislative act if it is thought to violate the principle of keeping government decision making close to the citizens concerned, is the basis of a lengthy new protocol to the Lisbon Treaty. Yet the Court of Justice retains jurisdiction on establishing violations of subsidiarity.

At present the EU's highly proceduralist, consensus building system does away with the need for a nullification device. Reasoning by analogy, however, the nullification debate in US political development suggests that EU democratization is apt to provoke acute constitutional conflicts concerning competence allocation and competency over competences. Thus a transformation in representation that would see supranationalism replace national vetoes will probably require a stronger safeguard than that currently offered by subsidiarity. Nullification offers precisely such a mechanism, one that is, moreover, political rather than purely judicial and, if grounded in a referendum or special convention, is also linked to popular sovereignty at the national level.

Existing instruments of flexibility – notably policy 'opt-outs' – negotiated to render integration palatable give further credence to this claim. On the understanding that framework treaties can produce many unintended consequences, member states willing to countenance voluntary centralization would still seek to retain control over the progress of integration to avoid becoming locked into a process without guarantees or an emergency brake.[19] Thus it seems likely that the EU would have to adopt a mechanism, probably applied to a restricted set of sensitive policy areas, akin to Calhoun's nullification principle, whereby legislation could be blocked by either one or a certain threshold of member states until a specified majority (or unanimity) of the total units agreed that the original law was constitutional. A nullification mechanism could thus be one way of pursuing further integration while avoiding merely reconstituting sovereignty at the European level. Indeed, the tendency among certain proponents of integration to revere the EU as a 'post-sovereign' entity (MacCormick, 1997) implies that a nullification device designed to promote flexibility, dialogue and ultimately compromise would appeal to opponents and supporters of integration alike.

Notwithstanding this putative exploration of how a change in representation could be managed at the EU level, it is important to remember that such a fundamental transformation in the rules of the game would require the unanimous agreement of all EU member states: a veritable unanimity trap. The sorry fate of the Constitutional Treaty, although ratified by a majority of member states, underlies how unlikely it is that the EU member states will be faced with a Philadelphian moment, where the confederated states awoke one morning to find their delegates had – without any mandate to do so – decided to do away with the unanimity principle for adopting the constitution that would replace the Articles of Confederation. The immutability of the unanimity principle thus means that a radical reform of the rules of the game is parasitic on the successful justification of an integration project demanding more supranational decision making and representation.

In this context the analogy with the relationship between the units and the union in the antebellum US continues to illuminate. The inability of the US compound polity to remain viable as changes in the nature of political representation threatened to undermine the existence of slavery suggests that *viable voluntary centralization requires that a change in the purposes of the union take place before there is a recalibration of representation promoting the cross-unit representation of individuals*, not vice versa. Hence the viability of voluntary centralization is more than a question of finding appropriate institutional innovations, such as nullification, to manage the functioning of a more supranational EU. It is also a question of how such supranationalism could be justified in the first place in order to transform expectations about the nature of integration. The concluding section thus sketches how this justification could be articulated and argues that, so as to be viable, the inspiration to renegotiate the rules of the game in this way would have to originate at the level of member state politics.

6.5 The political process needed for justifying voluntary centralization

Most studies reveal that EU citizens have until very recently tended largely to be underwhelmed by the process of integration. Neither what Bartolini calls constitutive (competences and rules) nor isomorphic (policy preferences) issues concerning the EU are a day-to-day priority for them (2006: 34). As a treaty-based political system, however, the periodic revision of the treaties produces inbuilt critical junctures concerning the fate and purpose of integration. At these moments the EU compound polity re-examines its rules of the games, including the purposes behind integration itself. This constitutes a rare opportunity for national politics to tackle squarely the political issues surrounding integration in a way that European parliamentary elections, with their abysmal turnout and low exposure, and national elections, where domestic priorities dominate, do not. Moreover, treaty moments also have profound effects on domestic political parties. These parties often find it difficult to contain the debate over the merits and demerits of integration and during the course of ordinary politics are likely to agree to disagree internally. In this way the cleavage over integration is not structured through ordinary party competition[20] and can emerge with a vengeance during treaty ratification if it is subjected to a popular vote.

Evidence from voting studies suggests referendums on treaties afford perhaps the best means of engaging a wider public in a debate on EU politics (Gallagher et al., 1995: 119; cf. Hainsworth, 2006). The most recent scholarship reveals that direct democracy increases citizens' understanding of and participation in politics (Benz and Stutzer, 2004; Smith and Tolbert, 2004) and that in referendums on European integration issue-voting will tend to prevail over second-order voting given an effective campaign.[21] Since political elites in most countries have been found to be more pro-European than their electorates (Van der Eijk and Franklin, 2004), referendums also force the political class to confront and respond to arguments over Europe that are often marginalized in ordinary circumstances. However, the debate over referendums has largely focused on vaunting the merits of allowing the people of Europe to decide. Considerably less explored is how referendums can be moments for changing the rules of the game by establishing new political objectives for the EU.

Traditionally, referendums on treaty reforms are ratificatory moments in which the public is asked to approve or disapprove of an agreement negotiated by their political elites. Hence, as Runciman (2003) argues, these have hitherto been plebiscitary referendums whereby the electorate 'can put an issue to bed, but only if they vote with their political masters', as further demonstrated by the ratification problems encountered by both the Constitutional Treaty and its successor. Moreover, these referendum debates have proved deficient for articulating a clear debate about what the EU is for, let alone allowing the public to choose between different conceptions of pooled sovereignty. Rather, the debate concerns how the various treaty changes are (mis)interpreted. Often, therefore, the struggle over ratification is marked by a campaign where the differences are 'largely of interpretation rather than principle' (Hayward, 2003: 128), sidelining substantive discussion of the objectives of political union and requisite institutional design.

The example of France in 1992 is highly illuminating here. With voters being called upon to ratify a treaty that launched an ambitious new economic project, EMU, as well as a framework for policy initiatives in CFSP and Justice and Home Affairs (JHA), it might have been expected that the debate would centre on arguments justifying the need for this particular evolution in integration. In reality, French citizens were given the usual assurances by supporters of Maastricht that national sovereignty and identity were safeguarded, a claim obviously disputed by their opponents.[22] Indeed, it was the spectre of German resurgence that provided one of the best means of justifying this new project. Demonstrating the enduring power of European integration's initial objectives of containing German might and strengthening its own democratic trajectory, discussion about newly reunified Germany played a central role in the referendum debate. A host of political leaders from across the spectrum urged voters to ratify the treaty as a means of securing peace and democracy in Europe. Former Prime Minister Michel Rocard spoke of the need 'to preserve Germany from its demons', the then premier Pierre Bérégovoy prophesied that the collapse of the treaty would break the Franco-German axis, leaving Germany eastern-looking and 'probably encouraging an anti-democratic ferment', while former President Valéry Giscard D'Estaing warned of Germany going it alone, meaning that 'a no [vote] would ensure German preponderance over Europe' (Criddle, 1993: 234–5). Finally, during the live television debate between Mitterrand and the leader of the no campaign, Helmut Kohl intervened via satellite precisely to dispel fears of German domination.

Statistics from the French vote show how nugatory the discussion of competing visions of what the EU is actually for turned out to be. Among Yes voters, 72 per cent voted to assure a lasting peace in Europe, 63 per cent as an indispensable means for building Europe and 21 per cent through fear of German domination in Europe. Among No voters, 57 per cent were motivated by fears of a loss of sovereignty while 40 per cent feared German domination (ibid., p. 238). In other words, both sides were more preoccupied with debating the evolution of the rules of the game in relation to questions of peace, identity and sovereignty than trying to justify the merits and demerits of different kinds of polity per se. A similar tale can be told about subsequent referendums. In Ireland's two referendums on the Nice Treaty, which tweaked institutional design and paved the way for dramatic eastern enlargement, arguments over whether this new project was justified took second place to bland general preferences for or against integration. As Richard Sinnott has shown, in the two Nice referendums more than 40 per cent and 50 per cent of Yes voters, respectively, declared they supported the treaty because of a belief that integration 'is generally a good thing' compared to the 22 per cent and 29 per cent of voters who thought enlargement 'was a good thing' (2003: 47).

Such residual justifications for integration proved insufficient to convince Dutch or French voters to accept the Constitutional Treaty in 2005. A highly complex treaty – the product of an overarching compromise between supranational and intergovernmental visions of Europe – this latest step in the integration project lacked a persuasive justification for the majority of voters in these two countries. The major impediment to discussing the EU compound polity in terms of why it is justifiable to pool certain elements of sovereignty is the fact that from the outset integration has been considered as a project with an undefined end, an end in itself, rather than a means to an end. This is a peculiar state of affairs since federation, like all projects of political union between states, is ordinarily 'conceived as a means toward an end' (De Vree, 1972: 28). As a result, integration has been supported somewhat surreptitiously, as a federalism that dare not speak its name. Majone calls this phenomenon 'cryptofederalism' (2006: 610–12), which prefers to focus on the momentum of the process – the metaphor of riding a bicycle – rather than fixing a determinate end goal with a clear justification. With proponents of integration assuming that this project is *ipso facto* desirable and couching their support in abstract terms relating to peace and prosperity, it is not surprising that critics of the EU respond with equally vague ideological counterclaims. Moravcsik portrays this paucity of justificatory debate well, explaining that the integration debate 'inevitably comes to be dominated by "symbolic extremists" of a Euro-enthusiastic or Eurosceptic persuasion' (2006: 237) leaving little middle ground for re-evaluating the purposes behind the process itself.

European integration is marked, therefore, by a notable path-dependency regarding the nature of the debate over justifying the process in terms of political objectives. Not only do European political issues often lack national salience as well as an overlap with domestic cleavages; the justificatory framework for pursuing integration – perpetual peace and economic growth – has not evolved since the launch of the EEC. Moreover, these two objectives are difficult to interpret as substantive purposes entailing a certain form of political organization. Peace, as Terry Nardin explains, 'is better regarded as a constraint rather than as a purpose, for to respect the value of peace is not to achieve an end so much as the avoidance of all force' (Nardin, 1983: 13). Whereas the pursuit of economic growth is constitutive of what Oakeshott calls a *societas cupiditatis*, wherein although mutual benefit 'may be common to many or even to all, there is no common substantive want the satisfaction of which they may all be supposed to be seeking' (1975: 287–95). Thus neither peace nor economic growth necessarily implies supranational integration rather than intergovernmentalism. Indeed, as Craig Parsons (2003) has shown, the emergence of the supranational community method for achieving these twin goals was a very contingent event that hinged on precarious political coalitions in France, which more often than not united for pragmatic domestic reasons rather than enthusiasm for supranationalism.

Hence the path-dependency of justifications for integration makes it increasingly difficult to refocus public debate on what the EU is actually for and what kind of institutional structure and competence regime is necessary to accomplish its tasks. While the limited and abstract basis for justifying the EU is certainly no barrier to dynamic equilibrium – indeed it constitutes an asset for this scenario of renegotiating the rules of the game by allowing elites not to dwell on the finality of integration – this is not the case for voluntary centralization. Without a clearly justified project for greater integration, voluntary centralization cannot emerge from within national politics to play a role in treaty renegotiation and subsequent ratification.

The evaluation of the proper content of such justifications for greater supranational integration would warrant a study in its own right. Abstaining from such a discussion, it is necessary to conclude instead with a consideration of the political process through which these justifications could arise. Currently the rules of the game of EU politics evolve almost exclusively through treaty reform, a largely intergovernmental, elite process. Electorates are sometimes asked to give their assent to the new treaty. Nevertheless, referendums need not be *ex post* devices, coming on the back of treaty reform, since they could also be proposed as a way to mandate a renegotiation of the rules of the game. Given the increasing willingness to submit European issues to referendum votes – in total, there have been 42 national referendums on integration[23] – it is not too far-fetched to imagine the future use of national referendum initiatives to signal public preference prior to debating a new integration project requiring treaty reform. Potentially – as Schmitter has already recognized (2000: 120–3) – this method represents a better way of grounding justification of a new integration project in national politics as it would link change in the purposes of union with a mechanism for engendering non-objection by the citizens of member states.

In fact, there is a precedent for a bottom-up initiative procedure originating within the units (dependent on reaching a certain threshold of states) that would then trigger an extraordinary convention to discuss this proposal. This unusual device can still be found in the US Constitution as an alternative to congressional amendment[24] but was in fact better spelled out, and with a much lower threshold than the two-thirds required in the US Constitution, in the Constitution of the Confederate States of America (1861). Among the confederated states, amendment worked thus:

> Upon the demand of any three States, legally assembled in their several conventions, the Congress shall summon a convention of all the States, to take into consideration such amendments to the Constitution as the said States shall concur in suggesting at the time when the said demand is made; and should any of the proposed amendments to the Constitution be agreed on by the said convention, voting by States, and the same be ratified by the Legislatures of two-thirds of the several States, or by conventions in two-thirds thereof, as the one or the other mode of ratification may be proposed by the general convention, they shall thenceforward form a part of this Constitution.[25]

A similar mechanism in the EU would at least have spared European citizens the top-down process of treaty reform which culminated in the needlessly grandiloquent Treaty Establishing a Constitution for Europe. Significantly, one of the few EU-specialists who warned that 'the moment for a dramatic act of "self-constitutionalization" has long since passed' (Schmitter, 2000: 118) is also an advocate of using a bottom-up referendum procedure to ascertain expectations about integration by calling for a referendum where it would be possible for citizens to signal whether they want to participate in a supranational Europe or remain in a confederal arrangement (ibid., pp. 120–3). In Schmitter's bold plan, national treaty referendums could be used creatively to determine the contours of EU constitutionalism by allowing citizens to choose between sticking to the current intergovernmental treaty system or else mandating their governments to construct a supranational polity based on a new treaty. Grasping the inherent connection between popular sovereignty and the problem of justifying further integration, Schmitter seeks to use the former to settle the latter – a novel method of escaping the unanimity trap for EU treaty reform. The resulting twin treaty system – assuming citizens in certain countries would refuse to countenance participation in a more supranational Europe – appears a more convincing way out of the current integration impasse than the hitherto seldom used mechanism for 'enhanced co-operation'.[26] Whereas the latter would first have to be negotiated by elites, the former would be mandated from the start by citizens.

Indeed, even if referendum initiatives, originating from within member states, for reforming the treaties were unsuccessful they could have the important function of introducing new arguments into the integration debate as well as indicating to – often internally divided – party elites voter preferences. Furthermore, existing research on referendum initiatives shows that this procedure favours the introduction of proposals that 'seek policy changes that the government refuses to provide' (Lupia and Matsusaka, 2004: 475). Thus national initiative referendums on integration projects could begin to engender a popular debate about the EU as a means to certain ends, that is, as a mandated project for the pursuit of certain objectives.

In other words, it seems possible to introduce politicization in the sense of a mandate for certain broad policy objectives through a treaty amendment procedure anchored in domestic political representation rather than in transnational processes. National politicization of the foundational principles of the EU thus represents a compelling alternative to the transnational politicization of day-to-day governance suggested by Hix (2006, 2008). Such a national method of politicization would not only respect the character of the EU as a voluntary association of member states whose objectives are determined on the basis of national not supranational representation. This discussion of mandated objectives would also increase the salience of debates over integration in the domestic arena and in addition overcome the problem of sustaining partisan alignments across the Commission, Council and European Parliament as assumed by Hix's model for introducing limited democratic politics into EU policymaking (Bartolini, 2006: 40). More importantly, this kind of political debate would reverse the perverse trend in European politics whereby the institutionalization of the EU is contested more during European Parliament elections than in national representation even though only the latter is competent to determine such matters (Mair, 2004, 2005).

Thus the conditions for viable voluntary centralization in the EU are very demanding. In order to succeed in advancing voluntary centralization, referendum initiatives would have to give rise to a successful justification of changes in the rules of the game anchored in a new understanding of the purposes of integration. This task is made all the more difficult since even the viability of the current dynamic equilibrium cannot be taken for granted, as explained in section 6.2. Without an exogenous shock it seems difficult to believe that a pellucid and persuasive justification for voluntary centralization will emerge as the mere possibility of holding referendums to mandate renegotiation of the rules of the game is no guarantee for the emergence of adequate justifications for supranational integration. Finally, any new treaty agreement conceding new powers of sovereignty based on a new justification for integration would, as argued in section 6.4, still necessitate the construction of complex safeguards on reserved policy areas or *ex post facto* means of oversight as member states try to control for unintended consequences. Given these two necessary conditions, therefore, it seems highly implausible to expect voluntary centralization in the EU even in the medium term.

6.6 Conclusion

This study has consistently pointed out the need to understand that the EU is viable because it follows a process of dynamic equilibrium when negotiating the rules of the game of politics. The inability of the EU to transform itself into a fully supranational entity has given rise to many proposals for enhancing the kernel of supranational representation already present in its institutional architecture. Such transformations are typically considered a boon for EU effectiveness and democratic legitimacy. Yet the analysis presented here, using an analogy with the antebellum US compound polity, has revealed that such a move will adversely affect the viability of integration: it would mark a departure from dynamic equilibrium without meeting the conditions needed for viable voluntary centralization.

Hence this conclusion differs significantly from the usual shrill pleas for democratizing or politicizing the EU. A union of people, or a union with multiple *demoi*, does not mean that a supranational Europe is by definition impossible. Yet the voluntary centralization required for these kinds of political projects can only be accomplished by the legitimacy furnished through domestic politics. Before this can even be contemplated, however, the EU would have to be considered a means to an end rather than an end in itself. Likewise, member states would have to experience a revolution in the debate over the future of Europe; integration would have to be justified in terms of radical new purposes, which the nation state alone could be shown not to be in a position to accomplish. In reality, we are a long way from such a transformation.

Conclusion: Implications for EU Studies and the Debate over the Future of Integration

This book addressed a crucial yet currently undertheorized research question: what makes the EU viable? Such a task was shown to matter not only because of the succession of crises, resulting at times in inanition, that the European integration project has endured in the past six decades. Understanding viability is also essential in order to judge the merits of the current plethora of schemes for reforming the EU order. The Janus-faced nature of the viability problem was reflected in the twofold analytical concern with, firstly, explaining the historical evolution of successful integration before, secondly, considering how certain transformative changes would affect this compound political system. The former was seen to follow, in the conceptual vocabulary of this study, a path of dynamic equilibrium; the second, a process theorized as voluntary centralization, was revealed as fraught with danger.

The connecting thread throughout this analytical endeavour was the conceptualization of viability in terms of contestation over four 'rules of the game of politics'. Moreover, these contested rules of the game that came under scrutiny — institutional competences, expectations about the union, competency over competences and political representation — are specific to the nature of the EU political system as opposed to traditional nation states. Yet as a union of states and citizens, the EU shares these characteristics with another compound political system: the antebellum US republic. Hence the evolution of disputes over the rules of the game, and the success or otherwise of attempted solutions, in the US antebellum provided the foil for the analysis of EU viability.

Although transatlantic comparisons are becoming a mainstay of EU studies, two features of the analytical framework deployed in this book stand out from more conventional comparative work. Above all, studying contestation over the rules of the game in both compound systems required a thoroughly interdisciplinary approach. Historical analysis — albeit with the usual caveats that apply to an enquiry broached from within the discipline of political science (Lustick, 1996) — was combined with a focus on the institutional and ideational sources of political contestation, without neglecting the legal-constitutional dimension of change in both polities. At the same time, the study also broke with the formulaic understanding that relations between states are structured according to the principle of anarchy whereas politics within a state conforms to a pellucid logic of hierarchy (Waltz, 1979).

Sovereignty, rendered as the problem of establishing competency over competences, was thus treated as only one component of the rules of the game of politics in both compound systems. That is to say, sovereignty – the organization of a clear hierarchy of political authority – was not treated as a *precondition* of viability. Indeed, this gambit allowed for a more nuanced understanding of how disputes over the rules of the game emerged and came to be managed or not. For instance, in both the antebellum and the EU it was shown that disputes over the sovereign status of the units were intimately tied to changes and proposals for altering the basis of political representation. This was the case with the contest over state nullification of federal legislation, as a practical remedy as well as a theoretical doctrine, in the US. Supporters of such a mechanism claimed it was necessary in order to reinforce the representation of states, while its opponents argued that this ran contrary to republican principles of government. Likewise, debates over accepting ECJ jurisprudence or amending treaties by EU-wide referendum majorities entail more than respect for the symbols of sovereignty: they reflect contrasting visions of the proper calibration of political representation between states *qua* states and citizens *qua* EU citizens.

Furthermore, neither democracy nor federalism was presented as a short cut solution for solving the problem of EU viability. The democracy debates engulfing EU studies have become so conceptually unwieldy as to make it very doubtful that one triumphant ontological definition of democracy could ever provide a successful blueprint for further integration. In a similar vein, the principle of federalism always bespeaks a certain particularism because the compromise upon which federation is always founded 'indicates the existence of a problem to which no one yet possesses the solution' (Rosanvallon, 2006: 228–9). The fourfold nature of the rules of the game framework thus provides a potent alternative to a priori visions of a democratically sound or federally well-organized EU by revealing which political struggles need to be managed or overcome for the sake of viability. In particular, the analysis revealed that changed expectations about the nature of the integration project will have to be justified at the domestic level, rather than imposed through pan-European majorities, in order to be workable. After all, it was exactly such a transformation in expectations about the nature of the US republic, lacking a justification established at the unit level, in the antebellum US political system that heralded its downfall.

Naturally, there may be disagreement over the appropriateness of the rules of the game identified in this study as the crucial components of political contestation in compound political systems. Rather than pre-empt such debate, which in any event I believe would be profitable for enhancing the understanding of what makes the EU system hang together, it seems more pertinent to address a potential shortcoming in the comparison of differences in how these rules of the game were contested. More realist-minded scholars of international politics are apt to raise the question as to the unequal importance of security considerations underlying disputes over the rules of the game in the respective compound systems.

Notably, thanks to NATO, the EU has been shielded from the security imperative of integrating in response to the minatory nature of international anarchy, often seen as the impetus for federation (Riker, 1964). To paraphrase Winston Churchill, the EU is the sturdy child of the safety provided by the US-led alliance. By contrast, the US compound system, which expanded territorially as an 'empire of liberty' in Jefferson's famous phrase, was all too aware of the looming spectre of anarchic self-help should the Philadelphian republican system break down (Onuf and Onuf, 1993). The potential disintegration of the federal republic into competing geographical sections still nestled amid European states' petty power rivalries – amply demonstrated by the French intervention in Mexico during the US Civil War – raised the stakes of preserving the American union. A collapse in the understanding of the rules of the game in the EU is devoid of any such negative consequence for states' security. Yet ultimately the significance of such differing security considerations is limited. The fact is that a definitive rupture in the rules of the game in the EU, secession of a member state, would nonetheless spell the demise of the viability of the current framework of integration, which is supposed to be a broad church, one 'united in diversity'. The withdrawal of a unit would thus become a critical juncture after which, besides the likely contraction of the EU motto of 'united in diversity', expectations about the nature of the integration process will have changed radically.

Applying the insights of this study

Given the analogical examination of the EU and the antebellum US compound political systems, the arguments put forward in this book speak to two different scholarly readerships. On the one hand, they contribute to the increasingly sophisticated international relations literature on the US federal union. On the other hand, they imply a challenge to some of the preconceptions regarding how to conduct a transatlantic comparison between the EU and the US systems.

Traditionally, historical and political analysis has interpreted the weakness and ultimate breakdown of the federal union as the result of clashing competences, *imperium in imperio*, exacerbated by expansion and industrialization, which could no longer be contained by existing political institutions (Stampp, 1978; Aldrich, 1995; Foner, 1995; Goldstein, 2001). This constitutional and institutional explanation of the throes of the early republic neglects, as scholars of international relations have recently pointed out (Onuf and Onuf, 1993; Deudney, 1995; Hendrickson, 2003; Fritz, 2008), the significance of republican ideas of how the sovereignty of the people ought to be expressed in the federal union. Seen in this light, the problem of divided sovereignty provides only a partial explanation of the travails of the antebellum, which must be complemented by a proper understanding of how conceptions of republican freedom shaped constitutional debates over the nature of federalism.

This study has further vindicated the validity of applying this republican perspective in order to understand the dynamics of antebellum political contestation. In particular, it demonstrated that the politics of sovereignty in this period constituted an interlocking and inseparable dispute between conceptions of the proper constitutional nature of the federal system and the legitimate institutionalization of popular sovereignty within it. It was shown that both types of argument, constitutional and republican, were invariably invoked as mutually supportive by proponents and opponents of the contested principle of states' rights. Wrangles between the state and the federal level regarding competency over competences and expectations about what the nature of the union entailed for the units took the form of disputed claims over the constitutional status of the states. Yet these claims also necessitated grounding in a republican notion of popular sovereignty. In this way Webster's theory of majoritarianism, which presupposed the populist changes of the Jacksonian era, battled Calhoun's doctrines of nullification and concurrent majorities that were deliberate attempts to respond to these innovations.

This argument about the insufficiency of explanations linking the crises of the antebellum solely to the contradiction of divided competences, resulting in clashing spheres of governance triggered by policy disputes, is also highly relevant to the EU studies context. The origin of such clashes over the rules of the game in both compound polities was shown to involve questions of representing popular sovereignty as much as of constitutional allocation of competences. Consequently, this analysis casts doubt on the belief that such disputes can be resolved simply by a pellucid demarcation of the respective powers of each level of government. This means it is necessary to be wary of calls to fix the sources of EU political contestation by establishing a competence catalogue or by specifying once and for all where *Kompetenz-Kompetenz* lies.

Such propositions fail to acknowledge the manner in which forming a union of states and citizens implies a thorny and shifting struggle between the units' and the union's rival claims to represent best the interests of citizens. These clashes over the nature of political representation are thus a constitutive component of the rules of the game in their own right and not an epiphenomenon of policy disputes. This is precisely why abstract proposals for specifying competences according to the logic of so-called subsidiarity – the principle that governmental action should take place at the level where it is most efficacious – are not viable. Instead, if a shift in political representation, whereby the EU would be able to claim to represent citizens better, is to be successful, the analysis presented in this book suggests this transformation will have to be legitimated first at the level of domestic politics. In this sense, the future viability of integration is not a function of mimicking the nation state's coercive apparatus. Waltz argues (1979: 88) that for supranationalism to work requires such institutions to 'acquire some of the attributes and capabilities of states', meaning a monopoly of legitimate coercion. However, the argument developed in this book was that a more supranational EU will rather have to replicate the nation states' monopoly of popular sovereignty in a way that is acceptable to the units. Eventually, the federal level in the US compound system was able to gain such a monopoly – albeit only after the Civil War – but the obstacles to achieving this feat in the EU are very high.

In relation to the existing corpus of transatlantic comparisons, this argument thus implies the need for developing broader contrasts, extending beyond the current predilection for comparative studies of policy or decision making. In particular, it appears necessary to understand more about the contestation over judicial authority engendered by the Supreme Court and the ECJ as well as the part played by issues of political representation in such disputes. So far there is only one book-length study of this topic (Goldstein, 2001). However, perhaps the more fundamental implication of this study is that future transatlantic comparisons will have to pay more attention to the caesura represented by the Civil War. Putting an end to the claimed sovereign status of the states had a tremendous centripetal effect on the compound political system that has rarely been properly acknowledged in the literature.

One of the major components of the comparative analysis in this study focused on the changes wrought by Jacksonian democracy to the original system of compound political representation. The Civil War prevented the (southern) states' growing challenge to these transformations from taking effect and determined that such challenges would henceforth be illegitimate. Hence this settlement secured the role of the presidency as the embodiment of popular sovereignty throughout the union, a situation that was to serve Roosevelt so much in his confrontation with the Supreme Court over the New Deal. Yet there is another change relating to the presidency that lies outside the scope of this work but whose significance should also lead to its incorporation into the future agenda of transatlantic comparisons. Woodrow Wilson, in his guise as a political scientist, was probably the first to note this change. Following the 1898 war with Spain in which the US acquired extensive overseas territories, he remarked that the president would 'henceforth be one of the great powers of the world' (Wilson, 1908: 78). Despite the novelty of this situation, Wilson was certain that it marked a radical and long-lasting development in the federal system: 'we have but begun to see the presidential office in this light; but it is the light which will more and more beat upon it, and more and more determine its character and its effect upon the politics of the nation' (ibid.). However, the impact of this new aspect of the presidency upon the politics of representation in the US has so far received little attention in the existing transatlantic comparisons.

Consequently, despite the growing willingness to forsake nostrums of EU and US exceptionalism, there remains much to explore about the process of creating and maintaining a union of states and citizens by comparing these two cases. Indeed, these potential avenues of research are all the more pertinent in light of current developments in integration. Firstly, increased reliance on the adjudicatory role of the ECJ is to be expected once the Charter of Fundamental Rights is at last given legal status when member states apply EU legislation. Secondly, there is a strong tendency to believe that the success of future integration depends on the EU's ability to coordinate member state foreign policy more closely. Such a move is seen as a way of legitimizing integration by responding to citizens' supposed demands for the EU to become a stronger actor in international politics. This is why the Constitutional Treaty and its successor placed so much emphasis on the creation of a (member-state appointed) President of the Council: to allow the EU to represent more powerfully its foreign policy ambitions to its own citizens. The presupposition is that such a move will bolster the integration project by establishing a new method of representing the interests of citizens *qua* EU citizens, demonstrating the benefits of EU-level decision making in foreign policy. In other words, this institutional innovation appears designed to replicate the effects Wilson thought would inevitably stem from the US president's new international role.

In this twin context of resorting more frequently to the ECJ in sensitive issues of competence and the attempted presidentialization of EU foreign policy, there are obvious parallels with the evolution of the US federal system. It is safe to assume, therefore, that further analysis of the transatlantic analogy is likely to try to establish what such moves may entail for the continued success of integration. At the same time, however, this study has repeatedly demonstrated the pitfalls of invoking this analogy to identify supposed preconditions that specify how integration must invariably fare given the US precedent. To overcome this temptation requires a more sophisticated grasp of how both compound systems evolved and the reasons for differences in their respective paths. The hope is that the present study will provide a starting point for such endeavours by furnishing scholars with the first, but certainly not the last, word on what makes the EU viable.

Notes

Introduction: Questioning What Makes the EU Viable

1. The EU itself likes to emphasize its uniqueness. In the famous ENEL case, the ECJ referred to the creation of 'an independent legal order', *Costa v. ENEL* (1964).
2. For a withering critique of the hubris behind such claims see Anderson (2007).
3. One exception is McKay's (1999) discussion of the viability of European Monetary Union.
4. The major exception is Goldstein's (2001) innovative book-length study of the process of establishing federal supremacy over the legal system of the units.
5. In natural science, dynamic equilibrium is used to describe a chemical reaction whereby two opposing processes occur at the same rate, meaning there is no net change but since the reaction is continuous the equilibrium is dynamic.
6. I am thus using an idiosyncratic definition of political culture, not one beholden to Almond (1956).

1 The Problem of Viability in a Compound Polity

1. It was Publius, the pseudonym used by John Jay, Alexander Hamilton and James Madison when writing the federalist papers, who coined the term 'the compound republic' in Federalist 39; cf. Ostrom (1987).
2. This canonical interpretation is Weber's. For him the state is 'a compulsory organization with a territorial base. Furthermore ... the use of force is regarded as legitimate only so far as it is either permitted by the state or prescribed by it' (Weber, 1983: 56).
3. In sheer numerical terms, if the evacuation of 8500 Israeli settlers from the Gaza strip in 2005 required the mobilization of 50,000 troops it is obvious that no state can govern simply by employing its agents of coercion every time legislation provokes resistance.
4. Machiavelli's favourite, Cesare Borgia, was hailed for his decision to turn against the man he had appointed to render the Romagna 'obedient to the sovereign authority' when his lieutenant grew overzealous. 'Remirro [de Orco]'s body,' as Machiavelli delights in describing, 'was found cut in two pieces on the piazza at Cesena, with a block of wood and a bloody knife beside it. The brutality of this spectacle kept the people of the Romagna at once appeased and stupefied' (Machiavelli, 1961: 24).
5. 'Coercion does not define them (governments); every time they can do without it they do without it' (Guizot, 1985: 137).

6. In the antebellum period, the bounding of power through negarchical federal arrangements has been shown to have prevented a series of international crises from escalating into open hostilities, which competing realist and liberal theories cannot explain (Silverstone, 2004).
7. Federalism as a response to threat was Riker's (1964) original explanatory theory; cf. Forsyth's (1981) notion of confederation as an alternative to hegemony and balance of power as a form of interstate guarantee.
8. Marks (1993) even suggests that external threats contributed greatly to the impetus for replacing the American confederation with a more national government.
9. For an illuminating study of EU viability as a function of survival in the international arena see Haldén (2006).
10. This explains why an empire, which is based on a centre/periphery hierarchy, cannot be a compound polity, cf. Wæver (1996).
11. In a pure confederation, the unit of political representation is solely a collective one (a people, a state) and legal acts fall on states in their 'corporate or collective capacities' (Hamilton et al., 2003: 67). It is thus 'a contractual union of states' (Forsyth, 1981: 3) lacking the representation of individuals as citizens of the union itself. Conversely, in a federal order, individuals are represented alongside territorial units for the purposes of decision making and legislation touches citizens directly (Hamilton et al., 2003).
12. *Decentralization* is discounted as a possible scenario of viability because, when considered as a process, this notion implies a pre-existing centralization not pertinent in either the US or the EU case.
13. In theory at least, this process of voluntary centralization could ultimately result in a unitary state, meaning that a compound polity contains the potential for self-abolition. This is presumably what Chopin (2002) or McDonald (1988) would argue has happened to US federalism.
14. The latter corresponds to Bacharach and Baratz's (1962: 948) definition of power as not simply the ability to make decisions that affect others but also 'limit[ing] the scope of the political process to public consideration of only those issues that are relatively innocuous' to one actor.
15. Moravcsik (2002: 605) makes a similar point about the relationship between lamentations over the EU's democratic failings and the a priori conceptualization of democracy. By adopting a somewhat different yardstick of democracy, one that gives a certain precedence to horizontal separation of powers, 'then the widespread criticism of the EU as democratically illegitimate is unsupported by the existing empirical evidence'.
16. 'The powers not delegated to the United States by the Constitution, nor prohibited by it to the States, are reserved to the States respectively, or to the people.'
17. 'This Constitution, and the Laws of the United States which shall be made in Pursuance thereof ... shall be the supreme Law of the Land ... any Thing in the Constitution or Laws of any State to the Contrary notwithstanding.'
18. The federal government has the right to 'make all laws necessary and proper for carrying into execution'. Publius called this the need for a 'vigorous' national government.
19. So-called anti-federalists opposed ratification of the federal constitution, seeking instead to maintain a purely confederal arrangement between the former colonies. See Storing (1985).

20. For instance, Glyn Morgan (2005, 13–14) somewhat confusingly distinguishes between a 'federal polity', with a dual system of representation of both units and citizens, and a 'federation' where only units are represented. Yet the latter is precisely the definition of a confederation (Forsyth, 1981).
21. Regional separatism is much more viable in the context of European integration since it offers access to a large free market as well as security guarantees, thereby explaining the resurgence of regionalism at a time of growing supranational integration (Alesina and Spolaore, 2003; Jolly, 2007).
22. The single political institution supposed to transcend the divide between linguistic communities is the monarchy.
23. Although formalized in the Lisbon Treaty, the possibility of withdrawal was thought to exist previously de facto (De Witte, 2004b).
24. Admittedly, the failure to apply economic sanctions for excessive budget deficits despite the terms of the stability and growth pact occurred after the publication of Goldstein's study.

2 Developing an Analogical Comparison between the EU and the Antebellum US Republic

1. A more sophisticated historical perspective would link this process to the struggle between revolution and counter-revolution, as well as a struggle between France and Germany for control of Western Europe, and the struggle between Germany, Austria and Russia over Central and Eastern Europe (Pocock, 1999).
2. Indeed, social science itself is often considered bounded by 'national traditions' (Wagner, 2004).
3. This thesis needs to be prefaced with Hendrik Spruyt's (1994: 178) point that size and population are not straightforward predictors of military muscle and that 'the ability to wage war [is] a function of institutional arrangements'. In this crucial respect the territorial, sovereign state's competitors proved much 'less effective and less efficient in mobilizing resources' (ibid.).
4. Terrorism does not present states with a threat in comparison to which all previous threats pale into insignificance – it cannot even come close to equalling the insanity of mutually assured destruction – rather it is the threat itself that cannot really be evaluated. As Runciman (2004) explains, 'terrorism confronts us with risks that cannot be measured on any reliable scale, because the evidence is always so uncertain'. For a curious argument that terrorism provides a sufficiently compelling motive for deepening integration, see Morgan (2005).
5. The EU's institutional identity is largely defined in opposition to that of the nation state. According to the guidebook produced by the Delegation of the European Commission to the US, 'the EU is a unique, treaty-based, institutional framework that decides and manages economic and political cooperation among its member countries'.
6. Comparisons are even drawn with empires (Wæver, 1996; Zielonka, 2006).
7. Even anecdotally there is plenty with which to dispute this claim, starting with the point that 'as late as 1892, the United States had no ambassadors abroad and only a handful of ministers, most in the important capitals of Europe' (Robin, 1992: 18).

8. The lineage of this scholarship, characterized as it is by careful attention to political culture and ideology, can be traced back to Bernard Bailyn's (1971) work on redefining the American revolution as an 'ideological transformation' and the insights generated are worthy of this intellectual heritage.
9. Or, as Lowi (2006: 102) puts it, 'the United States of 1789 was neither united nor a state'.
10. Deudney (1995: 220) calls it the 'war of Southern secession'. In fact, this is exactly how it is known in most major European languages: *guerre de sécession, Sezessionskrieg, guerra di secessione*.
11. The origin of this misinterpretation is probably Publius, who declared in Federalist 22 that 'all nations have found it necessary to establish one court paramount to the rest, possessing a general superintendence, and authorized to settle and declare in the last resort a uniform rule of civil justice' (Hamilton et al., 2003: 104).
12. The constitutional legality of this amendment is open to question (McDonald, 1991).
13. This ruling was handed down in the infamous Slaughterhouse Cases (McDonald, 2000: 219-20; cf. Zuckert, 1992: 89). The latest scholarship on this infamous decision in fact suggests this restrictive interpretation of the amendment was part of a strategy to help reconstruction states control armed white militias by denying them protection under the Second Amendment, which thus required the Supreme Court to deny the incorporation of the Bill of Rights to the state level (Goldstein, 2007).
14. The 'Virginia Plan' discussed during the Philadelphia convention proposed a federal veto of state legislation (Robertson, 2005: 95–8).
15. This act made the federal trial courts 'the primary and powerful reliances for vindicating every right given by the Constitution, the laws, and treaties of the United States' (Frankfurter and Landis, 1928: 109).
16. The two most significant crises of twentieth-century American political development, the New Deal and Civil Rights, illustrate this point. Whereas the former was a conflict over the ability of the Supreme Court to fetter the will of a popularly-elected federal government – a federal-level conflict over institutional competences – the latter gave rise to a half-baked attempt to resurrect the discredited notion of nullification, which failed in the face of robust executive action.
17. This notion of cumulative knowledge based on falsifiability is of course that of Karl Popper. See Davis (2005: 92-131) for a critique of deductive logical positivism when applied to the social sciences.
18. The actual number of these debates is contested but the paradigm case is the 'second debate' between the historical school and the proponents of a positivist approach. Unsurprisingly, now that the methods of comparative politics are being used to study the EU, doubts have been raised over the usefulness of studying the EU from an IR perspective. One of the leading comparativists, McKay (2005: 530), claims the 'concepts and approaches borrowed from international relations and its sub-disciplines look less and less appropriate'.
19. The capacity of the integration question to wreak havoc with domestic politics is well illustrated by the 2005 French referendum on the constitutional treaty (Ivaldi, 2006; cf. Schmidt, 2007).

20. However, Schmidt (2006) argues that federal states find it easier to adapt to the democratic practices of the EU.
21. A chronicle cannot fall into the 'Whig' trap since, as White (1975: 7) explains, it contains no 'inauguration' nor any 'culmination or resolution; [it] can go on indefinitely'.
22. L. Strauss believed that modern political philosophy was post-Machiavellian as it had abandoned the task of finding out how man ought to live. He remarked somewhat bitterly that 'by lowering the standards of political excellence one guarantees the actualisation of the only kind of political order that in principle is possible' (1987: 300).
23. 'I am', Tocqueville wrote, 'of the opinion that absolute perfection is rarely to be found in any system of laws' (1994: 14).
24. Philosophy, in the Aristotelian sense, is the highest form of *theoria* and is the striving to interpret the world through reason, which is why Marx pointed out that philosophers before him had never changed the world they observed.
25. Of course, this does not mean that the member states of the EU do not suffer from serious political crises and indeed credible doubts on both their effectiveness and legitimacy. For an insightful round-up of the challenges to the capacities of nation states see Dunn (1996).
26. The Jerusalem Center for Public Affairs holds an online database of Elazar's papers, where the title has been changed from the original Jerusalem Post article entitled 'Federalism will preserve Yugoslavia' to one a little less presumptive: 'Will Federalism Preserve Yugoslavia?'. See http://www.jcpa.org/dje/articles2/yugoslavia.htm (accessed 22 December, 2007).
27. The actual wording is the: 'informal pre-conditions of the success of American federalism' (Siedentop, 2000: 11).
28. Other scholars note the exceptionalism of the American case but interpret this as an illustration of 'the essential independence of nationality from geo-political and ethnic factors' rather than as the success of a post-national project (Greenfeld, 1992: 23).
29. 'Preconditions which were identified and explored by Tocqueville' (Siedentop, 2000: 11).
30. Etzioni is not an altogether reliable guide on the EU. He claims that 'the Commission is composed of national representatives' (2001, xxix). Yet before exercising their functions commissioners must take an oath which commands that they are 'neither to seek nor to take instruction from any government or body'.
31. Of course, a line can always be drawn between two points. Thus the realm of the comparable is infinite. One recent study has even attempted an analogy between American secessionism and the problem of the Mezzogiorno in Italy (Doyle, 2002).

3 Comparing How the Rules of the Game are Contested

1. Morris (1974: 1068) argues that 'the historical evidence indicates that a national government was in operation before the formation of the states'. However, the argument that national government and thus national sovereignty predates that of the states is forcefully disputed by Van Tyne (1907).

2. This explains why the secondary sources – because scholars of politics cannot pretend to do the historian's job and delve into the primary material (Lustick, 1996) – this study relies on are predominantly volumes of political history with unfolding political narratives of state and sectional interests, parties, elections, leaders and ideologies. However, I also make some use of cultural history emphasizing the symbolic or ritualistic function of political life to understand the less institutionalized nature of the rules of the game.
3. One notable exception to this scholarly consensus is a recent work that recasts the narrative of secession as the product of sectional strife based on competing visions of commercial policy that turned into a struggle between two rival states. See Onuf and Onuf (2006).
4. For a subtle and synoptic overview of the protean understanding of the constitution over the last two centuries see Hendrickson (2003: 281–97). Intellectual historians share this inability to furnish a settled analysis of the intellectual heritage that inspired the politics of revolutionary America. For some the hero of the story is Locke, while according to J. G. A. Pocock (1975: 462) this event ought to be thought of as 'the last great act of the renaissance' due to the influence of the ideology of civic humanism.
5. One user remarked of this curious fact that 'it was evident that the former document was an object of interest to very few visitors of Washington' (quoted in Kammen, 1986: 127).
6. It reads: 'The Judicial power of the United States shall not be construed to extend to any suit in law or equity, commenced or prosecuted against one of the United States by citizens of another State, or by Citizens or Subjects of any Foreign State.' This means the states are liable to a suit by the US or from other states but not citizens of other states, the precedent being the English system where no writ could be brought against the sovereign (Orth, 1987).
7. Andrew Jackson's victory in the battle of New Orleans, January 1815, came *after* peace terms (the Treaty of Ghent) had been agreed to, which makes this war particularly tricky to date.
8. The war ended soon after the Hartford Convention met, thereby removing its very *raison d'être*.
9. Daniel Webster, the famous orator who defended the union against states rights advocates, most notably in his Senate 1830 debate with Robert Hayne, was counsel for McCulloch.
10. This expression was originally coined by Charles and Mary Beard in 1930. See Ransom (1999).
11. A Supreme Court ruling confirmed that unilateral secession was unconstitutional because what had been created at Philadelphia was 'an indestructible Union, composed of indestructible states'. *Texas v. White*, 47 U.S 700 (1869).
12. For an in-depth study of the various evocations of the Civil War in its aftermath, see Blight (2001). Blight also describes the existence of a southern vision of the war as a 'lost cause', led by chivalrous but outnumbered forces trying to protect their liberty and supposedly noble way of life.
13. 'The Revolution', Barry Schwartz (1982: 387) notes in his study of collective memory in this period, 'was the only event which expressed the unity of the new nation and which could serve as a basis of national tradition'.

The heroic age of colonization and revolution provided almost all the scenes and images for antebellum art celebrated in Washington: 'of the 69 images placed in the Capitol before the Civil War, 60 represented men and events of the revolutionary and pre-revolutionary periods' (ibid., p. 385).
14. In his study on American political architecture, Robin (1992: 32) explains this policy whereby: 'Federal officials consistently discouraged the public erection of statues of generals and other Union heroes within these national shrines. The eclectic sanctuary at Gettysburg and other sites bore witness to the limited success of this effort. The Quartermaster General [Montgomery Meigs] did, however, succeed in preserving the rows of tombstones as the central motif of this celebration of nationhood. These grave markers provided the building blocks for an abstract monument celebrating ideals rather than valiant leadership.'
15. In her essay on the frontier hero in American literature, Calder (1977: 86) notes that 'the process of America's westward expansion produced its myth and its legendary figures, but not until after the Civil War, the last phase of settlement, was there consolidated a compelling representative hero'.
16. Already in 1873 the Supreme Court's ruling in the *Slaughterhouse Cases* greatly attenuated the provisions of the Fourteenth Amendment through a highly restrictive interpretation of the 'privileges and immunities of citizens of the United States' (McDonald, 2000: 219–21).
17. *Commission of the European Communities v. Council of the European Union* (2004).
18. In order to reflect the modern interlocking of federal, state and municipal government the theory of 'co-operative' or 'marble-cake' federalism has now replaced that of dual federalism. However, Elazar (1962) contends that the cooperative phase of intergovernmental relations in US history began already in the early nineteenth century. More recently, Kincaid (1990) has described the US as a 'coercive federal' arrangement. For a review of all these concepts see Zimmerman (2001).
19. McKay (2001: 24) notes that these powers 'in contemporary eighteenth-century terms, amounted to the equivalent of the sort of powers exercised by the unitary governments of the time'.
20. It does, however, have its 'own resources', consisting of revenue from the common external tariff and a percentage of national value added tax.
21. The Treaty of Amsterdam (1997) provided for the renumbering of both the EEC and Maastricht treaties. I have kept the original treaty numbering to avoid anachronism; the number in square brackets refers to the article number as amended by Amsterdam.
22. The Lisbon Treaty specifies the principle of conferral in its revision of Article 5 of the TEU.
23. The Lisbon treaty specifies 11 such areas of shared competence: internal market; social policy for the aspects defined in the treaty; economic, social and territorial cohesion; agriculture and fisheries, excluding the conservation of marine biological resources; environment; consumer protection; transport; trans-European networks; energy; area of freedom, security and justice; common safety concerns in public health matters.
24. Not in all: The German and Italian constitutions both prohibit the use of referendums to ratify international treaties.

25. Functionalist spillover theory was predicated in part on the belief in the emergence of transnational political entrepreneurs who would mobilize constituencies in favour of greater integration.
26. These territories were acquired by purchase or through belligerence. The Northwest Ordinance adopted under the last months of the Articles of Confederation prohibited slavery in the territory northwest of the Ohio river and east of the Mississippi (Onuf, 1987).

4 The Struggle to Maintain a Compound System: Creating and Contesting the Rules of the Game in European Integration

1. Jean Monnet linked the Schuman plan directly to the Ruhr problem, which depended on finding an arrangement that would both satisfy French economic interests and assuage their fears of being the perpetual underdog. 'Ruhr production', he argued, 'should be utilized not only for Germany or as the result of bilateral arrangements, but it should contribute to the production of the whole of Europe' (quoted in Beloff, 1963: 57).
2. Joseph Weiler (1994) proposes three founding ideals: peace, prosperity and supranationalism. By overlooking the fears surrounding the future status of Germany and the project's relationship with democracy, Weiler's three ideals tell only a part of the integration story.
3. In this sense, the contest over the Ruhr was a successor to previous centuries' conflicts over the Lowlands in northwestern Europe, which ceased only after the British guarantee of Belgian neutrality (Lukacs, 1976: 62).
4. In this study I take federal to be synonymous with supranational and use confederal as a synonym for intergovernmental.
5. Gillingham (1991: 313–4) claims that Monnet subsequently referred to the ECSC Treaty as 'Europe's first antitrust law'. It is clear that the liberal thrust of the treaty fitted with the free trade agenda of America's vision for the post-war international order.
6. 'Members [of the Consultative Committee] are appointed by the Council of Ministers for two-year terms, upon nomination by "representative" trade associations and trade unions, after the Council of Ministers has determined which groups shall be considered "representative"' (Haas, 1968: 43).
7. Speech at the University of Zurich. Available online at www.churchill-society-london.org.uk/astonish.html (accessed 22 December 2007).
8. Konrad Adenauer, the Federal Republic's first chancellor, was not prepared to accept West Germany's return to sovereign status at any cost. But he nevertheless acquiesced to signing a treaty 'that was supposed to redress the imbalances of nature and organization between coal-rich Germany and the remaining six [sic] fuel-importing nations' (Gillingham, 1991: 280) and which the Ruhr producers had rejected.
9. In 1950 the Americans threatened to cut off funds for European defence, at a time when the US financed a quarter of the entire French defence budget (Harrison, 1981: 33; 240, n. 78).
10. Primary sources concerning the European Political Community can be found at http://www.ena.lu/?lang=2&doc=382 (accessed 18 August 2008).

11. For a comprehensive legal comparison of the two treaties see Soulé (1958).
12. The ECJ's ruling in *Van Gend en Loos* referred to the creation of 'a Community of unlimited duration' as part of the rationale for why the EEC was not to be considered as an ordinary international treaty.
13. This expectation has proved true. See the table on increasing competences in Börzel (2005: 221–3).
14. Of course, the EEC did not replace the ECSC. Following the 1965 Merger Treaty, a single Council and Commission were created for the 'three communities': ECSC, EEC and European Atomic Energy Community (EURATOM). The ECSC treaty expired on 23 July 2002 and the international agreements it had made were devolved to the EU.
15. Under the terms of the EEC Treaty it was already specified that a 'regulation' would be 'binding in its entirety and directly applicable in all Member States' (Article 189).
16. *Syndicat général des fabricants de semoules de France*, 1968; *Ministre de l'Intérieur contre Cohn-Bendit*, 1978.
17. Nicolo (1989); Whereas the *Cour de Cassation* accepted EEC supremacy in *Administration des Douanes v. Société des cafés Jacques Vabre* (1975), the *Conseil d'État*.
18. As one noted legal scholar observes, this joining together of the ECJ and the national courts has a significant effect on compliance. As a result, the supranational element of ever closer union is strengthened by the integration of European juridical decisions into national court systems: 'The national Courts and the European Court of Justice are thus integrated into a unitary system of judicial decision-making. What is important – indeed crucial – is the fact that it is the national court acting in tandem with the European Court which gives the formal final decision on the compatibility of the national measure with Community law. The main result of this procedure is the binding effect and enforcement value which such a decision will have on a Member State – coming from its own courts – as opposed to a similar decision handed down from Luxembourg by the European Court of Justice' (Weiler, 1982: 55).
19. The ECSC treaty was similarly open to new members. Article 98 declared that 'any European State may request to accede to the present Treaty'.
20. This article was subsequently repealed during the Amsterdam negotiations. Currently it is the 'Copenhagen Criteria' that govern the eligibility of candidate countries.
21. The UK, Denmark, Norway, Sweden, Austria, Switzerland and Portugal.
22. De Gaulle had some good reasons to doubt that the UK could use nuclear weapons independently since the failure of the Blue Streak missile project meant that the UK became dependent on US nuclear technology.
23. The new French President, Georges Pompidou, unilaterally announced he would hold a referendum on enlargement in April 1972. Pompidou's gamble has largely been forgotten; if it is remembered at all it is usually treated as an instrument of domestic political positioning. Yet it was also intended as a means of strengthening France's negotiating hand at the Paris summit scheduled for later that year, where the details of EMU were to be discussed (Criddle, 1993).
24. It is no coincidence that the first round of enlargement in 1973, which heralded the use of referendums, corresponded with the creation by the

Commission of regular, standardized public opinion surveys – called Eurobarometer – in all member states.

25. Fellow-applicants Ireland, Denmark and Norway, all held popular consultations on the subject of joining the common market; Norway voted against, in Denmark two-thirds voted yes and in Ireland the figure was 83 per cent in favour.
26. The mechanism only applied if a state suffered from a balance of payments deficit, something the UK's North Sea oil revenues soon made improbable.
27. The first was in 1932 when the Liberal government debated whether to abandon the principle of free trade.
28. In Denmark's accession referendum, for instance, an anti-EEC party was formed from splinter politicians from the main party formations who later rejoined them, while in France both the Maastricht Treaty poll (1992) and the vote on the Constitutional Treaty (2005) have produced unlikely alliances between offshoots of mainstream parties.
29. The economic justification for integration often relates to the notion of the costs of 'non-Europe'. This argument works both *ex post facto*, to explain the benefits of the SEA's deregulations, as well as *ex ante* in the case of the single currency that was often sold on the basis of the size of the expected savings on conversion charges and lower prices.
30. In the 1971 White Paper that set out the advantages of joining the Community, the government claimed 'there is no question of any erosion of essential national sovereignty; what is proposed is a sharing and an enlargement of individual national sovereignties in the general interest' (HMG, 1971: 8).
31. These are known as the Copenhagen Criteria named after the 1993 European Council held in the Danish capital, which specify 'the stability of institutions guaranteeing democracy, the rule of law, human rights and respect for and protection of minorities' as paramount criteria for admission.
32. For a constructivist account emphasizing the rhetoric of liberal democracy in enlargement, see Schimmelfennig (2003).
33. For a survey of the arguments as they stood in the 1980s see Weiler (1988).
34. As befits the history of integration, with its invariably bathetic moments, parliamentary ratification passed smoothly in every country with one exception. During the debate in the French national assembly, where competition from another heavily agricultural country was causing a stir, 'references to the Acropolis, Solon and Greek culture were mixed with expressions of fear about pears, aubergines and courgettes' (Tsoulakis, 1981: 142).
35. Morgan (2005: 1–2) begins his study with the classic British avatar of this struggle, the case of a greengrocer prosecuted for selling a pound of bananas.
36. After all, the Rome Treaty 'does not contain a supremacy clause and does not provide for the direct effect of directives or treaty provisions' (Stone Sweet, 2005: 48).
37. An added advantage for the French was that since under the exchange rate mechanism the Franc was pegged to the Deutschmark 'decisions on interest rates made by the Bundesbank simply had to be accepted by the French if they wanted to keep the link' between the two currencies. Thus for the French EMU was also 'an attempt to reassert some control over their own monetary policy' (George, 1998: 226).

38. Dehousse (2005: 116) claims the equation between federalism and centralization is 'an ahistorical reading, certainly, but now so deeply ingrained in British culture that it has become a factor to be taken into account'. Yet this is an inherently ideological claim since political science literature clearly distinguishes federation from confederation. The former consists of 'communities of both individuals and polities and is committed to protect the liberties of both, but with a greater emphasis on the liberties of individuals than on the liberties of the constituent polities. Confederations, on the other hand, place greater emphasis on the liberties of the constituent polities, since it is the task of each polity to protect individual liberty, more or less as each defines it, within its own borders' (Majone, 2005: 221).
39. 'Since mid-1989 Kohl had argued that the Bundestag would demand progress on foreign policy and the powers of the Parliament in exchange for ratification of a monetary agreement' (Moravcsik, 1998: 447).
40. These were: European citizenship, visa policy, education, culture, public health, consumer protection, development cooperation, transport, telecommunications and energy infrastructures and industry.
41. Besides the Court's unwillingness to become a tool for the member states to strike down unwanted legislation, there is also a practical reason inhibiting this potential role of arbiter between European and national power. As a result of the complex interrelationship in the joint federal structure that connects the EU with the member states, it is also difficult to disentangle the two levels of government to determine the comparative effectiveness and efficiency of each.
42. Included in the treaty was also a protocol protecting Ireland's constitutional principle of the 'right to life of the unborn' against EU encroachment. Ireland felt threatened by an undesired legal precedent: a 1990 case brought before the ECJ had to rule on whether abortion was a service and thus whether Irish students could freely distribute information about clinics performing terminations in the UK. The protocol was designed to secure a cross-party coalition for the upcoming referendum.
43. There was a precedent for this in the SEA. A declaration annexed to the treaty specified that the goal of completing the internal market by 31 December 1992 did not 'create an automatic legal effect' thereby depriving the ECJ of the ability to force the pace of integration.
44. In reality, the identity agenda pre-dated Maastricht by several years. Already in the mid-1980s the Commission had pursued a policy in the symbolic sphere – albeit a shallow one. It persuaded the Council to celebrate 'Europe Day' on the anniversary of the Schuman declaration, to adopt a flag (purloined from the Council of Europe), a hymn (likewise borrowed from the Council of Europe), a common burgundy-coloured passport and a stylistically identical driving licence.
45. For the sake of simplicity I have deliberately omitted a discussion of the Amsterdam Treaty (1997) as well as the Nice Treaty (2001). The former transferred immigration and asylum policy to the first pillar with certain caveats, while the latter changed the voting rules for QMV. However, both fell well short of fundamentally reconstituting the rules of the game as understood in this study.

200 Notes

46. Although extraneous to the treaties and ordinary legislation, the EU's courts did not wait for its status to be resolved by political agreement and made reference to the Charter, thereby implying it is already binding on the actions of the union. The first time was in *max.mobil Telecommunikation Service* v. *Commission* case T-54/99.
47. As the French political philosopher Ferry (2000: 123) remarks, 'perhaps moreover it is partly to prevent the actual emergence of the crucial question "who is sovereign in the Union?" that the decision-making processes of community and intergovernmental bodies are subjected to such extreme proceduralism, with the need for much consultation and toing and froing'.
48. There is also a provision for 'enhanced cooperation' (first present in the Nice Treaty), which is the opposite of the opt-out mechanism: it allows for a pioneer group of states to pool more sovereignty in new areas.

5 Contrasting and Explaining the Viability of Two Compound Systems

1. President Andrew Jackson, reacting to a Supreme Court decision declaring Georgia's expropriation of Cherokee lands, wrote to one of his generals that 'if order were issued tomorrow one regiment of militia could not be got to march to save [the Cherokee] from destruction and this the opposition know' (quoted in Friedman, 1998: 400, fn 269).
2. 'Chisolm was a citizen of South Carolina and his suit was based upon a claim for the delivery of goods to the state for which no payment had been made ... In deciding that Georgia was subject to suit, the Court was rejecting the claim that the state was vested with the traits of sovereignty. "As to the purposes of the Union", to repeat the declaration of Justice Wilson, "Georgia is not a sovereign state"' (quoted in Bernard Schwartz, 1993: 20–2).
3. As the Kentucky resolution of 1798 affirms, the US is a compact in which certain precise powers are delegated but with each state reserving 'the residuary mass of right to their own self-government; and that whensoever the general government assumes undelegated powers, its acts are unauthoritative, void, and of no force' (Rabun, 1956: 51).
4. 'In the partitionment of governmental functions between nation and state, the state gets the most but the nation the highest' (Bryce, 1995: 378).
5. This illustrates how far removed modern cooperative federalism is from the original constitutional design.
6. Certain member states, of course, are notorious foot-draggers when it comes to implementing European directives or complying with ECJ rulings. This explains the introduction in the Maastricht Treaty (Article 228) of a regime of fines for non-compliance, a change fought for by probably the most euro-sceptic member state, the UK.
7. Thomas Jefferson, prior to his participation in federal politics, had vituperated that 'such addiction [to a political party] is the last degradation of a free and moral agent. If I could not go to heaven but with a party, I would not go there at all' (quoted in Aldrich, 1995: 93).

8. According to Moravcsik (2002: 65) 'if we adopt reasonable criteria for judging democratic governance, then the widespread criticism of the EU as democratically illegitimate is unsupported by the existing empirical evidence'.
9. As Bruce Ackerman (1991: 68–9) explains, 'the [electoral] College was a clever device to avoid the plebiscitarian Presidency ... since the President was supposed to gain the White House on the basis of his past service, it was unthinkable for him to claim that his (nonexistent) "mandate" allowed him to transform his office into a functional equivalent of a third house of the legislature'.
10. It should not be forgotten, however, that the separate states passed resolutions in favour of the Declaration so as to give it their binding assent (Van Tyne, 1907: 537).
11. The American constitution has no formal requirement that the Electoral College should be appointed by the people; the organization of the college is left to the states' discretion.
12. As Magnette (2007: 1076) explains, 'the Parliament may lean to the centre-right whilst the European Council is for the most part centre-left or the converse. In addition a President of the European Commission may see the European Council drift gradually towards the centre-right as national elections occur'.
13. This popular mobilization distinguishes Switzerland from other European consociations and consensus democracies.
14. The Lisbon Treaty does contain a right for a citizen's initiative. Under Article 8 B, a million citizens from across the EU – the number of states has not yet been specified – may petition the Commission for legislative action 'for the purpose of implementing the treaties'. This back door approach to supranationalism via direct democracy is unlikely to change the rules of the game much since the petition – which itself is non-binding – could only refer to a policy area already within the existing powers of the Commission.
15. The typical complaint of British euro-sceptics is that whereas a treaty providing for a common market was ratified by referendum in 1975 this decision certainly did not equate to a sanction for later developments in integration.
16. According to one leading law scholar, the 'undoubted attraction of the convention method lies in the way it broadens participation in the constitutional conversation and thereby allows a public *débat d'idées*' (De Witte, 2003: 215).
17. A similar gambit for expanding public debate on integration by bringing together national and European parliamentarians was tried prior to Maastricht. The brainchild of President Mitterrand, an *'assises'* met in late 1990 to prepare a declaration on their expectations of the Intergovernmental Conference (IGC). The whole experiment is now almost entirely forgotten. See Corbett (1993: 23–6).
18. See the table on increasing competences in Börzel (2005: 221–3). Hooghe and Marks (2008: 124 n. 11) point out that 'formal rules may not capture the practice of policy in fields such as agricultural policy and cohesion policy where, arguably, there has been some renationalization'.
19. Nor could the EU function under two different legal regimes in the absence of ratification by one or more member states. For the significance of this point see De Witte (2004a). However, Schmitter (2000) has proposed a two-treaty structure to meet different states' preferences, whereby a confederal

arrangement among certain states would coexist alongside a more federal treaty for the rest.
20. Recognizing the pitfalls of a lapse to regionalism, George Washington had referred to the 'cement of interest' as a necessary component of the success of the extended republic. On the idea of economic interest as a central component of federal union see Matson and Onuf (1985); cf. Minicucci (2001).
21. Lincoln (1991: 58) would also refer to the need for government to be founded on a majority in the inaugural address of his first term: 'unanimity is impossible; the rule of a minority, as a permanent arrangement, is wholly inadmissible; so that, rejecting the majority principle, anarchy or despotism in some form is all that is left'.
22. This distinguished Lincoln from the Whig understanding whereby liberty, although derived from the union, 'had to be regulated in ways consistent with the preservation of the Union' (Orren and Skowronek, 2004: 70).
23. Morgan himself sees the finality argument as a three-way contest between defenders of the nation state, advocates of a post-sovereign EU polity and proponents, like himself, of a unitary European superstate.
24. For an unconventional dissenting interpretation, see Onuf and Onuf (2006).
25. There was also an enormous financial incentive in spreading the slave economy since after 1815 'cotton became the most valuable staple commodity in the Atlantic world', with production doubling between 1815 and 1820 and again in the following five-years (Wilentz, 2005: 221).
26. James K. Polk is said to have offered Spain $100 million in 1848 to purchase Cuba to bring another slave-holding state into the union (Hart A., 1917: 330; May, 1973).
27. Wilentz (2005: 585) argues that in expanding the union the naive Polk 'wanted to supplant sectional jealousies with nationalist unity' as his 'vision of Manifest Destiny was as an emollient on sectional discord, and not a sectional ploy'. The project backfired spectacularly as it only enflamed existing tensions.
28. As Wilentz (2005: 648) points out, 'the most doctrinaire state-rights slave-holders were perfectly willing to invoke robust federal power to protect slavery'. In fact, by the 1850s a role reversal had taken place, with the Northern states de facto nullifying federal fugitive slave legislation (McDonald, 2000: 172–5).
29. This can be seen in the 2006 'Bolkestein' directive on liberalizing services, which provoked the fury of socialist MEPs and irked several important member states. To placate these critics the final version was much watered down, notably the 'country of origin' principle that would have allowed firms to offer services transnationally while being subject to only their home country's rules and regulations rather than meeting separate national standards.
30. Aldrich (1995: 106) also draws attention to developments in national infrastructure that made national mass parties 'technologically feasible'.
31. 'As a result, although the percentage of white males who voted in 1828 was about double that in 1824, the absolute number of voters tripled in 1828, breaking the one million mark, up from 365,000 in 1824' (Aldrich, 1995: 106-7).
32. 'This last vestige of the old form of national parties ended in 1824 in the face of the weak showing of its nominee' (Aldrich, 1995: 99).

33. Remini described his programme as 'neo-Jeffersonian and conservative, leaning toward states' rights and the economics of laissez faire but so bland and inoffensive that those previously disposed to follow him could not seriously object to a single point' (quoted in Aldrich, 1995: 110).
34. 'The disruption of the second American party system started with the collapse of Whiggery in several states of the Lower South' (Fehrenbacher, 1980: 48).
35. The Republicans also managed to appeal to northern fears of immigration by linking the threat of wage competition from new citizens and the supposedly anti-republican proclivities of Irish and German immigrants' Catholicism to the economic and political threat coming from the South (Freehling, 1994: 205–6).
36. Nativism was a highly successful anti-immigrant creed that spawned the Know-Nothing party as the second party system collapsed (Foner, 1995: 226–60).
37. The case was in fact engineered by abolitionists (McDonald, 2000: 177).
38. However, none of these were slave holders (McDonald, 2000: 179).
39. In 1857-8 the South sought Kansas' admission as a slave state despite a majority of its citizens having voted to enter it as a free state. Kansas entered the union as a free state in 1861.
40. C-147/03 *Commission* v. *Austria* [2005] ECR I-5969.
41. *Numerus clausus* systems fix a limit on admissions and are thus associated with stringent entry examinations.
42. There is a similar situation in Belgium, where the parliament of the French-speaking community (competent in matters of education) recently passed a law (*le décret Simonet*) requiring that 70 per cent of students in certain health-related degree programmes be Belgian residents. This legislation was adopted as a response to the number of students from France electing to study in French-speaking Belgian universities because of lower fees and less demanding entrance examinations.
43. Foner (1995: 9) takes this as proof that 'government by majority rule works best when political issues involve superficial problems, rather than deep social divisions'.

6 The Future Evolution of the EU Compound Polity: The Obstacles to Voluntary Centralization

1. I follow Majone's (1996: 52-4) distinction between social policy, which provides 'merit goods' that could also be supplied although perhaps inadequately by the market, such as pensions or unemployment benefit, and social regulation, which delivers 'public goods' that markets cannot provide, such as environmental protection or consumer safety.
2. 'There was, and continues to be, a consensus on basic liberal premises that state intervention should remain limited in economic and social spheres' (Della Sala, 2005: 134).
3. Bartolini (2005: 177–247), drawing on the work of Stein Rokkan, prefers to conceptualize this antinomy as boundary-removing and boundary-building.
4. *Barber* v. *GRE* (1990).

5. The possible costs of the decision were minimized by a protocol inserted into the Maastricht Treaty that forbade the awarding of retrospective compensation for gender inequality in pensionable age.
6. Recent case. See *Laval v. Svenska Byggnadsarbetareförbundet* (2007).
7. Analysing the 1984 *Marshall* ruling, Arnull (2006: 645) comments that this constituted a 'leading example of the Court's capacity for restraint'.
8. Paradoxically, early in his political career, Calhoun was more often to be found advocating the cause of the federal government rather than rallying behind states' rights (McDonald, 2000: 75–6).
9. 'Many came to despair of being able to block the Wilmot proviso by regular legislative methods or by the veto of the president; they therefore considered it bad policy to wait till the dreaded and final blow was struck by Congress before a finger should be raised by way of warning or defense' (Cole, 1914: 376).
10. 'The first great principle of all republican liberty ... is that the majority must govern' (Webster, 1833: 33).
11. I take this theory of concurrent majorities and his proposal for a dual presidency to be the work of a profound reflection on the nature of the American compound system and what made it viable rather than a crude scheme for preserving slavery by a disgruntled southerner. For a survey of Calhoun's political philosophy see Lerner (1963).
12. The text of Article II.I reads: 'The person having the greatest number of votes shall be the President, if such number be a majority of the whole number of electors appointed; and if there be more than one who have such majority, and have an equal number of votes, then the House of Representatives shall immediately choose by ballot one of them for President; and if no person have a majority, then from the five highest on the list the said House shall in like manner choose the President. But in choosing the President, the votes shall be taken by States, the representation from each state having one vote; a quorum for this purpose shall consist of a member or members from two thirds of the states, and a majority of all the states shall be necessary to a choice. In every case, after the choice of the President, the person having the greatest number of votes of the electors shall be the Vice President.' Following the hotly contested election of Jefferson in 1800, the Twelfth Amendment was passed, which made electors nominate the candidates for one office or the other.
13. 'The practice of representation does not need to become bogged down in the independence/mandate controversy: genuine representation is possible in the absence of explicit instructions from the voters, so long as it coincides with the absence of explicit objections from the voters' (Runciman, 2006: 10).
14. The comparative federalism literature has shown the usefulness of constitutional ambiguity for defusing conflict (Erk and Gagnon, 2000).
15. As Bartolini (2005: 266) explains, integration 'was driven by the growing pressure deriving from the slow but significant economic peripheralization of Europe in the post-Second World War world economy and the corresponding perception of the inadequacy of the European state as a unit of economic organization in world competition'.
16. Hix's argument builds on the introduction in 2001 of qualified-majority voting for electing the Commission president and the college of

Commissioners, who are then subject to a majority vote in the European Parliament. Consequently, there can now be a linkage between all three branches of EU government as the Commission is selected by a majority of both governments and MEPs. This method of linking the supranational with the domestic level is the platform for 'an EU-version of "government-opposition" politics' (2008: 108), which will produce a policy mandate for the Commission that was precisely impossible under the previous system where the president was chosen purely by unanimous agreement between the member states.
17. The lack of anything resembling an integrated EU public sphere also hampers the court's ability to gauge public opinion on a matter, whereas the US Supreme Court has seldom remained at odds with public consensus on important issues (Miller and Howell, 1956: 3).
18. A nullifying convention was convened in 1832 by South Carolina in the course of the Tariff dispute. Of course, this method mimicked the convention through which the state had accepted the US Constitution (McDonald, 2000: 104–10).
19. Another tool would be the exit option, or at least the threat of withdrawal. It is important to note that the Lisbon Treaty for the first time creates a formal legal avenue of withdrawal from the EU although this is obviously not a flexible instrument.
20. 'The lack of any party thematization of EU issues leaves the mass public attitudes towards the EU largely unstructured' (Bartolini, 2005: 385).
21. For a review of the debate over second- and first-order voting in EU referendums see Garry et al. (2005); Glencross and Trechsel (2007).
22. 'Mitterrand contended that national governments would always be able to safeguard national interests ... Mitterrand played the sovereignty card well and emerged from the exchange [a TV debate with Philippe Séguin] the clear winner' (Criddle, 1993: 234).
23. This sum includes eight referendums in three non-EU member states: Norway, Liechtenstein and Switzerland.
24. This mechanism has never been used although the threat of calling such a convention to impose union-wide direct election of senators encouraged Congress to pass the Seventeenth Amendment (Wirls, 1999: 4).
25. Article V. Since originally there were only seven confederate states the threshold for an amendment convention was nearly 50 per cent of states; by the end of 1861 13 states had seceded.
26. Provided, however, that the treaty binding certain member states to a more supranational polity did not affect the rights granted to all EU citizens under the current treaty arrangement. This is the same problem as for enhanced co-operation, which has led one EU lawyer to conclude that such moves are impossible since the further integration of a group of states 'would unavoidably affect the rights which the other member states have under current EU law' (De Witte, 2004b: 12).

Bibliography

Abrams, R. (1996) 'The Relevance of American Federalism to the European Union: From Confederation to Federal Union to Nation-State', in R. Herr and S. Weber (eds), *European Integration and American Federalism: A Comparative Perspective* (Berkeley: University of California Press), pp. 14–18.
Ackerman, B. (1991) *We the People: Foundations* (Cambridge, MA: Belknap).
——. (1998) *We the People: Transformations* (Cambridge, MA: Belknap).
——. (2005) 'The Art of Stealth', *London Review of Books*, 17 February.
Adler-Nissen, R. (2008) 'Organized Duplicity? When States Opt Out of the European Union', in R. Adler-Nissen and T. Gammeltoft-Hansen (eds), *Sovereignty Games: Instrumentalizing State Sovereignty in a European and Global Context* (New York: Palgrave Macmillan), pp. 81–103.
Aldrich, J. (1995) *Why Parties? The Origin and Transformation of Political Parties in America* (Chicago: University of Chicago Press).
Alesina, A. and E. Spolaore (2003) *The Size of Nations* (Cambridge, MA: MIT Press).
Almond, G. (1956) 'Comparative Political Systems', *The Journal of Politics*, 18 (3), pp. 391–409.
Alter, K. (1998) 'Who Are the "Masters of the Treaties"? European Governments and the European Court of Justice', *International Organization*, 52 (1), pp. 121–47.
——. (2001) *Establishing the Supremacy of European Law: The Making of an International Rule of Law in Europe* (Oxford: Oxford University Press).
——. (2008) 'Agent or Trustee: International Courts in their Political Context', *European Journal of International Relations*, 14 (1), pp. 33–63.
Altschuler, G. and S. Blumin (2000) *Rude Republic: Americans and their Politics in the Nineteenth Century* (Princeton: Princeton University Press).
Andersen, S. and K. Eliassen (eds), (1996) *The European Union: How Democratic Is It?* (London: Sage).
Anderson, P. (2007) 'Depicting Europe', *London Review of Books*, 20 September.
Aristotle (1982) *The Poetics* (Cambridge, MA: Harvard University Press).
Arnull, A. (2006) *The European Union and Its Court of Justice* (Oxford: Oxford University Press).
Aron, R. (1991) *Main Currents in Sociological Thought* (Harmondsworth: Penguin).
Auer, A. (2007) 'National Referendums in the Process of European Integration: Time for a Change', in A. Albi and J. Ziller (eds), *The European Constitution and National Constitutions: Ratification and Beyond* (The Hague: Kluwer Law International), pp. 261–72.
Bacharach, P. and B. Baratz (1962) 'Two Faces of Power', *American Political Science Review*, 56 (4), pp. 947–52.
Bagehot, W. (1963) *The English Constitution* (London: Fontana).
Bailyn, B. (1971) *The Ideological Origins of the American Revolution* (Cambridge, MA: Belknap).

Baker, L. (1974) *John Marshall: A Life in Law* (New York: Macmillan).
Bartolini, S. (2004) 'Tra formazione e trascendenza dei confini. Integrazione europea e stato-nazione', *Rivista Italiana di Scienza Politica*, 34 (2), pp. 167–96.
——. (2005) *Restructuring Europe: Centre Formation, System Building and Political Structuring Between the Nation-State and the European Union* (Oxford: Oxford University Press).
——. (2006) 'Should the Union Be Politicised? Prospects and Risks', in S. Hix and S. Bartolini, 'Politics: The Right or the Wrong Sort of Medicine for the EU?', Notre Europe Policy Paper, n. 19, pp. 29–50.
Beloff, M. (1963) *The United States and the Unity of Europe* (Westport: Greenwood Press).
Belz, H. (1969) 'The Constitution in the Gilded Age: The Beginnings of Constitutional Realism in American Scholarship', *American Journal of Legal History*, 13 (2), pp. 110–25.
——. (2000) (ed.), *The Webster-Hayne Debate on the Nature of the Union: Selected Documents* (Indianapolis: Liberty Fund).
Benz, M. and Stutzer (2004) 'Are Voters Better Informed When They Have a Larger Say in Politics? Evidence from the EU and Switzerland', *Public Choice*, 119 (1–2), pp. 31–59.
Beyme, K. von (1987) *America as a Model: The Impact of American Democracy in the World* (Aldershot: Gower).
Blight, D. W. (2001) *Race and Reunion: The Civil War in American Memory* (Cambridge, MA: Harvard University Press).
Blondel, J. (1998) 'Il modello svizzero: un futuro per l'Europa?', *Rivista Italiana di Scienza Politica*, 2 (August), pp. 203–28
Bogaards, M. (2002) 'Consociational Interpretations of the European Union', *European Union Politics*, 3 (3), pp. 357–81.
Boom, S. J. (1995) 'The European Union After the Maastricht Decision: Is Germany the Virginia of Europe?', *The American Journal of Comparative Law*, 43 (2), pp. 177–226.
Börzel, T. (2005) 'Mind the Gap! European Integration between Scope and Level', *Journal of European Public Policy*, 12 (2), pp. 217–36.
Boucher, D. (2005) 'The Rule of Law in the Modern European State', *European Journal of Political Theory*, 4 (1), pp. 89–107.
Bryce, J. (1995) *The American Commonwealth* (Indianapolis: Liberty Fund).
Buiter, W. (2006) 'The "Sense and Nonsense of Maastricht" Revisited. What Have We Learnt about Stabilization in EMU?', *Journal of Common Market Studies*, 44 (4), pp. 687–710.
Búrca, G. de (1998) 'The Principle of Subsidiarity and the Court of Justice as an Institutional Actor', *Journal of Common Market Studies*, 36 (2), pp. 217–35.
Burgess, M. (2006) *Comparative Federalism: Theory and Practice* (London: Routledge).
Butler, D. and U. Kitzinger (1976) *The 1975 Referendum* (London: Macmillan).
Butler, N. M. (1923) *Building the American Nation: An Essay of Interpretation* (New York: C. Scribner's Sons).
Butler, N. M. (1939) *Building the American Nation: An Essay of Interpretation* (New York: C. Scribner's Sons).
Calder, J. (1977) *Heroes: From Byron to Guevara* (London: Hamilton).

Calhoun, J. C. (1978) 'Letter to Governor James Hamilton Junior', in C. Wilson (ed.), *The Papers of John Calhoun* (Columbia: University of South Carolina Press), vol. xi.
——. (1992) 'A Discourse on the Constitution and Government of the United States', in R. M. Lence (ed.), *Union and Liberty: The Political Philosophy of John C. Calhoun* (Indianapolis: Liberty Fund), pp. 79–284.
Calleo, D. (2001) *Rethinking Europe's Future* (Princeton: Princeton University Press).
Caporaso, J. (1996) 'The European Union and Forms of State: Westphalian, Regulatory or Post-Modern?', *Journal of Common Market Studies*, 34 (1), pp. 29–52.
Cassesse, S. and G. della Cananea (1992) 'The Commission of the European Economic Community: The Administrative Ramifications of its Political Development', *Jahrbuch für europäische Verwaltungsgeschichte*, 4, pp. 75–94.
Cecchini, P., M. Catinat and A. Jacquemin (1988) *The European Challenge 1992: The Benefits of a Single Market* (Aldershot: Gower).
Chopin, T. (2002) *L'Héritage du fédéralisme? États-Unis/Europe* (Paris: Fondation Robert Schuman).
Chryssochoou, D. (1994) Democracy and Symbiosis in the European Union: Towards a Confederal Consociation?', *West European Politics*, 17 (4), pp. 1–14.
Cole, A. C. (1914) 'The South and the Right of Southern Secession in the 1850s', *Mississippi Valley Historical Review*, 1 (3), pp. 376–99.
Collier, D. and S. Levitsky (1997) 'Democracy with Adjectives: Conceptual Innovation in Comparative Research', *World Politics*, 49 (3), pp. 430–51.
Conan Doyle, A. (1985) *Sherlock Holmes: The Complete Illustrated Short Stories* (London: Chancellor).
Corbett, R. (1993) *The Treaty of Maastricht. From Conception to Ratification: A Comprehensive Guide* (Harlow: Longman).
Corwin, E. S. (1934) *The Twilight of the Supreme Court* (New Haven: Yale University Press).
Costa, O. and P. Magnette (2003) 'The European Union as a Consociation? A Methodological Assessment', *West European Politics*, 26 (3), pp. 1–18.
Criddle, B. (1993) 'The French Referendum on the Maastricht Treaty September 1992', *Parliamentary Affairs*, 46 (2), pp. 228–38.
Cronin, B. (2002) 'The Two Faces of the United Nations: The Tension Between Intergovernmentalism and Transnationalism', *Global Governance*, 8, pp. 53–71.
Cronin, C. (2003) 'Democracy and Collective Identity: In Defence of Constitutional Patriotism', *European Journal of Philosophy*, 11 (1), pp. 1–28.
Davis, J. W. (2005) *Terms of Inquiry: On the Theory and Practice of Political Science* (Baltimore: Johns Hopkins University Press).
Dehousse, R. (1994) 'Community Competences: Are There Limits to Growth?', in R. Dehousse (ed.), *Europe After Maastricht. An Ever Closer Union?* (Munich: Beck), pp. 103–25.
——. (1995) 'Constitutional Reform in the European Community: Are there Alternatives to the Majoritarian Avenue?', *West European Politics*, 18 (3), pp. 118–36.
——. (ed.), (1997) *Europe: The Impossible Status Quo* (Basingstoke: Macmillan).
——. 2005) 'We the States: Why the Anti-Federalists Won', in N. Jabko and C. Parsons (eds), *With Us or against US? European Trends in American Perspective* (New York: Oxford University Press), pp. 105–21.

——. (2006) 'The Unmaking of a Constitution: Lessons from the European Referenda', *Constellations*, 13 (2), pp. 151–64.

Della Sala, V. (2005) 'European Polity-Building: Searching for Legitimacy Between Economic and Social Europe', in S. Fabbrini (ed.), *Democracy and Federalism*, pp. 133–47.

Denton, G. (1984) 'Re-Structuring the EC Budget: Implications of the Fontainebleau Agreement', *Journal of Common Market Studies*, 23 (2), pp. 117–40.

Deudney, D. (1995) 'The Philadelphian State System: Sovereignty, Arms Control, and Balance of Power in the American State System', *International Organization*, 49 (2), pp. 191–229.

——. (2004) 'Publius Before Kant: Federal-Republican Security and Democratic Peace', *European Journal of International Relations*, 10 (3) pp. 315–56.

——. (2005) and N. Suveges 'First in Freedom: American Martial Liberal Exceptionalism and International Context', Paper presented at the Annual Conference of the American Political Science Association, Washington DC, 1–4 September.

De Vree, J. (1972) *Political Integration: The Formation of Theory and its Problems* (Mouton: The Hague).

De Witte, B. (2003) 'Entry into Force and Revision', in B. de Witte (ed.), *Ten Reflections on the Constitutional Treaty for Europe* (San Domenico di Fiesole: European University Institute), pp. 203–19.

——. (2004a) 'Treaty Revision in the European Union: Constitutional Change Through International Law', *Netherlands Yearbook of International Law*, 35, pp. 51–84.

——. (2004b) The Process of Ratification of the Constitutional Treaty and the Crisis Options: A Legal Perspective', EUI Working Paper, LAW 04/16.

Diamond, J. (2004) *Collapse: How Societies Choose to Fail or Succeed* (London: Allen Lane).

DiLorenzo, T. (1998) 'Yankee Confederates: New England Secession Movements Prior to the War between the States', in D. Gordon (ed.), *Secession, State and Liberty* (New Brunswick: Transaction), pp. 135–54.

Donahue, J. D. and M. A. Pollack (2001) 'Centralization and its Discontents: The Rythmns of Federalism in the United States and the European Union', in K. Nicolaïdis and R. Howse (eds), *The Federal Vision. Legitimacy and Levels of Governance in the United States and the European Union* (Oxford: Oxford University Press), pp. 73–117.

Doyle, D. H. (2002) *Nations Divided: America, Italy and the Southern Question* (Athens, GA: University of Georgia Press).

Duff, A. (1994) 'Ratification', in A. Duff, J. Pinder and R. Pryce (eds), *Maastricht and Beyond. Building the European Union* (London: Routledge), pp. 53–70.

Dunn, J. (1996) 'Is There a Contemporary Crisis of the Nation State?', in J. Dunn (ed.), *The History of Political Thought and Other Essays* (Cambridge: Cambridge University Press), pp. 196–210.

EC (1993) European Council in Edinburgh, 11–12 December, 1992: Conclusions of the Presidency (Luxembourg: Office for Official Publications of the European Communities).

EEC (1981) *Bulletin of the European Communities* (Luxembourg: Office for Official Publications of the European Communities).

Van der Eijk, C. and M. Franklin (2004) 'Potential for Contestation on European Matters at National Elections in Europe', in G. Marks and M. R. Steenbergen (eds), *European Integration and Political Conflict* (Cambridge: Cambridge University Press), pp. 32–50.

Elazar, D. J. (1962) *The American Partnership* (Chicago: University of Chicago Press).

———. (1986) and I. Greilsammer 'Federal Democracy: The USA and Europe Compared. A Political Science Perspective', in M. Cappelletti, M. Secombe and J. Weiler (eds), *Integration Through Law. Europe and the American Federal Experience* (Berlin: Walter de Gruyter), vol. 1, bk 1, pp. 71–149.

———. (1991) 'Federalism Will Preserve Yugoslavia', *Jerusalem Post*, 18 July.

———. (2001) 'The United States and the European Union: Models for their Epochs', in K. Nicolaïdis and R. Howse (eds), *The Federal Vision* (Oxford: Oxford University Press), pp. 31–53.

Elliot, J. (1836) *Elliot's Debates* (Washington DC: Taylor & Mauray).

Erk, J. and J.-A. Gagnon (2000)'Constitutional Ambiguity and Federal Trust: The Codification of Federalism in Belgium, Canada and Spain', *Regional and Federal Studies*, 10 (1), pp. 92–111.

Etzioni, A. (2001) *Political Unification Revisited. On Building Supranational Communities* (Oxford: Lexington).

Eulau, H. (1974) 'Polarity in Representational Federalism: A Neglected Theme of Political Theory', in D. J. Elazar (ed.), *The Federal Polity* (New Brunswick: Transaction).

Fabbrini, S. (2001) 'The Puzzle of the Compound Republic: The US, EU and the Implications of Federalism', in S. Fabbrini (ed.), *Nation, Federalism and Democracy. The EU, Italy and the American Federal Experience* (Bologna: Editrici Compositori), pp. 55–65.

———. (2003) 'A Single Western State Model?: Differential Development and Constrained Convergence of Public Authority in Europe and America', *Comparative Political Studies*, 36 (6), pp. 653–78.

———. (2004) and D. Sicurelli, 'The Federalization of the EU, the US and "Compound Republic Theory": The Convention's Debate', *Regional and Federal Studies*, 14 (2), pp. 232–54.

———. (2005a) 'Is the EU Exceptional? The EU and the US in Comparative Perspective', in S. Fabbrini (ed.), *Democracy and Federalism in the European Union and the United States. Exploring Post-National Governance* (Abingdon: Routledge), pp. 3–24.

———. (2005b) 'Building a Market without a State: The EU in an American Perspective', in S. Fabbrini (ed.), *Democracy and Federalism in the European Union and the United States. Exploring Post-National Governance* (Abingdon: Routledge), pp. 119–32.

———. (2005c) 'Madison in Brussels: The EU and the US as Compound Democracies', *European Political Science*, 4 (2), pp. 188–98.

———. (2007a) 'Constitutionalization of a Compound Democracy: The European Union in American Perspective', Paper presented at From Spinelli to the Reform Treaty: Ideas, Successes and Failures of European Federalism and Constitutionalism Conference, European University Institute, Florence, Italy, 12 October.

———. (2007b) *Compound Democracies: Why the United States and Europe Are Becoming Similar* (Oxford: Oxford University Press).

Fehrenbacher, D. E. (1980) *The South and Three Sectional Crises* (Baton Rouge: Louisiana State University Press).
Ferguson, N. (2001) *Colossus: The Price of America's Empire* (London: Penguin).
Ferry, J.-M. (2000) *La Question de l'Etat Européen* (Paris: Gallimard).
Filippov, M., P. Ordeshook and O. Shvetsova (2004) *Designing Federalism: A Theory of Self-Sustainable Federal Institutions* (Cambridge: Cambridge University Press).
Fiorina, M., S. J. Adams and J. C. Pope (2004) *Culture War? The Myth of a Polarized America* (New York: Longman).
Foner, E. (1995) *Free Soil, Free Labour, Free Men: The Ideology of the Republican Party Before the Civil War* (New York: Oxford University Press).
——. (2001) Book Review, *New York Times*, 4 March.
——. (2002) *Reconstruction: America's Unfinished Revolution, 1863–1877* (New York: Harper).
Ford, L. K. Jnr. (1994) 'Inventing the Concurrent Majority: Madison, Calhoun, and the Problem of Majoritarianism in American Political Thought', *Journal of Southern History*, 60 (1), pp. 19–58.
Forsyth, M. (1981) *Unions of States: The Theory and Practice of Confederation* (Leicester: Leicester University Press).
Franck, T. M. (ed.), (1968) *Why Federations Fail: An Inquiry into the Requisites for Successful Federalism* (New York: New York University Press).
Frankfurter, F. and J. Landis (1928) *The Business of the Supreme Court: A Study in the Federal Judicial System* (New York: Macmillan).
Franklin, M., M. Marsh and L. McLaren (1994) 'Uncorking the Bottle: Popular Opposition to European Unification in the Wake of Maastricht', *Journal of Common Market Studies*, 32 (4), pp. 455–72.
Freehling, W. W. (1994) *The Reintegration of American History: Slavery and the Civil War* (New York: Oxford University Press).
Friedman, B. (1998) 'The History of the Countermajoritarian Difficulty, Part One: The Road to Judicial Supremacy', *New York University Law Review*, 73 (2), pp. 333–433.
Fritz, C. (2008) *American Sovereigns* (Cambridge: Cambridge University Press).
Fursdon, E. (1992) 'The Role of the European Defence Community in European Integration', in F. Heller and J. Gillingham (eds), *NATO: The Founding of the Atlantic Alliance and the Integration of Europe* (Basingstoke: Macmillan).
Gallagher, M., M. Laver and P. Mair (1995) *Representative Government in Modern Europe* (New York: McGraw Hill).
Garry, J., M. Marsh and R. Sinnott (2005) '"Second-Order" versus "Issue-Voting" Effects in EU Referenda. Evidence from the Irish Nice Treaty Referendums', *European Union Politics*, 6 (2), pp. 201–22.
Garton Ash, T. (2001) 'The European Orchestra', *New York Review of Books*, 48 (8).
George, S. (1998) *An Awkward Partner: Britain in the European Community* (Oxford: Oxford University Press).
Van Gerven, W. (2005) *The European Union: A Polity of States and Peoples* (Oxford: Hart Publishing).
Gienapp, W. E. (1996) 'The Political System and the Coming of the Civil War', in G. S. Boritt (ed.), *Why the Civil War Came* (New York: Oxford University Press).
Gillingham, J. (1991) *Coal, Steel, and the Rebirth of Europe, 1945–1955. The Germans and French from Ruhr Conflict to Economic Community* (Cambridge: Cambridge University Press).

———. (2003) *European Integration, 1950–2003. Superstate or New Market Economy?* (Cambridge: Cambridge University Press).

Glencross, A. and A. H. Trechsel (2007) 'First or Second Order Referendums? Understanding the Votes on the Constitutional Treaty in Four EU Member States', Paper presented at the International Conference on Direct Democracy in Latin America, Buenos Aires, 14–15 March.

Glencross, A. (2008) 'Consensus to Contestation: Reconfiguring Democratic Representation in the European Union in the Light of Nineteenth Century United States Democratization', *Democratization*, 15 (1), pp. 123–41.

———. (2009a) 'Altiero Spinelli and the Idea of the US Constitution as a Model for Europe: The Promises and Pitfalls of an Analogy', *Journal of Common Market Studies*, 47 (1), pp. 287–307.

———. (2009b) 'The Difficulty of Justifying Integration as a Consequence of Depoliticization: Evidence from the 2005 French Referendum', *Government and Opposition*, 44 (2), pp. 243–61.

Goldstein, L. F. (2001) *Constituting Federal Sovereignty: The European Union in Comparative Context* (Baltimore: Johns Hopkins University Press).

———. (2007) 'The Specter of the Second Amendment: Rereading Slaughterhouse and Cruikshank', *Studies in American Political Development*, 21 (Fall), pp. 131–48.

Greenberg, S. B. (2004) *The Two Americas: Our Current Political Deadlock and How to Break It* (New York: Thomas Dunne Book).

Greenfeld, L. (1992) *Nationalism: Five Roads to Modernity* (Cambridge, MA: Harvard University Press).

Greenstone, J. D. (1993) *The Lincoln Persuasion: Remaking American Liberalism* (Princeton: Princeton University Press).

Griffiths, R. T. (1994) 'Europe's First Constitution: The European Political Community', in S. Martin (ed.), *The Construction of Europe: Essays in Honour of Emile Noël* (Dordrecht: Springer), pp. 19–40.

Guizot, F. (1985) *Histoire de la civilisation en Europe* (Paris: Hachette).

Haas, E. (1964) *Beyond the Nation-State: Functionalism and International Organization* (Stanford: Stanford University Press).

———. (1968) *The Uniting of Europe: Political, Social and Economic Forces, 1950–1957* (Stanford: Stanford University Press).

Habermas, J. (2000) 'Why Europe Needs a Constitution', *New Left Review*, 11 (September–October), pp. 5–26.

Hainsworth, P. (2006) 'France Says No: The 29 May 2005 Referendum on the European Constitution', *Parliamentary Affairs*, 59 (1), pp. 98–117.

Haldén, P. (2006) 'Compound Republics as Viable Political Systems: A Comparison of the Holy Roman Empire of the German Nation and the European Union', Ph.D. Thesis, European University Institute.

Hamilton, A. (1993) 'Conjectures about the New Constitution', in B. Bailyn (ed.), *The Debate on the Constitution: Federalist and Anti-Federalist Speeches, Articles and Letters during the Struggle over Ratification* (New York: Library of America), vol. 1, pp. 9–11.

———. (2003) with J. Jay and J. Madison *The Federalist with Letters of Brutus* (Cambridge: Cambridge University Press).

Harrison, M. (1981) *The Reluctant Ally: France and Atlantic Security* (Baltimore: Johns Hopkins University Press).

Hart, A. B. (1917) *New American History* (New York: American Book Company).

Hart, H. M. (1955) 'The Relations Between State and Federal Law', in A. MacMahon (ed.), *Federalism: Mature and Emergent* (Garden City: Doubleday).

Hayward, K. (2003) 'If at First You Don't Succeed: The Second Referendum on the Treaty of Nice', *Irish Political Studies*, 18 (1), pp. 120–32.

Heckly, C. and E. Oberkampf (1994) *La Subsidiarité à l'Américaine: quels enseignements pour l'Europe?* (Paris: L'Harmattan).

Heipertz, M. and A. Verdun (2004) 'The Dog that Would Never Bite? What We Can Learn from the Origins of the Stability and Growth Pact', *Journal of European Public Policy*, 11 (5), pp. 765–80.

Helfer, L. and A.-M. Slaughter (2005) 'Why States Create International Tribunals: A Response to Professors Posner and Yoo', *California Law Review*, 93 (3), pp. 899–956.

Hempel, C. and P. Oppenheimer (1948) 'Studies in the Logic of Explanation', *Philosophy of Science*, 15 (2), pp. 135–75.

Hendrickson, D. (2003) *Peace Pact: The Lost World of the American Founding* (Lawrence: University Press of Kansas).

Hesse, M. (1964) 'Aristotle's Logic of Analogy', *Philosophical Quarterly*, 15 (61), pp. 328–40.

Hix, S. (1999) 'Dimensions and Alignments in European Union Politics: Cognitive Constraints and Partisan Responses', *European Journal of Political Research*, 35 (1), pp. 69–106.

——. (2005) and A. Follesdal 'Why There is a Democratic Deficit in the EU: A Response to Majone and Moravcsik', *European Governance Papers* (EUROGOV), No. C-05-02.

——. (2006) 'Why the EU Needs (Left-Right) Politics? Policy Reform and Accountability are Impossible Without It', in S. Hix and S. Bartolini (eds), 'Politics: The Right or the Wrong Sort of Medicine for the EU?', Notre Europe Policy Paper, no. 19, pp. 1–28.

——. (2008) *What's Wrong with the European Union and How to Fix It?* (Oxford: Polity).

HMG (1971) *The United Kingdom and the European Communities* (London: HMSO).

——. (2003) *A Constitutional Treaty for Europe. The British Approach to the European Union Intergovernmental Conference 2003* (London: HMSO).

Hoffmann, S. (1966) 'Obstinate or Obsolete? The Fate of the Nation-State and the Case of Western Europe', *Daedalus*, 95 (3), pp. 862–915.

——. (2005) Book Review, *Foreign Affairs*, 84 (1), pp. 189–90.

Hofstadter, R. (1970) *The Idea of a Party System. The Rise of Legitimate Opposition in the United States, 1780–1840* (Berkeley: University of California Press).

Holmes, S. (1988). 'Gag Rules or the Politics of Omission', in J. Elster and R. Slagstad (eds), *Constitutionalism and Democracy* (Cambridge: Cambridge University Press, 1988), pp. 19–58.

Holt, M. F. (1999) *The Rise and Fall of the American Whig Party: Jacksonian Politics and the Onset of the Civil War* (Oxford: Oxford University Press).

Hooghe, L., and G. Marks (2008) 'European Union?', *West European Politics*, 31 (1 and 2), pp. 108–29.

Hume, D. (1994) *Political Essays* (Cambridge: Cambridge University Press).

Hunter, J. D. (1992) *Culture Wars: The Struggle to Define America* (New York: Basic Books).

Ivaldi, G. (2006) 'Beyond France's 2005 Referendum on the European Constitutional Treaty: Second-Order Model, Anti-Establishment Attitudes and the End of the Alternative European Utopia', *West European Politics*, 29 (1), pp. 47–69.

Jabko, N. (2007) 'The Constitution as a Repertoire: The Power and Limits of Symbolic Politics', Paper presented at the First Annual Research Conference of the EU Centre of Excellence, Dalhousie University, 22 May.

Jackson, R. (1999) 'Sovereignty in World Politics: A Glance at the Conceptual and Historical Landscape', *Political Studies*, 47 (3), pp. 431–56.

James, H. (1879) *Hawthorne* (London: Macmillan).

Jolly, S. (2007) 'A Europe of Regions? Regional Integration, Sub-National Mobilization and the Optimal Size of States', Ph.D. Dissertation, Duke University

Judt, T. (2005) *Postwar: A History of Europe since 1945* (London: Heinemann).

Kaczorowski, R. (1986) 'Revolutionary Constitutionalism in the Era of the Civil War and Reconstruction', *New York University Law Review*, 61, pp. 863–940.

Kammen, M. (1986) *A Machine that Would Go of Itself. The Constitution in American Culture* (New York: Alfred Knopf).

Kassim, H. (2005) 'Le Royaume-Uni et le Traité constitutionnel européen', *Critique Internationale*, 29 (Oct–Dec), pp. 113–33.

Katz, R. (2000) 'Models of Democracy: Elite Attitudes and the Democratic Deficit in the European Union', Paper presented at the ECPR Joint Sessions, Copenhagen, 14–19 April.

Kelemen, R. D. (2003) 'The Structure and Dynamics of EU Federalism', *Comparative Political Studies*, 36 (1–2), pp. 184–208.

——. (2004) *The Rules of Federalism: Institutions and Regulatory Processes in the EU and Beyond* (Cambridge, MA: Harvard University Press).

——. (2006) 'Federalism and Democratization: The United States and European Union in Comparative Perspective', in A. Menon and M. Schain (eds), *Comparative Federalism: The European Union and United States in Comparative Perspective* (Oxford: Oxford University Press), pp. 221–42.

Keohane, R. and L. Martin (1995) 'The Promise of Institutional Theory', *International Security*, 20 (1), pp. 39–51.

Khanna, P. (2004) 'The Metrosexual Superpower', *Foreign Policy* (July/August).

Kincaid, J. (1990) 'From Cooperative to Coercive Federalism', *The Annals of the American Academy of Political and Social Science*, 509, pp. 139–52.

——. (1999) 'Confederal Federalism and Citizen Representation in the European Union', in J. Brzinski, T. Lancaster and C. Tuschhoff (eds), *Compounded Representation in Western Europe* (London: Frank Cass), pp. 34–58.

Kipling, R. (1940) 'The English Flag', in R. Kipling (ed.), *Verse: Definitive Edition* (Garden City: Doubleday), pp. 221–3.

Koch, A. (ed.), (1969) *Notes of Debates in the Federal Convention of 1787* (New York: Norton).

Koslowski, R. and F. Kratochwil (1994) 'Understanding Change in International Politics: The Soviet Empire's Demise and the International System', *International Organization*, 48 (2), pp. 215–47.

Kratochwil, F. (1978) *International Order and Foreign Policy: A Theoretical Sketch of Post-War International Politics* (Boulder: Westview Press).

——. (1991) *Rules, Norms, and Decisions: On the Conditions of Practical and Legal Reasoning in International Relations and Domestic Affairs* (Cambridge: Cambridge University Press).

Kreppel, A. (2006) 'Understanding the European Parliament from a Federalist Perspective: The Legislatures of theUnited States and European Union Compared', in A. Menon and M. Schain (eds), *Comparative Federalism: The European Union and United States in Comparative Perspective* (Oxford: Oxford University Press), pp. 245–74.

Lacroix, J. (2002) 'For a European Constitutional Patriotism', *Political Studies*, 50 (5), pp. 944–58.

Laffan, B. (ed.), (1996) *Constitution-Building in the European Union* (Dublin: Brunswick Press).

Lehman, E. W. (1992) *The Viable Polity* (Philadelphia: Temple University Press).

Leigh, M. (1975) 'Linkage Politics: The French Referendum and the Paris Summit of 1972', *Journal of Common Market Studies*, 14 (2), pp. 157–70.

Lemco, J. (1991) *Political Stability in Federal Governments* (New York: Praeger).

Leonard, M. (2005) *Why Europe Will Run the Twenty-First Century* (London: Fourth Estate).

Lerner, R. (1963) 'Calhoun's New Science of Politics', *The American Political Science Review*, 57 (4), pp. 918–32.

Lijphart, A. (1975) 'Comparable-Cases Strategy in Comparative Research', *Comparative Political Studies*, 8 (2), pp. 158–77.

Lincoln, A. (1991) *Great Speeches* (New York: Dover).

Lindberg, L. and S. Scheingold (eds), (1970) *Europe's Would-Be Polity: Patterns of Change in the European Community* (Englewood Cliffs: Prentice Hall).

——. (eds), (1971) *Regional Integration. Theory and Research* (Cambridge, MA: Harvard University Press).

Lowi, T. (2006) 'Eurofederalism: What Can European Union Learn from the United States?', in A. Menon and M. Schain (eds), *Comparative Federalism: The European Union and United States in Comparative Perspective* (Oxford: Oxford University Press), pp. 93–119.

Lukacs, J. (1976) *Decline and Rise of Europe. A Study in Recent History, with Particular Emphasis on the Development of a European Consciousness* (Westport: Greenwood Press).

Lupia, A. and J. Matsusaka (2004) 'Direct Democracy: New Approaches to Old Questions', *Annual Review of Political Science*, 7, pp. 463–82.

Lustick, I. (1996) 'History, Historiography and Political Science: Multiple Historical Records and the Problem of Selection Bias', *American Political Science Review*, 90 (3), pp. 605–18.

MacCormick, N. (1997) 'Democracy, Subsidiarity, and Citizenship in the "European Commonwealth"', *Law and Philosophy*, 16 (4), pp. 331–56.

——. (1999) *Questioning Sovereignty: Law, State and Nation in the European Community* (Oxford: Oxford University Press).

Machiavelli, N. (1961) *The Prince* (Harmondsworth: Penguin).

Madison, J. (1840) *The Papers of James Madison* (Washington DC: Langtree and O'Sullivan).

——. (1962) 'Letter to Thomas Jefferson, 4 February 1790', in W. T. Hutchinson, W. M. E. Rachal and R. A. Rutland (eds), *Papers of James Madison* (Chicago: University of Chicago Press), vol. 13, pp. 19–21.

Magnette, P. (2005) *What is the European Union? Nature and Prospects* (Basingstoke: Macmillan).

——. (2006) 'Comparing Constitutional Change in the United States and the European Union', in A. Menon and M. Schain (eds), *Comparative Federalism* (Oxford: Oxford University Press), pp. 149–76.

——. (2007) 'Vers un changement de régime?', in G. Amato, H. Bribosia and B. de Witte (eds), *Genèse et destinée de la Constitution Européenne: commentaire du Traité établissant une Constitution pour l'Europe à la lumière des travaux préparatoires et perspectives d'avenir* (Brussels: Bruylant), pp. 1065–80.

Mair, P. (2004) 'Popular Democracy and the Construction of the European Union Political System', Paper presented at the ECPR Joint Sessions, Uppsala, 13–18 April.

——. (2005) 'Popular Democracy and the European Union Polity', *European Governance Papers* (EUROGOV) no. C-05-03.

Majone, G. (1996) (ed.), *Regulating Europe* (London: Routledge).

——. (2001) Two Logics of Delegation: Agency and Fiduciary Relations in EU Governance, *European Union Politics*, 2 (1), pp. 103–22.

——. (2005) *Dilemmas of Integration: The Ambiguities and Pitfalls of Integration by Stealth* (Oxford: Oxford University Press).

——. (2006) 'The Common Sense of European Integration', *Journal of European Public Policy*, 13 (5), pp. 607–26.

Maletz, D. J. (1998) 'The Union as Idea: Tocqueville on the American Constitution', *History of Political Thought*, 19 (4), pp. 599–620.

Marks, F. W. (1993) *Independence on Trial: Foreign Affairs and the Making of the Constitution* (Baton Rouge: Scholarly Resources).

Marquand, D. (1979) *Parliament for Europe* (London: Jonathan Cape).

——. (1997) Book Review, *Political Quarterly*, 68 (1), pp. 120–1.

Marshall, T. H. (1992) *Citizenship and Social Class* (London: Pluto).

Matson, C. and P. Onuf (1985) 'Toward a Republican Empire: Interest and Ideology in Revolutionary America', *American Quarterly*, 37 (4), pp. 496–531.

May, R. E. (1973) *The Southern Dream of a Caribbean Empire, 1854–1861* (Louisiana: Baton Rouge).

McCormick, R. (1975) 'Political Development and the Second Party System', in W. N. Chambers and W. D. Burnham (eds), *The American Party Systems: Stages of Political Development* (New York: Oxford University Press), pp. 90–116.

McDonald, F. (1988) 'Federalism in America: An Obituary', in F. and E. McDonald (eds), *Requiem: Variations on Eighteenth-Century Themes* (Lawrence: University of Kansas Press), pp. 195–206.

——. (1991) 'Was the Fourteenth Amendment Legally Adopted?', *Georgia Journal of Southern Legal History*, 1, pp. 5–11.

——. (2000) *States' Rights and the Union: Imperium in Imperio, 1777–1876* (Lawrence: University Press of Kansas).

McKay, D. (1999) *Federalism and European Union: A Political Economy Perspective* (Oxford: Oxford University Press).

——. (2001) *Designing Europe. Comparative Lessons from the Federal Experience* (Oxford: Oxford University Press).

——. (2004) 'The EU as a Self-Sustaining Federation', in L. Dobson and A. Follesdal (eds), *Political Theory and the European Constitution* (London: Routledge), pp. 23–39.

——. (2005) 'Economic Logic or Political Logic? Economic Theory, Federal Theory and EMU', *Journal of European Public Policy*, 12 (3), pp. 528–44.
McPherson, James (1984) Book Review, *The American Journal of Legal History*, 28 (4), pp. 377–9.
——. (1991) *Abraham Lincoln and the Second American Revolution* (New York: Oxford University Press).
——. (1994) *What They Fought For, 1861–1865* (Baton Rouge: Louisiana State University Press).
Melville, H. (1991) 'Misgivings', in H. Cohen (ed.), *Selected Poems* (New York: Fordham University Press), p. 3.
Mendez, F. (2007) 'The Governance and Regulation of the Internet in the European Union, the United States and Switzerland: A Comparative Federal Approach', Ph.D. Thesis, European University Institute, Florence, Italy.
Menon, A. and M. Schain (2006) *Comparative Federalism: The European Union and United States in Comparative Perspective* (Oxford: Oxford University Press).
Miller, A. and R. Howell (1956) 'Interposition, Nullification and the Delicate Division of Power in a Federal System', *Journal of Public Law*, 5 (1), pp. 2–48.
Miller, D. (2000) *Citizenship and National Identity* (Oxford: Polity).
Millon-Delsol, C. (1992) *L'Etat subsidiaire* (Paris: Presses Universitaires de France).
Milward, A. (2000) *The European Rescue of the European Nation-State* (London: Routledge).
Minicucci, S. (2001) 'The Cement of Interest: Interest-Based Models of Nation-Building in the Early Republic', *Social Science History*, 25 (2), pp. 247–74.
Mitrany, D. (1943) *A Working Peace System: An Argument for the Functional Development of International Organization* (London: Royal Institute of International Affairs).
Moravcsik, A. (1998) *The Choice for Europe: Social Purpose and State Power from Messina to Maastricht* (Ithaca: Cornell University Press).
——. (2002) 'In Defence of the "Democratic Deficit": Reassessing Legitimacy in the European Union', *Journal of Common Market Studies*, 40 (4), pp. 603–24.
——. (2005) 'Europe Without Illusions: A Category Error', *Prospect*, 112.
——. (2006) 'What Can We Learn from the Collapse of the European Constitutional Project?', *Politische Vierteljahresschrift*, 47 (2), pp. 219–41
Morgan, E. (1988) *Inventing the People: The Rise of Popular Sovereignty in England and America* (New York: Norton).
Morgan, G. (2005) *The Idea of a European Superstate: Public Justification and European Integration* (Princeton: Princeton University Press).
Morgenthau, H. (1985) *Politics Among Nations. The Struggle for Power and Peace* (New York: Alfred Knopf).
Morris, R. (1974) 'The Forging of the Union Reconsidered: A Historical Refutation of State Sovereignty over the Seabeds', *Columbia Law Review*, 74 (6), pp. 1056–93.
Nardin, T. (1983) *Law, Morality and the Relations of States* (Princeton: Princeton University Press).
Nichols, R. F. (1972) *The Invention of the American Political Parties* (New York: Free Press).
Nicholson, F. and R. East (1987) *From the Six to the Twelve: The Enlargement of the European Communities* (Harlow: Longman).

Nicolaïdis, K. and R. Howse (eds), (2001) *The Federal Vision. Legitimacy and Levels of Governance in the United States and the European Union* (Oxford: Oxford University Press).
——. (2004) 'We the Peoples of Europe ... ', Foreign Affairs, 83 (6), pp. 97–119.
Nietzsche, F. (1990) *Beyond Good and Evil* (London: Penguin).
Norris, P. (1997) 'Representation and the Democratic Deficit, *European Journal of Political Research*, 32, pp. 273–82.
Nugent, N. (2003) *The Government and Politics of the European Union* (Durham, NC: Duke University Press).
——. (ed.), (2004) *European Enlargement* (Basingstoke: Palgrave Macmillan).
Oakeshott, M. (1975) *On Human Conduct* (Oxford: Clarendon Press).
——. (1977) *Rationalism in Politics and Other Essays* (London: Methuen).
Onuf, N. (1991) 'Sovereignty: Outline of a Conceptual History', *Alternatives*, 16 (4), pp. 425–66.
Onuf, P. (1987) *Statehood and Union. A History of the Northwest Ordinance* (Bloomington: Indiana University Press).
——. (1991) 'Sovereignty', in J. Greene and J. R. Pole (eds), *Blackwell Encyclopedia of the American Revolution* (Oxford: Blackwell, 1991), pp. 661–8.
——. (1993) and N. Onuf, *Federal Union, Modern World. The Law of Nations in an Age of Revolutions, 1776–1814* (Madison: Madison House).
——. (2006) and N. Onuf, *Nations, Markets and War: Modern History and the American Civil War* (Charlottesville: University of Virginia Press).
Orren, K. and S. Skowronek (2004) *The Search for American Political Development* (Cambridge: Cambridge University Press).
Orth, J. V. (1987) *The Judicial Power of the United States: The Eleventh Amendment in American History* (New York: Oxford University Press).
Ostrom, V. (1987) *The Political Theory of a Compound Republic. Designing the American Experiment* (Lincoln: University of Nebraska Press).
Parsons, C. (2003) *A Certain Idea of Europe* (Ithaca: Cornell University Press).
Pierson, P. (1998) 'Social Policy and European Integration', in A. Moravcsik (ed.), *Centralization or Fragmentation? Europe Facing the Challenges of Deepening, Diversity and Democracy* (New York: Brookings Institution), pp. 124–58.
Pinder, J. (1963) *Europe Against De Gaulle* (London: Pall Mall).
Pitkin, H. (1972) *The Concept of Representation* (Berkeley: University of California Press).
Plattner, M. (2003) 'Competing Goals, Conflicting Perspectives', *Journal of Democracy*, 14 (4), pp. 42–56.
Pocock, J. G. A. (1975) *The Machiavellian Moment: Florentine Political Thought and the Atlantic Republican Tradition* (Princeton: Princeton University Press).
——. (1999) 'Enlightenment and Counter-Enlightenment, Revolution and Counter-Revolution; A Eurosceptical Enquiry', *History of Political Thought*, 20 (1), pp. 125–39.
Pollack, M. A. (1994) 'Creeping Competence: The Expanding Agenda of the European Community', *Journal of Public Policy*, 14 (2), pp. 95–145.
——.(1997) 'Delegation, Agency and Agenda-Setting in the European Community', *International Organization*, 51 (1), pp. 99–134.
——. (2001) 'International Relations Theory and European Integration', *Journal of Common Market Studies*, 39 (2), pp. 221–44.

———. (2005) 'Theorizing the European Union: International Organization, Domestic Polity, or Experiment in New Governance', *Annual Review of Political Science*, 8, pp. 357–98.

Pollak, J. and P. Slominski (2004) 'The Representative Quality of the EU: A Comparison Between the IGC and the Convention', *Journal of European Integration*, 26 (3), pp. 201–26.

Preuss, U. (1995) 'Citizenship and Identity: Aspects of a Political Theory of Citizenship', in R. Bellamy, V. Bufacchi, and D. Castaglione (eds), *Democracy and Constitutional Culture in the Union of Europe* (London: Lothian Foundation Press).

Rabun, J. (1956) 'Documents Illustrating the Development of the Doctrine of Interposition', *Journal of Public Law*, 5 (1), pp. 49–89.

Rakove, J. (1996) *Original Meanings: Politics and Ideas in the Making of the Constitution* (New York: Alfred Knopf).

Ransom, R. L. (1999) 'Fact and Counterfact: The "Second American Revolution" Revisited', *Civil War History*, 45 (1), pp. 28–60.

Remini, R. V. (1998a) *Andrew Jackson: The Course of American Freedom, 1828–1832* (Baltimore: Johns Hopkins University Press).

———. (1998b) *Andrew Jackson: The Course of American Democracy, 1833–1845* (Baltimore: Johns Hopkins University Press).

———.(2001) *The Life of Andrew Jackson* (New York: Pernnial).

Rifkin, J. (2004) *The European Dream: How Europe's Vision of the Future is Quietly Eclipsing the American Dream* (Oxford: Polity Press).

Riker, W. H. (1955) 'The Senate and American Federalism', *American Political Science Review*, 49 (2), pp. 452–69.

———. (1964) *Federalism: Origin, Operation, Significance* (Boston: Little).

Robertson, D. (2005) *The Constitution and America's Destiny* (Cambridge: Cambridge University Press).

Robin, R. (1992) *Enclaves of America. The Rhetoric of American Political Architecture Abroad, 1900–1965* (Princeton: Princeton University Press).

Rokkan, S. (1999) *State Formation, Nation-Building and Mass Politics in Europe: The Theory of Stein Rokkan* (Oxford: Oxford University Press).

Rosamond, B. (2007) 'European Integration and the Social Science of EU Studies: The Disciplinary Politics of a Subfield', *International Affairs*, 83 (1), pp. 231–52.

Rosanvallon, P. (2006) *Democracy Past and Future* (New York: Columbia University Press).

Ruggie, J. (1998) *Constructing the World Polity: Essays on International Institutionalization* (London: Routledge).

Runciman, D. (2003) 'Politicians in a Fix', *London Review of Books*, 4 September.

———. (2004) 'The Precautionary Principle', *London Review of Books*, 1 April.

———. (2006) 'The Paradox of Political Representation', Paper presented at the Princeton Political Philosophy Consortium, 30 March.

Sarkozy, N. (2006) Discours devant les Amis de l'Europe et la Fondation Robert Schuman, Brussels, 8 September.

Sbragia, A. (ed.), (1992) *Euro-Politics: Institutions and Policy Making in the 'New' European Community* (Washington DC: Brookings Institution).

———. (2000) 'The European Union as Coxswain: Governance by Steering', in J. Pierre (ed.), *Debating Governance* (Oxford: Oxford University Press), pp. 219–40.

——. (2005) 'Post-National Democracy as Post-National Democratization', in S. Fabbrini (ed.), *Democracy and Federalism* (London: Routledge), pp. 167–82.
Schain, M. (2006) 'Immigration Policy', in A. Menon and M. Schain (eds), *Comparative Federalism: The European Union and the United States in Comparative Perspective* (New York: Oxford University Press), pp. 339–64.
Scharpf, F. (1995) 'Federal Arrangements and Multi-Party Systems', *Australian Journal of Political Science*, 30, pp. 27–39.
——. (1999) *Governing in Europe: Effective and Democratic?* (Oxford: Oxford University Press).
——. (2000) 'The Viability of Advanced Welfare States in the International Economy: Vulnerabilities and Options', *Journal of European Public Policy*, 7 (2), pp. 190–228.
Schimmelfennig, F. (2003) *The EU, NATO and the Integration of Europe: Rules and Rhetoric* (Cambridge: Cambridge University Press).
Schlesinger, A. (1977) 'America: Experiment or Destiny', *American Historical Review*, 82 (3), pp. 505–22.
Schmidt, V. (2006) *Democracy in Europe: The EU and National Polities* (Oxford: Oxford University Press).
——.(2007) 'Trapped by their Ideas: French Elites' Discourses of European Integration and Globalization', *Journal of European Public Policy*, 14 (7), pp. 992–1009.
Schmitt, C. (1992) 'The Constitutional Theory of Federalism', *TELOS*, 91 (Spring), pp. 26–56.
Schmitt, H. and J. Thomassen (eds), (1999) *Political Representation and Legitimacy in the European Union* (Oxford: Oxford University Press).
Schmitter, P. (1996) 'Imagining the Future Euro-Polity with the Help of New Concepts', in G. Marks, F. Scharpf, P. C. Schmitter and W. Streeck (eds), *Governance in the European Union* (London: Sage), pp. 121–50.
——. (2000) *How to Democratize the European Union – And Why Bother?* (Lanham: Rowman & Littlefield).
Schwartz, B. (1982) 'The Social Context of Commemoration: A Study In Collective Memory', *Social Forces*, 61 (2), pp. 372–402.
Schwartz, B. (1993) *A History of the Supreme Court* (New York: Oxford University Press).
Sewell, W. H., Jr. (1967) 'Marc Bloch and the Logic of Comparative History', *History and Theory*, 6 (2), pp. 208–18.
Shefter, M. (1994) *Political Parties and the State: The American Historical Experience* (Princeton: Princeton University Press).
Sidjanski, D. (1992) *L'Avenir fédéraliste de l'Europe. La communauté européenne, des origines au traité de Maastricht* (Paris: Presses Universitaires de France).
Siedentop, L. (2000) *Democracy in Europe* (London: Allen Lane).
Silverstone, S. (2004) *Divided Union: The Politics of War in the Early American Republic* (Cornell University Press).
Sinnott, R. (2003) 'Attitudes and Behaviour of the Irish Electorate in the Second Referendum on the Treaty of Nice', University College Dublin Working Paper.
Siotis, J. (1983) 'Characteristics and Motives for Entry', in J.-L. Sampedro and J.-A. Payno (eds), *The Enlargement of the European Community: Case Studies of Greece, Portugal and Spain* (London: Macmillan).

Skocpol, T. and Somers M. (1994) 'The Uses of Comparative History in Macrosocial Inquiry', in T. Skocpol (ed.), *Social Revolutions in the Modern World* (Cambridge: Cambridge University Press), pp. 72–98.

Skowronek, S. (1982) *Building a New American State: The Expansion of National Administrative Capacities, 1877–1920* (Cambridge: Cambridge University Press).

Smith, D. and C. Tolbert (2004) *Educated by Initiative: The Effects of Direct Democracy on Citizens and Political Organization in the American States* (Ann Arbor: University of Michigan Press).

Smith, J. (1998) 'The 1975 Referendum', *Journal of European Integration History*, 5 (1), pp. 41–56.

Smith, R. M. (1993) 'Beyond Tocqueville, Myrdal and Hartz: The Multiple Traditions in America', *American Political Science Review*, 87 (3), pp. 549–66.

Soulé, Y.-P. (1958) 'Comparaison entre les dispositions institutionnelles du Traité CECA et du Traité CEE', *Revue du Marché Commun*, 1 (2), pp. 95–102, and 1 (4), pp. 208–16.

Spinelli, A. (1966) *The Eurocrats: Conflict and Crisis in the European Community* (Baltimore: Johns Hopkins University Press).

——. (1993) 'Il modello costituzionale americano e i tentavi di unità europea', in M. Albertini (ed.), *Il Federalismo: Anthologia e definizione* (Bologna: Il Mulino).

Spruyt, H. (1994) *The Sovereign State and Its Competitors: An Analysis of Systems Change* (Princeton: Princeton University Press).

Stampp, K. (1978) 'The Concept of a Perpetual Union', *Journal of American History*, 65 (1), pp. 5–33.

Steed, M. (1977) 'Landmarks of the British Referendum', *Parliamentary Affairs*, 30 (1), pp. 130–3.

Stefanova, B. (2006) 'The "No" Vote in the French and Dutch Referenda on the EU Constitution: A Spillover of Consequences of the Wider Europe', *PS: Political Science and Politics*, 39 (2), pp. 251–55.

Stein, E. (1981) 'Lawyers, Judges and the Making of a Transnational Constitution', *American Journal of International Law*, 75 (1), pp. 1–27.

Stepan, A. (1999) 'Federalism and Democracy: Beyond the U.S. Model', *Journal of Democracy*, 10 (4), pp. 19–34.

Stone Sweet, A. (2004) *The Judicial Construction of Europe* (New York: Oxford University Press).

——. (2005) 'The Constitutionalization of the EU: Steps Towards a Supranational Polity', in S. Fabbrini (ed.), *Democracy and Federalism*, pp. 44–56.

Storing, H. (1985) *The Anti-Federalist: An Abridgement* (Chicago: University of Chicago Press).

Stråth, B. (2005) 'Methodological and Substantive Remarks on Myth, Memory and History in the Construction of a European Community', *German Law Journal*, 6 (2), pp. 255–71.

Strauss, D. (2005) 'Pop Con', *Legal Affairs*, March/April.

Strauss, L. (1987) Entry on Machiavelli, in L. Strauss and J. Cropsey (eds), *History of Political Philosophy* (Chicago: Rand McNally), pp. 247–76.

Swift, E. K. (1996) *The Making of an American Senate: Reconstitutive Change in Congress, 1787–1841* (Ann Arbor: University of Michigan Press).

Thatcher, M. (1988) Speech to the College of Europe, Bruges, 20 September.

Tilly, C. (1984) *Big Structures, Large Processes, Huge Comparisons* (New York: Russell Sage Foundation).
——. (1992) *Coercion Capital, and European States, AD 990–1992* (Cambridge, MA: Blackwell).
Tipton, D. (1969) *Nullification and Interposition in American Political Thought* (Albuquerque: University of New Mexico Press).
Tocqueville, A. de (1990) *De la démocratie en Amérique, édition historico-critique, revue et augmentée par Eduardo Nolla* (Paris: J. Vrin).
——. (1994) *Democracy in America*, trans. H. Reeve (London: David Campbell).
Torbiörn, K. (2003) *Destination Europe: The Political and Economic Growth of a Continent* (Manchester: Manchester University Press).
Trechsel, A. H. (2005) 'How to Federalize the EU ... and Why Bother', *Journal of European Public Policy*, 12 (3), pp. 401–18.
Tsoulakis, L. (1981) *The European Community and Its Mediterranean Enlargement* (London: Allen and Unwin).
Tushnet, M. (1999) *Taking the Constitution Away from the Courts* (Princeton: Princeton University Press).
Van Tyne, C. (1907) 'Sovereignty in the American Revolution: An Historical Study', *The American Historical Review*, 12 (3), pp. 529–45.
Wæver, O. (1996) 'Europe's Three Empires: A Watsonian Interpretation of Post-Wall European Security', in R. Fawn and J. Larkins (eds), *International Society after the Cold War* (Basingstoke: Macmillan), pp. 220–60.
Wagner, P. (2004) 'Formes d'état et formes de savoir social. Les traditions nationales en sciences sociales et la pluralité d'interprétations de la modernité', in B. Zimmermann (ed.), *L'Etat et les sciences sociales* (Paris: Seuil).
Waltz, K. N. (1979) *Theory of International Politics* (Reading, MA: Addison-Wesley).
Warren, C. (1913) 'Legislative and Judicial Attacks on the Supreme Court', *American Law Review*, 47 (1), pp. 1–34.
Weber, M. (1983) *Economy and Society: An Outline of Interpretive Sociology* (Berkeley: University of California Press).
Webster, D. (1833) *Speech in Reply to Mr Calhoun's Speech on the Bill 'Further To Provide for the Collection of Duties on Imports'* (Washington: Gales & Seaton).
Weiler, J. (1982) 'Community, Member States and European Integration: Is the Law Relevant?', *Journal of Common Market Studies*, 21 (2), pp. 39–56.
——. (1988) 'Parlement Européen, Intégration Européenne et Légitimité', in J.-V. Louis and D. Waelbroeck (eds), *Le Parlement Européen dans l'évolution institutionnelle* (Bruxelles: Editions de l'Université de Bruxelles), pp. 325–48.
——. (1994) 'Fin-de-siècle Europe', in R. Dehousse (ed.), *Europe after Maastricht. An Ever Closer Union?* (Munich: Beck), pp. 203–16.
——. (1997) 'The European Union Belongs to its Citizens: Three Immodest Proposals', *European Law Review*, 22 (2), pp. 150–6.
——. (1999) *The Constitution of Europe: Do the New Clothes Have an Emperor? And Other Essays on European Integration* (Cambridge: Cambridge University Press).
——. (2001) 'Federalism Without Constitutionalism: Europe's *Sonderweg*', in K. Nicolaïdis and R. Howse (eds), *The Federal Vision. Legitimacy and Levels of Governance in the United States and the European Union* (Oxford: Oxford University Press), pp. 54–70.
Weingast, B. R. (1998) 'Political Stability and Civil War: Institutions, Commitment and American Democracy', in R. Bates, A. Greif, M. Levi, J.-L. Rosenthal and

B. Weingast (eds), *Analytic Narratives* (Princeton: Princeton University Press), pp. 148–93.

Werner, W. G. and J. H. de Wilde (2001) 'The Endurance of Sovereignty', *European Journal of International Relations*, 7 (3), pp. 283–313.

White, H. (1975) *Metahistory: The Historical Imagination in Nineteenth-Century Europe* (Baltimore: Johns Hopkins University Press).

Wieland, J. (1994) 'Germany in the European Union – The Maastricht Decision of the Bundesverfassungsgericht', *European Journal of International Law*, 5, pp. 1–8.

Wilentz, S. (2005) *The Rise of American Democracy: Jefferson to Lincoln* (New York: Norton).

Wilson, W. (1908) *Constitutional Government in the United States* (New York: Columbia University Press).

Wind, M. (2001) *Sovereignty and European Integration: Towards a Post-Hobbesian Order* (Basingstoke: Palgrave Macmillan).

Winders, R. (2002) *Crisis in the Southwest: The United States, Mexico, and the Struggle Over Texas* (Wilmington: Scholarly Resources).

Wirls, D. (1999) 'Regionalism, Rotten Boroughs, Race and Realignment: The Seventeenth Amendment and the Politics of Representation', *Studies in American Political Development*, 13 (Spring), pp. 1–30.

Wood, G. S. (1969) *The Creation of the American Republic, 1776–1787* (New York: Newton).

Yack, B. (2001) 'Popular Sovereignty and Nationalism', *Political Theory*, 29 (4), pp. 517–36.

Zielonka, J. (2006) *Europe as Empire: The Nature of the Enlarged European Union* (Oxford: Oxford University Press).

Zimmerman, J. (2001) 'National-State Relations: Cooperative Federalism in the Twentieth Century', *Publius*, 31 (2), pp. 15–30.

Zweifel, T. (2002) 'Who is Without Sin Cast the First Stone: The EU's Democratic Deficit in Comparison', *Journal of European Public Policy*, 9 (5), pp. 812–40.

Zuckert, M. (1992) 'Completing the Constitution: The Fourteenth Amendment and Constitutional Rights', *Publius*, 22 (2), pp. 69–91.

Index

absolutism, 33, 34
Ackerman, Bruce, 22, 123
acquis communautaire, 67, 89, 171
Adams, John Quincy, 121, 140
Aldrich, John, 142
Alien and Sedition Acts (1798), 56, 115, 162
Alter, Karen, 102
analogy
  between EU and antebellum US, 1–6, 8, 10, 12, 16, 19, 20, 23, 31, 64, 65, 66, 112, 151, 153, 161, 169, 173, 180, 184
  general use of, 51–2, 54, 64,
antebellum United States, 23, 30, 37–43, 54–62, 67–8, 69, 70–1, 115–6, 125, 126–8, 131–7, 138–47, 153, 161–7, 171, 183, 184, 185
  see also United States of America
anti-federalists, 22, 107
anti-majoritarianism, 15, 18
  in EU, 138, 150, 153, 168, 169
  in US, 121, 161, 163, 170
Aristotle, 46, 47, 51
Arkansas, 134
Articles of Confederation, *see under* United States of America
Atlantic Alliance, 34, 156
  see also NATO
Atlanticism, 89
Australia, 27
Austria, 27
  Commission v. Austria (2005), 147–8

Bagehot, Walter, 16, 22, 102
Barber ECJ decision (1990), 158
Barron v. Baltimore case (1833), 41
Bartolini, Stefano, 49, 173
Basque Country, 25
Belgium, 2, 29, 149

Bérégovoy, Pierre, 175
bicameralism, 127
Bill of Rights, *see* United States Constitution
Bridge, Nigel (Lord), 92
Bryce, James, 116
Butler, Nicholas, 60

Calhoun, John, 40, 117, 128, 161, 170, 171
  proposal for dual presidency, 165
  theory of concurrent majorities, 163–6, 169, 185
  theory of nullification, 118, 153, 172, 185
California, 135
Canada, 27
centralization, coercive, 10, 15, 16
centralization, voluntary, 4, 5, 6, 15–19, 29–31, 64, 72–3, 75, 107, 109, 112, 114, 118, 144, 151, 153–4, 156, 167–9, 172–3, 177–180, 182
  see also dynamic equilibrium
Cecchini Report (1988), 126
Charter of Fundamental Rights, 109–11, 123, 129, 149, 158, 187
Chisolm v. Georgia case (1793), 56, 115
Christianity, 49
Churchill, Winston, 77, 184
Clay's Compromise (1850), 58, 142
Clay, Henry, 135
Cold War, 10
Committee of the Regions, 25
Common Agricultural Policy, 89
Common Foreign and Security Policy, 111, 130, 155–6
Commonwealth, British, 87, 90, 91
Community Charter of Fundamental Social Rights of Workers, 102

competency over competences, 4, 13, 14, 15, 18, 29, 40, 41, 43, 53, 55, 57, 60, 63, 64, 76, 86, 107, 108, 109, 112, 147, 148, 149, 164, 172, 182, 183, 185
compound polity, 3, 54, 73, 161, 171
　antebellum US as, 5, 32, 42, 54–5, 58–60, 66, 126, 131–3, 137, 147, 150–1, 153–4, 161, 165, 173, 180
　EU as, 3, 4, 54, 63–4, 66, 68, 109, 112–3, 118, 121, 137, 148–9, 150–1, 153–5, 160, 168, 174, 176
　theory of, 20–31, 51–2
　viability in, 8–20, 54, 65
Conan Doyle, Arthur, 32, 45
concurrent majorities
　in EU, 166, 168–70
　in US, *see under* Calhoun, John
confederalism, 24–6, 79, 103, 114
confederation, 9, 10, 24–6, 51, 99
　economic confederation, 9
Conscription Bill (1812), 57, 162
constitutionalization of EU, 37, 80, 81, 113, 178
constitutional law, 85
constitutional patriotism, 19
constitutional politics, 16, 17, 42
Constitutional Treaty, *see under* European Union
Convention on the Future of Europe, 65
Costa v. ENEL case (1964), 82–5
Council of Ministers, 25, 26, 72, 77, 78, 92, 94, 138, 147, 148, 160, 169
customs union, 67, 79, 81, 87, 88, 94
Cyprus, 94

Davis, James W., 8
Delaware, 139
Delors, Jacques, 98
democracy, 1, 4, 12–3, 19, 65, 69, 74, 93, 100, 102, 105, 112, 130, 160, 171, 175, 183
　American, 30, 46, 49, 51, 59, 144, 167
　as criterion for membership of EEC/EU, 93–6, 99, 109
　democratic deficit, 1, 6, 94, 96, 105, 153

　direct, 28, 40, 91, 122, 126, 174
　Jacksonian, 31, 141, 143, 163, 187
　liberal, 33, 75–6, 93, 95, 130, 167
　majoritarian, 153, 161
　parliamentary, 90
　representative, 166
　suggested solutions to, 19
　supranational, 153
democratization, 1, 5, 6, 54, 66, 153, 162, 167–70, 172
'*demoi-cracy*', 35
Denmark, 91, 92, 106, 155
Deudney, Daniel, 10, 28, 38, 39
District of Columbia, 135
Dred Scott case (1857), 41, 59–60, 146, 151
dynamic equilibrium, 4–5, 15, 17–9, 29–31, 75, 104, 107–9, 112, 114, 118, 123, 125, 131, 133, 135, 137–8, 144, 146–7, 149–54, 161, 168, 177, 180, 182
　see also rules of the game

Economic and Financial Affairs Council, 63–4
Elazar, Daniel, 69
elites, 7, 11, 19, 68, 85, 155, 160, 177, 179
　European political, 2, 73, 124
　national political, 73
　pro-integration, 66, 69
　tension with citizens over European integration, 70, 107, 174
empire, 33, 86
"empty chair crisis", *see* European Economic Community
English language, 49
Etzioni, Amitai, 50
European Coal and Steel Community
　creation of, 75–9
　importance for expectations about European integration, 76, 77, 81
　institutions of, 76, 80
European Commission, 1, 28, 63–4, 66, 80, 82–5, 87, 94, 103, 105, 110, 122, 148, 169, 179
European Council, 25, 28, 72, 97, 106, 112, 160

226 *Index*

European Court of Justice, 17, 63–4, 97, 101–3, 109–12, 151, 158–9, 183, 186–8
　effects of jurisprudence on EU member states, 25–6, 30, 72, 80, 82–6, 92–3, 122, 137, 160
　as fiduciary or trustee institution, 148
　impact of decisions on rules of the game, 147, 149–50
　ruling on education policy, 148–9
European Defence Community
　failure of, 78–9, 97, 108, 155, 167
European Economic Community, 10, 14, 17, 24, 79–81, 82, 98, 177
　British accession to, 86–93
　"empty chair crisis", 14, 96, 97
　Mediterranean enlargement, 93–7
　relation to European Coal and Steel Community, 79–82
European Free Trade Area, 86–7
European integration
　choice of term, 74
　conflicting views, 138, 153
　expectations of, 75, 77, 80–1, 86, 108, 168
　founding objectives of, 75, 130, 164
　French attitudes to, 77–8, 88
　negative *v.* positive, 157, 158
　objectives of, 75, 92, 125, 180
　principle of "ever closer union", 69, 74, 79, 86, 95, 99, 123, 125, 131, 167
　process of, 79, 106
　referendums on, 89–92, 174, 177–9
　as *Sonderweg*, 13
　as subject of contestation in national politics, 45, 76, 86, 147, 174
　supranational *v.* intergovernmental visions of, 152, 158–9, 173, 177, 180
　UK attitudes to, 86, 92–3
European Monetary Union, 99, 102, 107, 175
European Parliament, 1, 26, 27, 36, 91, 96, 97, 119, 147, 160, 169, 170, 179

European Union
　as confederal consociation, 9, 36
　Constitutional Treaty, 15, 65, 68, 70, 79, 85, 99, 109–111, 122, 124, 154–5, 173–4, 176, 187
　enlargement of, 25, 30, 81, 86–8, 93, 95–8, 108, 154–5, 176
　Excessive Deficit Procedure, 63
　exit mechanism, 29, 68, 162
　harmonization in, 103, 110, 117, 149
　internal market, 67, 158–9
　as inter-state consociation, 9
　as non-state, 35–6
　power of veto in, 18, 25, 76, 87–8, 91–3, 96, 102, 109–10, 112, 116–7, 130, 147, 160, 168–70, 172
　regional fund, 89, 95
　as *sui generis*, 1, 3, 9, 36, 44
　treaty reform, 27, 30, 68, 71–3, 91, 107–9, 126, 131, 138, 147–8, 153–5, 161, 174, 177–9
　treaty system in, 67–8, 118, 122–5, 138, 179
euro zone, 63
　see also European Monetary Union

Fabbrini, Sergio, 27, 65, 153
Factortame case (1990), 92–3, 96
fascism, 17
federalism, 2, 27, 33, 183, 185
　comparative federalism, 4, 10, 20, 23–4, 27, 29, 48
　comparison between EU and Switzerland, 27–8
　comparison between EU and US, 49–50, 71
　distinction between federalism and confederalism, 24–6, 103, 107–8, 114
　dual, 22, 116
　dual *v.* joint, 66–7, 115–8
　in US, 32, 36–43, 49, 116, 163
Federalist, The, 15, 20, 21
　see also Publius
federal state, 11, 107
　Belgium as, 2
　EU as, 25, 99, 105–6, 114, 167

Index 227

US as, 3, 21–4, 56–8, 60, 62, 67, 113, 119–21, 124, 126–9, 131–6, 138–44, 147, 150, 162–5, 170–1, 184–88
Fehrenbacher, Don, 133, 145
Ferguson, Niall, 33
Fischer, Joschka, 79
Florida, 132, 134
Foner, Eric, 61, 136
Ford, Lacy, 164
Fouchet Plan, 87–8, 99
France, 14, 38, 46, 47, 50, 51, 56, 63, 64, 65, 79, 91, 94, 104, 106, 107, 133, 156, 157, 175, 177
Conseil d'état, 85
Cour de cassation, 85
l'exception française, 129
Franck, Thomas, 48
French Revolution, 10
intervention in Mexico, 184
referendum on Constitutional Treaty, 65, 176
referendum on Treaty of Maastricht, 106, 175
Franco-German relations, 76, 78, 79, 175
free market, 71, 77, 80, 81, 11, 124, 129, 138, 152, 167

Garton Ash, Timothy, 1
Gaulle, Charles de, 14, 88, 97
George, Stephen, 90
Georgia (USA), 115
German Democratic Republic, 98
Germany, 27, 63, 64, 75, 76, 77, 78, 86, 99, 105, 106, 148, 175
abandonment of Deutschmark, 98
Berlin Wall, fall of, 48
Bundesbank, 63
Bundestag, 105, 106
Constitutional Court ruling on Maastricht Treaty, 105–6
Deutscher Bund, 26
Grundgesetz, 105
re-armament, 76, 78
reunification, 63, 64, 98
Ruhrgebiet, 75
see also Franco-German relations
Gillingham, John, 44, 81

Giscard D'Estaing, Valéry, 175
Goldstein, Leslie F., 16, 30, 62,
Greece, 64,
accession to EEC, 93–5
Greilsammer, Ilan, 69
Grimke, Frederick, 72,
Guadalupe Hidalgo, Treaty of (1848), 135
Guizot, François, 8

Hague Summit (1969), 88–9
Hallstein, Walter, 84
Hamilton, Alexander, 15, 21, 56, 58, 139
Hartford Convention, 57, 162
Hayes, Rutherford, 62
Hayne, Robert, 120
Heath, Edward, 89
Heckly, Christophe, 117
Hendrickson, David, 38
High Representative for the Common Foreign and Security Policy, 103
Hix, Simon, 169, 179
Hobbes, Thomas, 9
Hoffmann, Stanley, 45, 51
Hume, David, 9

imperium in imperio, 20, 22, 185
intergovernmentalism, 43, 79, 111, 114, 155–7, 167, 169, 177
Internationale Handelsgesellschaft case (1970), 85
Ireland, 71, 91, 110, 176
Italy, 64

Jabko, Nicolas, 68
Jackson, Andrew, 57, 67, 120–1, 126, 140–2, 161, 165
see also democracy, Jacksonian
James, Henry, 53
Jefferson, Thomas, 56–7, 124, 139, 184
Jenkins, Roy, 95
Jim Crow laws, 62
Judt, Tony, 80

Kansas-Nebraska Act (1854), 58–9, 149
Kentucky and Virginia Resolutions (1798), 56–7, 115, 162

Kincaid, John, 171
Kohl, Helmut, 99
Kompetenz-Kompetenz, 20, 29, 58, 63, 100, 103, 144, 186
  see also competency over competences
Korea, 76
Kratochwil, Friedrich, 9, 12
Ku Klux Klan, 62

Laval v. Svenska Byggnadsarbetareförbundet case (2007), 159
legitimacy, 4, 7, 28, 39, 64, 98, 107, 120–2, 141, 150, 156, 168, 171, 181
  democratic, 19, 75, 92, 100, 110, 114, 128–9, 180
  foundational, 68, 70, 123
  governing, 64, 68, 70, 123
Lehman, Edward, 12
Leigh, Michael, 89
Leonard, Mark, 35
Lincoln, Abraham, 61, 126–7, 136, 140, 146–7, 150
Lindberg, Leon, 87
Lisbon, Treaty of (2007), 2, 15, 28–9, 67, 79, 85, 109–12, 116, 130, 138, 149, 155, 158, 160, 172
Louisiana Purchase (1803), 57, 132
Luxembourg Compromise, 14
  see also EEC "empty chair" crisis

Maastricht, Treaty of (1992), 26, 81, 96, 97–107
  Danish rejection of, 106–7
  debate over f-word, 99
  extension of qualified majority voting, 104
  French referendum on, 106
  German Constitutional Court ruling on, 105–6
  pillar structure of, 99, 103
  protocol on social policy, 104–5
  United Kingdom opt-outs, 102, 104
  see also subsidiarity
Macmillan, Harold, 87
Madison, James, 3, 20–1, 42, 56, 61, 124, 167

Magnette, Paul, 102–3, 126
Maine, 133
Majone, Giandomenico, 25–6, 157, 176
Major, John, 102
majoritarianism, 6, 137, 139, 153, 161, 163, 165, 170
  Webster's theory of, 127, 185
  see also anti-majoritarianism
Maletz, Donald, 150
Marshall, John, 57–8, 68, 119
Marquand, David, 96, 157
Massachusetts, 126, 133
McCormick, Richard, 142, 144
McCulloch v. Maryland case (1819), 58, 119
McDonald, Forrest, 39
McPherson, James, 42, 60, 128
Melville, Herman, 55
'metrosexual superpower', 35
Mexico, 58, 133–4, 162, 184
Michigan, 134
Milward, Alan, 80
Mississippi, 162
Missouri, 58, 132–3
Missouri Compromise (1820), 58–9, 134, 145–6
Mitterrand, François, 106, 175
Monnet, Jean, 84, 97
Montesquieu, Charles-Louis de Secondat, baron de, 8
Moravcsik, Andrew, 43, 65, 66, 81, 99, 176
Morgan, Glyn, 128
Morgenthau, Hans, 37

Napoleon, 34
Nardin, Terry, 177
Nashville Convention, 162
nationalism, 22, 33–5, 60, 97
nation state, 13, 19, 33–6, 48, 74, 79, 97, 101, 104, 119, 125, 129, 138, 156, 171, 181–2, 186
NATO, 11, 78, 125, 129, 152, 155–6, 184
  see also Atlantic Alliance
neo-functionalism, 43
Netherlands, 11, 65, 91
  referendum on Constitutional Treaty, 176

Index 229

New England, 57, 62
Nice, Treaty of (2001), 2, 109, 124, 149, 160, 176
Nichols, Roy F., 30, 31
Nietzsche, Friedrich, 7
negarchy, 10
New Mexico, 135
Northwest Ordinance (1787), 133, 145
Nugent, Neil, 137
nullification, 57
  see also Calhoun, John and South Carolina

Oakeshott, Michael, 47, 177
Oberkampf, Eric, 117
Onuf, Nicholas, 38
Onuf, Peter, 38, 120
opt-outs, 18, 25, 109, 117, 171–2
  for Denmark, 92, 107, 155
  for United Kingdom, 102, 111, 138, 149, 158–9

pan-European politics, 19, 49, 73, 96, 97, 105, 118, 121, 123, 149, 151, 153, 159, 183
Paris, Treaty of (1783), 24
Paris, Treaties of (1947), 75
Parsons, Craig, 177
Parti Québecois, 27
Pennsylvania Legislature, 57
'permissive consensus', 91
Philadelphia Convention, 21, 24, 38, 40, 61, 65, 131, 184
Pinder, John, 97
Pitkin, Hannah, 166
Plattner, Marc, 35
Pléven Plan, 78
Polk, James, 134
political elites, *see* elites
'popular constitutionalism', 40
popular sovereignty, 15, 19–20, 23–4, 28–9, 40, 42–3, 51, 59, 67–8, 70, 73, 75, 121, 137, 139, 145–6, 150, 171–2, 179, 185–7
  engaged *v.* recessed, 24, 28, 42
Portugal
  accession to EEC, 93–5
post-national theory, 19

Powell, Enoch, 91
praxis, 33, 43–4, 47
  contrasted with *theoria*, 47
proceduralism, 111, 117
public sphere, 19, 34, 91, 105, 122
Publius, 71, 137, 163

qualified majority voting, 27, 80–1, 92, 96, 101, 103–5, 110, 112, 137, 155

Randolph, Edmund, 21
Reconstruction, *see under* United States of America
referendums
  on Constitutional Treaty, 15, 65, 124
  Danish referendum on Treaty of Maastricht, 106–7
  effect on political parties, 90, 91–2, 93
  and European integration, 73, 88, 90, 91, 108, 126, 174, 177–9
  French referendum on UK accession to EEC, 87, 89
  French referendum on Constitutional Treaty, 154
  French referendum on Treaty of Maastricht, 106, 126, 175
  Irish referendum on Treaty of Nice, 176
  in Switzerland, 28, 122
  UK referendum on accession to EEC, 89–90, 92, 94
  see also democracy, direct
representation, 1, 4, 15, 24, 27, 73, 77, 79, 104, 109, 125, 130, 139, 152, 166, 171, 173, 186–7
  cross-national/supranational, 19, 93, 121, 153, 160, 168–70, 179–80
  cross-unit, 153, 161, 173
  dual system of, in antebellum US, 20, 161
  dual system of, in EU, 6, 161
  federal *v.* confederal principles of, 15, 107
  reconfiguration of, in EU, 27, 45, 151–3, 160, 168, 170, 172–3, 183, 186

representation (*Contd.*)
  as rule of the game of politics, 4, 5, 28, 41–2, 55, 59, 72, 76, 108, 138, 144, 154, 160, 163, 186
  of states *v.* citizens, 6, 13–8, 63, 153, 161, 164–6, 183
republican freedom, 61, 131
republican security project, 37
Riker, William, 143
Rocard, Michel, 175
Rome, Treaty of (1957), 70, 79, 88–2, 93, 95, 99, 102–4
Roosevelt, Franklin D., 187
rules of the game of politics, 4
  applicability to EU, 13
  applicability to US, 40
  comparison between EU and US, 33, 39, 52
  in compound polity, 161–173
  contestation of, in antebellum US, 54–62, 133–7, 138–47
  contestation of, in EU, 54, 19–20, 25–6, 28–30, 63–73, 74–82, 147–183
  definition of, 11–12
  effect of changes to, 18, 154
  evolution of, in EU, according to logic of dynamic equilibrium 154–61
  four contested rules of, in compound polity, 4, 5, 14, 17, 31, 74–112, 182–4
  impact of ECJ decisions on, 82–6, 147–9
  impact of US Civil War on, 41–3
  see also centralization *and* dynamic equilibrium
Runciman, David, 122, 166, 174

Sbragia, Alberta, 129
Scharpf, Fritz, 66
Schengen Agreement, 92
Scheingold, Stuart, 87
Schlesinger, Arthur, 55
Schmitter, Philippe, 35, 168–9, 178–9
Schuman Declaration, 97
Schuman, Robert, 84
Scott, Dred, *see* Dred Scott case

Scott, Winfield, 142, 145
Scotland, 25
secession, 2, 15, 48, 51, 55, 113, 126, 128, 147, 150, 162, 168, 170, 184
  threat of, 42, 162
separation of powers, 23, 54,
  vertical and horizontal, 11, 20, 27–8, 36
Shefter, Martin, 140
Sicurelli, Daniella, 27
Siedentop, Larry, 49–50
single currency, 98, 106
  see also European Monetary Union
Single European Act (1986), 81, 96–8
Sinnott, Richard, 176
social policy, 80–81, 104–5, 109–10, 112, 129, 156–60
  contrast between US and EU, 156–7
  contrasting views within EU on, 104, 137, 157–9
social protection, 77, 80, 105, 108–9, 157–8, 167
South Carolina, 139, 162
  nullification crisis, 115, 120, 126–7, 162–3
  Ordinance of Nullification (1832), 162
sovereignty, 8–10, 20, 26, 92, 104, 111–2, 164, 171, 175, 180, 183
  debates in antebellum US, 14, 38–40, 56, 59, 116, 120, 136, 185
  debates in EU, 30, 65, 76, 83, 85, 96, 129, 175
  divided, 22–3, 185
  locus of, 18, 22–3, 39, 58
  parliamentary, 92–3
  pooling of, 43, 96, 98, 102, 107, 130, 138, 175–6
  relation to representation, 43
  as status, 23–5
  UK defence of, 90–2
  see also popular sovereignty
Sozialstaat, EU as, 157
Spaak, Paul-Henri, 78
Spain, 132, 187
  accession to EEC, 93–5
Spinelli, Altiero, 65, 78, 97, 99
Staatenverbund, EU as, 106

Index   231

state-building, 32–5, 156
  see also nation state
state, definition of, 8
states-union, *see* compound polity
Steed, Michael, 91
Stone Sweet, Alec, 103, 106
subsidiarity, 100–2, 104, 109–10, 151, 171–2, 186
supranationalism, 79, 111, 114, 155–7, 159, 167, 169, 172–3, 177, 186
  see also intergovernmentalism
Switzerland, 4, 11, 27–8, 122

Tallmadge, James, 132–3
Taney, Roger, 59
tariff controversy, 116, 120, 126–7, 162
  see also South Carolina, nullification crisis
Texas, 133–4
Thatcher, Margaret, 97
  Bruges speech, 97
Thatcherism, 80
Tilly, Charles, 34
Tocqueville, Alexis de, 12, 22, 33, 46–7, 50–1, 71, 74, 150
traité de procédures, 81
traité de règles, 81
Turkey
  invasion of Cyprus, 94
  possible accession to EU, 2, 45, 154
Tyler, John, 134

United Kingdom, 149, 156
  accession to EEC, 87–93
  Labour Party, 89–90
Union of Soviet Socialist Republics, fall of, 97–8
  post-war threat from, 11, 75–6, 78
United Nations
  Security Council membership, 156
United States of America,
  antebellum period, *see* antebellum United States
  Articles of Confederation, 20, 29, 38, 39, 69, 133, 141, 143, 168, 173
  Civil War, 3, 14, 22, 32, 37, 39–41, 43, 55–6, 60–2, 67, 128, 139–40, 153, 184, 186–7

  Congress, 41–2, 57–8, 60, 62, 70, 115, 120, 127, 132–5, 139–40, 143, 145–6, 162, 165, 178
  Constitution, *see* United States Constitution
  Declaration of Independence, 56, 61, 69, 119, 125
  Democratic Party, 134, 141, 142
  Electoral College, 40, 67, 121, 132, 137, 139–41, 144, 146, 165
  exceptionalism, 3, 36, 187
  first party system, 139
  House of Representatives, 133–4, 140, 165
  Judiciary Act (1875), 43
  Mexican war (1846–1848), 61–2
  New Deal, 123, 187
  Reconstruction era, 31, 39–41, 60–2, 113, 123, 147
  Republican Party, founding of, 59, 145–6
  role of presidency, 28, 67–8, 141, 161, 187
  second party system, 140–44, 146, 167
  Senate, 58–9, 79, 116, 120, 126, 132–5, 143–4, 163, 169
  slavery issue, 5, 55, 58–60, 62, 70, 124, 131–7, 139, 142–7, 150, 154, 161–3, 167, 173
  Supreme Court, 39–43, 56–7, 59, 62, 71, 119, 138–9, 146, 164, 170, 186–7
  war with Britain (1812–14), 57, 61, 162
  War of Secession, *see under* Civil War
  Whig Party, 142, 144–5
United States Constitution, 17, 20, 22, 28–30, 38–40, 56–8, 60–1, 65, 67–70, 113, 115–20, 124–7, 136, 143, 147, 150, 162–3, 165, 167–8, 178
  amendments to, 16, 22, 40–2, 56–8, 62, 67, 71, 115, 120, 132–5, 139, 143, 146, 164, 168, 178
  Bill of Rights, 41, 56, 115
  compact theory of, 14, 40–2, 54–5, 56, 60, 116, 120, 163, 164
  ratification of, 24, 39, 120, 178

United States Constitution (*Contd.*)
  three-fifths rule, 124, 132, 142
  see also Philadelphia Convention
Utah, 135

Van Buren, Martin, 141–2, 165
Van Duyn case (1973), 83
Van Gend en Loos case (1963), 82–4
Venice, republic of, 34
viability
  as basis for comparison between EU and antebellum US, 5–6, 32–52
  definition of, 7–11, 15
  and dynamic equilibrium, 151, 160
  in EU, 1–4, 13, 16, 19, 23, 31, 87, 113–4, 153, 155, 160–1, 168, 173, 180, 182–4, 186
  and rules of the game, 23, 29, 54, 58, 68, 182
  scenarios of, 15–6, 18–9, 64–5
  see also compound polity
  in US, 4, 32, 147, 161, 165, 173
Vienna Convention on the Law of Treaties, 124

voting procedures, 16, 169–70
  first-order v. second-order, 73, 174
  see also qualified majority voting

Waltz, Kenneth, 186
Washington, George, 56
Webster, Daniel, 120, 126–7, 161, 163
  theory of majoritarianism, 127, 161, 185
Weiler, Joseph, 13, 35
welfare state, 156–7, 159
Whig interpretation of history, 49
Whig Party, *see* United States of America
White, Hayden, 46
Wilentz, Sean, 136
Wilmot Proviso (1846), 134–5
Wilson, Harold, 89–90, 95
Wilson, Woodrow, 187–8
Wood, Gordon S., 120

Yugoslavia, 48

Zuckert, Michael, 41